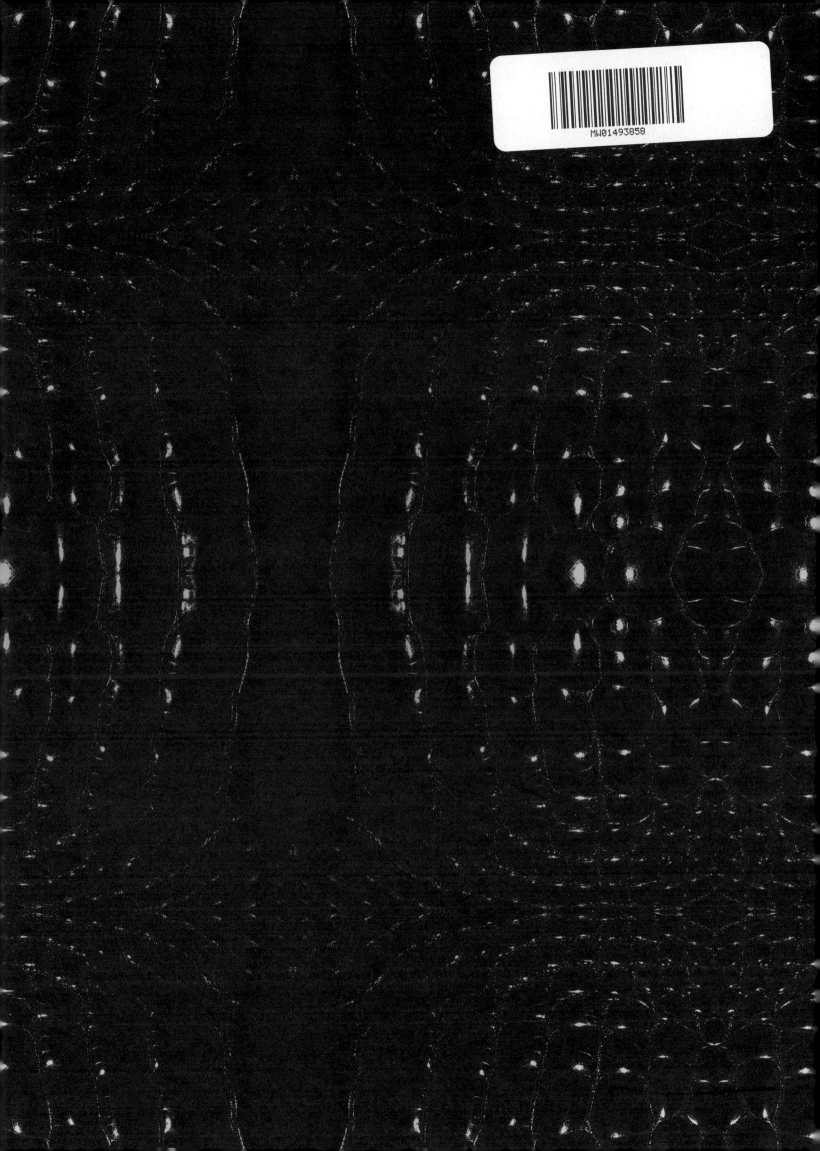

With best wishes
from Victoria
Stolof
Seattle 2010

Exotic Skin
ALLIGATOR AND CROCODILE
Handbags

The Ultimate Status Symbol to Wear and Collect

Victoria Stowe

Schiffer Publishing Ltd

4880 Lower Valley Road, Atglen, PA 19310

DEDICATION

Dedicated to my dear grandfather, my father, my baby-brother, my husband, and my son— men of wisdom, class and inspiration—and also to my Aunt Claudia, who believed that real beauty never grows old.

Other Schiffer Books on Related Subjects:
Passion for Purses: 1600-2005, Paula Higgins & Lori Blaser. ISBN:978-0-7643-2617-2 $49.95
Beads on Bags: 1880-2000. Lorita Winfield, Leslie Piña & Constance Korosec. ISBN:0-7643-1138-7 $49.95

Library of Congress Control Number: 2010921827

Cover photography: Victoria Stowe
Copy Editing, Logistics: Jim Stowe
Photography, Technical Support: Zack Davidov
Graphic Design, Set Design: Nina Passalaqua
Style and Design, Photography: Victoria Stowe

Disclaimer: The products pictured in this book are from the collection of the author. The book, which is not sponsored, endorsed, or otherwise affiliated with any of the companies whose products are represented herein, is derived from the author's independent research.

Designed by John P. Cheek
Cover design by Bruce Waters
Type set in Nadall/Zurich BT

ISBN: 978-0-7643-3477-1
Printed in China

Cover photo: Priceless, crocodile Porosus cocktail-purse. Adorned by 24K-gilded leaf, silver-glass Venetian beads, and rhinestones. Lined in champaign satin. (W 8-inch by H 6 ½ -inch by D 2-inch). Signed: Lucille de Paris Made in France; ca 1958.

Preface photo: Pike Market antique store in Seattle, USA, July 2009.

Schiffer Books are available at special discounts for bulk purchases for sales promotions or premiums. Special editions, including personalized covers, corporate imprints, and excerpts can be created in large quantities for special needs. For more information contact the publisher:

Published by Schiffer Publishing Ltd.
4880 Lower Valley Road
Atglen, PA 19310
Phone: (610) 593-1777; Fax: (610) 593-2002
E-mail: Info@schifferbooks.com

For the largest selection of fine reference books on this and related subjects, please visit our web site at
www.schifferbooks.com
We are always looking for people to write books on new and related subjects. If you have an idea for a book please contact us at the above address.

This book may be purchased from the publisher.
Include $5.00 for shipping.
Please try your bookstore first.
You may write for a free catalog.

In Europe, Schiffer books are distributed by
Bushwood Books
6 Marksbury Ave.
Kew Gardens
Surrey TW9 4JF England
Phone: 44 (0) 20 8392 8585; Fax: 44 (0) 20 8392 9876
E-mail: info@bushwoodbooks.co.uk
Website: www.bushwoodbooks.co.uk

CONTENTS

Acknowledgments 4

Preface 5

1. Why Collect Vintage? 6
    Hobby, Investment, or Fashion Necessity? 6
    Vintage vs. Second-hand 7
    The It Bag! 8

2. Piece of History to Wear 11
    Victorian 19th Century 12
    Edwardian Early 20th Century 16
    Flapper Twenties 21
    Ladylike Thirties 30
    Practical Forties 41
    Glamorous Fifties 51
    Youthful Sixties 64

3. Leading Makers 74
    Coblentz 76
    Deitsch 80
    Department Store Brands 86
    Dofan 92
    Evans 95
    Gucci 99
    Hermes 102
    Judith Leiber 104
    Koret 110
    Lederer de Paris 117
    Lesco 124
    Lucille de Paris 128
    Manon 140
    Mark Cross 144
    Martin Van Schaak 149
    Nettie Rosenstein 158
    Palizzio 163
    Rendl Original 167
    Rosenfeld, Harry 172
    South American Import 184
    Various Brands 190
     Bellestone 191
     Sterling USA 198
    Vassar 203

4. Exotic Skins 207
    Terminology 208
    American Alligator 210
    Crocodile 212
    Caiman 214
    Turtle 216
    Ostrich 218
    Lizard 220
    Snake 222
    Imitations 224
    Authenticity Test 226

5. Four Cs to Remember 227
    Circa 227
    Condition 238
    Craftsmanship 239
    Color 244

6. Three How-to's 252
    How to Buy 252
    How to Care 256
    How to Wear 257

7. Value and Price 266

Bibliography 269

Index 270

Acknowledgments

I am incredibly honored and grateful for the time and effort Judith Leiber and Jess Frost of the Leiber Museum contributed to this project. Judith Leiber kindly agreed to review the photos of her handbags featured in the book to confirm their production dates. Thank you!

My special gratitude goes to Jim Stowe for his endless commitment and support. His dedication was exactly what I needed to finish this book that took almost a decade to create.

The contribution of my photographer, Zack Davidov, simply cannot be overestimated. His fresh artistic vision and keen understanding of quality has defined the concept of the book, and his meticulous technical support made it real and feasible. Thank you from the bottom of my heart!

The ability of my set stylist and graphic designer, Nina Passalaqua, to "tune" into the atmosphere of period fashion added to the aura of its historical authenticity.

Finally, I must sincerely thank my friends, Karen Braun and Kathy Braun, who inspired me to go through with this project. They've always been there for me, through thick and thin, for almost two decades, and I am very grateful for that.

HERMÈS

HERMES
Most desired, crocodile Porosus pocketbook, with a turn-lock brass closure. (W 9 ¾ -inch by H 11 ½ -inch by D 2-inch). Signed (interior, back of the lock): Hermes Paris. 1959. Shown with an Hermes carre silk scarf (Les Cles pattern), and an Hermes leather bracelet.

Preface

Life is short. Time flies like a bullet. Days are packed with endless assignments, appointments, projects, and chores; and you feel you need more time for yourself. Most definitely, you need more passion, beauty, and excitement. Perhaps, a hobby would be a great idea. Something that would make you feel special and look fabulous. Something that could also become a smart investment. Collecting? Yes! Collecting vintage fashion? Absolutely!

That was what I was thinking, as I stood in front of a long row of glowing displays in an enchanting cove of Seattle's Pike Market antique store. Such an abundance! My eyes were gliding from one cabinet to another—when I suddenly gasped, "Oh, my gosh! I've never seen anything more beautiful—a true piece of art!"

That was when I first saw a vintage alligator handbag—a stunning piece by Lucille de Paris. Its beauty and the luxury of its skins captivated me. Since then, every spare minute I have—apart from my job—is devoted to collecting.

Collecting is fun. But, like any investment opportunity, it must be taken seriously. Not every old alligator purse is a valuable collectible, and to know the difference you have to do your homework. As I'm happy to share what I have learned over the years, it is my hope that this book will help you find the perfect handbag—the one you will cherish for years. The one you will carry with pride!

CHAPTER ONE
WHY COLLECT VINTAGE?

"A Thing of Beauty is a Joy Forever"

"If I should be allowed to choose one out of all the books that will be published a hundred years after my death, I would take a fashion magazine to see how the women were dressing a century after my decease. Their fripperies would tell me more about the society of that future day than all the philosophers, preachers and savants."—Anatole France

Collecting vintage exotic skin handbags is a relatively new and unusual phenomenon—unlike more established collecting areas, such as antique or vintage clothing, costume jewelry, beaded purses, or Lucite handbags. They attract not only fashion historians and experts who collect for preservation and research, but also millions of women mesmerized by the timeless elegance of these fine handbags.

Nostalgia for quality, luxury and sensible glamor of the past has created an unprecedented interest in vintage exotics among the fashion-conscious public. Rapid development of the Internet and online auctions have made vintage items accessible and affordable. A unique, finely crafted alligator handbag from the 1950s or 1960s—a great alternative to a new designer piece worth thousands of dollars—can now be acquired for a fraction of its original cost.

The motto of the 1950s, "More Taste Than Money," has become relevant once again. Today, owning a one-of-a-kind vintage alligator bag is a must among the young, hip crowd and in vogue with fashion-oriented women of all ages and walks of life. It is an affordable and tasteful way to create your own personal style.

These vintage handbags also offer a great opportunity to express your appreciation of classic designs, as Wan-Lin Horng, one of my friends and fellow collectors from Seattle, Washington, testifies:

> *I have always believed that I was born too late. I adore the fashion sense of Princess Grace Kelly, Audrey Hepburn, Greta Garbo, Jacqueline Kennedy Onassis, and Coco Chanel. It was by chance that while I was searching for a vintage Kelly-style handbag I stepped into a world that became a small obsession. The world of vintage exotics! I researched intensively in order to arm myself with enough knowledge to bid in auctions. And, over time, I came to appreciate these bags more than just fashion accessories. To me, they are works of art.*

Needless to say, an alligator handbag has never been about necessity. Its appeal is about the ultimate luxury to cherish for years and wear with pride. The wild beauty and scarcity of precious skins make every bag a unique piece of art to satisfy the most discriminating taste. The sense of historical importance that vintage brings into our lives makes it even more desirable. A piece of history to wear! Who wouldn't want to carry a tiny bit of it, especially if it doesn't break the bank?

HOBBY, INVESTMENT, OR FASHION NECESSITY?

"If a bag is attractive, it makes you feel good by default. More than that it's like you've gotta have it or you'll die."— Tom Ford, creative director, Gucci

Collecting vintage exotics has proved to be a smart investment opportunity that is rising in popularity worldwide, as rare pieces of museum quality can be worth thousands of dollars.

For almost a decade, the biggest Hollywood celebrities have been promoting the trend by carrying vintage to red-carpet events. Several museums worldwide display the finest vintage skin bags as an important part of their period fashion collections. Antique shops, regular department stores and leading auction houses have been doing good business selling vintage handbags as well.

When it comes to a fashion necessity, a classic vintage alligator handbag has become a statement and a conversation piece—perhaps the most unorthodox addition to any sophisticated wardrobe. I would hardly call myself a fashion plate, but having an extensive collection of vintage designer pieces makes me feel like I'm set for life and don't need to spend thousands of dollars on a current *It* bag. I can always find something similar—perhaps even better—at home.

Collecting vintage is practical and smart. Fairly often you can find absolutely fabulous, like-new pieces for very little money. Their quality, attention to detail and craftsmanship is superb. Their design is versatile and unique—truly the best choice toward creating your own, individual style. Or, if you'd rather not wear these bags, you could give them away as gifts, put them on display, or store them for investment purposes—and resell them when necessary for a healthy profit. Alligator handbags are relatively easy to take care of, especially if you have adequate space for proper storage.

Collecting vintage is informative. Some pieces have an intriguing history behind them that relates to the era in which they were crafted; it is always fun to imagine how their previous owners dressed and lived their daily lives.

Whichever reason appeals to you most—hobby, investment, or fashion necessity—collecting vintage is a smart idea. Plus, is the opportunity to join an exclusive club of people who own the ultimate status symbol: a precious alligator handbag!

Pair of smart, identical, miniature travel-bags; with removable, gold-plated watches, and hardware. Both made in France for Lederer de Paris, in late 1950s-early 1960s.

VINTAGE VS. SECOND-HAND

Not every older alligator handbag can be regarded as vintage. Instead, it could be merely an insignificant second-hand—worth little money as a collectible. That is why it is important to recognize the difference between *vintage* and *second-hand*. A collectible vintage may cost thousands, whereas a second-hand—merely hundreds. Only the second-hand pieces by renowned Hermes, Cartier, Chanel, Gucci, Dior, or Louis Vuitton—even the recent ones, regardless their age—are considered valuable collectibles.

Ultra-rare, genuine crocodile purse made in France by Cartier, in the 1960s. The so-called 'black tulip' color – the darkest shade of green that looks almost black – was first introduced in the 1960s by Christian Dior. (W 10-inch by H 7-inch by D 4-inch). Signed. Shown with a Cartier watch-box.

In the field of the exotic skin handbags, the term *vintage* defines the best examples produced by important makers during the period from the turn of the 20th century and to the late nineteen sixties, when the ban on selling alligator and some crocodile skins was enforced in the United States for over a decade, until the late nineteen eighties. To help determine whether a handbag is a valuable collectible, the details on leading design houses of the past is provided here, with numerous examples of their production. Similar pieces in mint or excellent condition are definitely the ones you want to acquire.

The reason a lot of people buy vintage is to save on luxury. Usually, vintage handbags cost less than brand-new designer bags, unless they are rare, museum-quality objects. Always do your homework to know the values, and never overpay. Hopefully, the values reference at the back of this book will help you master this task.

Be aware of caiman handbags recently produced in Asia, Germany or Italy to look like vintage crocodile. Made from inferior farmed skins, they are good for use, but not for a collection. To put it short, do your homework— and you will be successful in making a smart investment by buying a real, 100% authentic, vintage alligator handbag.

Caiman travel satchel, with combination locks and secret compartment. (W 10 ¼ -inch by H 10 ¼ -inch by D 4 ¼ -inch). Labeled: Carla Mancini Paris-Milano-New York. Ca late 1990s – great for everyday use, but not collectible, as yet.

THE IT BAG!

"Magic, mystery, and money are all wrapped up in the myth of a classic handbag."—Anna Johnson, Handbags: The Power of the Purse

As fashion historians have established, the idea of a classic *It* bag, an important handbag that conveys luxury and status, can be traced back to the 19th century. The idea was ultimately perfected in the 20th century by a handful of leading European fashion houses with long-standing traditions—such as Hermes, Louis Vuitton, Gucci, and Chanel—whose designs became distinct classics as a result of their established commercial success. The concept behind each trademark was a brilliant interpretation of old traditions. Their handbags were strictly practical in their application, and initially had nothing to do with status, luxury, or glamor.

At the beginning of the 20th century, the House of Hermes, a saddler to aristocracy, designed four basic shapes of handbags—triangle, square, barrel, and hobo—using the same simple and practical designs of saddlebags and feedbags that have been used for travel for centuries. Created under the pressures of time and circumstances, these still are the shapes on which most classic handbags of today are based.

Hermes merchandise ad April 27, 1929, France. (*L'Illustration*, 27 Avril 1929)

Louis Vuitton, one of the oldest French fashion houses that started as a maker of travel trunks for Napoleon III, recycled the idea of combining their branded canvas with leather by incorporating it into dozens of styles of lady's luggage and handbags. Soon, the concept caught on and transformed Louis Vuitton into one of the most prestigious brands in the world.

Louis Vuitton merchandise ad, March 21, 1931, France (*L'Illustration*, 21 Mars 1931)

In the late 1940s, when supplies were scarce after the Second World War, Gucci substituted leather and metal with cotton, canvas, and bamboo. In the 1950s, fashion designer Coco Chanel gave birth to the use of gilt chains as purse handles. Recognizable and commercially successful, both brands have become icons in modern fashion culture.

The recent revival of interest in the status bag has prompted old houses to reinvent their traditional designs. Over the last two decades, new colors and details have updated their look. Status handbags of today are presented as being young and hip. Their allure, fine quality and waiting lists have influenced many people to spend thousands of dollars for the *It* bags.

Alligator and crocodile have steadily been the ultimate materials among status handbags. Their high prestige was established in the late 19th century, when they first appeared in Europe and America as luxurious novelties prized for their wild beauty and durability. Always astronomically expensive, they became a part of the power-package of a privileged few, who were identified by their high social status. Royalty, celebrities, stars and fashion icons have worn them ever since as a staple of the status look. Jackie Kennedy validated their importance by consistently appearing with a fine alligator purse to accentuate the sleek simplicity of her signature look.

The Grand Duchess Marie – first cousin of the late Czar of Russia – in a dress of her own design, with an alligator handbag (*Vogue*, March 15, 1940).

"Classics, like a strong vintage, take time"—Anna Johnson

It took several decades for an alligator handbag to catch up with popular demand in America. In the post-war 1940s, it was transformed from an exclusive accessory into an All-American necessity suiting the needs of active, career-oriented women. Its casual elegance, which combines the luxury of genuine skins with the pragmatism of minimalist style, became a trademark of American tradition. Since then, alligator handbags became main-stream and their broad popularity as vintage goods has made it possible for millions of women of different means to own this status symbol for a reasonable price. The experience of wearing a fine vintage piece does not only represent the opportunity to join the club, but also imparts a thrill of learning their history, and what an exciting history it is!

CHANEL
Right: Glamorous, lipstick-red, baby-crocodile Porosus chain-clutch, with a famous, braided metal-and-leather strap, and 24K-plated hardware. (W 8 ½ -inch by H 5 ¼ -inch by D 2-inch). Left: Black lambskin quilted clutch. (W 10 ¼ -inch by H 6 ¼ -inch by D 2 ¼ -inch). Both made by Chanel France. Ca 1980s. Acquired from the Doyle auction house.

DARBY SCOTT
Understated, alligator-skin clutch treated with bombe finish, and adorned by a huge butterfly crafted of semi-precious gems by Brazilian artisans. Discreet zippered top; luxurious suede interior. (W 12 ¾ -inch by H 5 ¼ -inch by D 2-inch). Labeled: Darby Scott. Ca 2000s.

DOTTI
A true piece of modern art! Convertible frame-bag made of superbly textured java-lizard, with a removable, silk shell-cover, embroidered with genuine white and black coral, quartz, and onyx. Polished chrome hardware; pink leather interior, with black and mint-green trim. (W 8-inch by H 8-inch by D 2 ¾ -inch). Clasp stamped: Dotti. Labeled: Dotti Via Beisiana 26 – Roma. Italy, ca 1990s.

DOTTI

GUCCI
Iconic, front-flap purse, with a desirable bamboo top-handle, in superb matte alligator. Suede-lined; shoulder strap; 24K-plated trim. (W 7 ¼ -inch by H 8 ¼ -inch by D 2 ½ -inch). Signed: Gucci Made in Italy (serial number). Sold at Neiman-Marcus. Ca 1990s.

GUCCI

CHAPTER TWO
PIECE OF HISTORY TO WEAR

"Everything Old Is New Again"

Nobody expresses handbag history better than Anna Johnson, a well-respected vintage fashion collector and author of the witty book, *Handbags: The Power of the Purse*. She guesses that the very first skin handbag most likely was put together by a resourceful cave woman—a couple of small lizard or snake skins tied to a stick with grass strings—to form a provision carriage. *"From these simple beginnings, the bag has blossomed into every form, color and material imaginable,"* she remarks.

Anna Johnson further writes that over the centuries the primitive sack evolved into a drawstring pouch made from various materials. In the Middle Ages, a metal frame transformed it into a more structured bag that could be worn on the body.

Tiny, lavishly embroidered and gem-encrusted purses were a craze among ladies of means. In the 16th century, women hid small bags in the folds of voluminous skirts or up their sleeves. But by the 17th century, spacious yet discreet separate pockets, with an opening in the middle, were worn under petticoats and emerged as a prototype for the modern purse. That was an important turn in the course of handbags' history. With the introduction of sheer, flowing, Empire-style dresses in Paris in 1790, ladies could no longer hide anything under their skirts. Eventually, the pocket was put on a string to carry—and here we go, the handbag was born. In the 19th century, it was called a *reticule*.

Antique reticules, from late 19th century-early 20th century. **Left:** Made of leather – petite and flat – with a heavily embossed, engraved, and filigreed sterling silver frame. (W 6 ¾ - inch by H 5-inch). Hallmarked: London, England, Goldsmith & Silversmiths Co. Ltd., 1899. **Right:** Made of micro-beads with a drawstring closure, fully lined with silk. (W 9-inch by H 7-inch). Germany, ca 1890s. Based on information from the author of the book on German beaded purses, "Sabina Schürenberg Glasperlarbeiten. Taschen und Beutel, 1998", it was most likely made in Göppingen or Schwäbisch Gmünd, Germany, by Otto Hick, Fritz Schaupert & Cie, or Karl Seyfang. At the turn of the 20th century, Schaupert ran a shop in New York, at 31 Union Square.

VICTORIAN 19TH CENTURY

Later in the 19th century, the Industrial Revolution in Victorian England and subsequent development of railroads facilitated the rise of a new social class—working women—who needed a sturdy bag for travel. Such a bag—small and round made of leather and built on a strong metal frame with a secure closure, a lock, and a key—emerged around 1860.

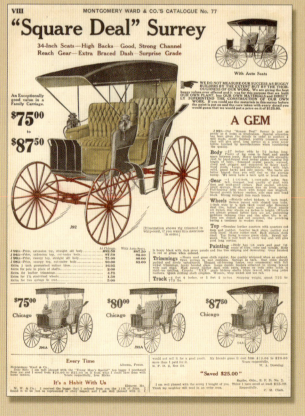

Sears, Roebuck & Co. Catalog cover and merchandise ads, 1897

Massive, hornback crocodile club-bag, with heavy-duty brass hardware (double-flange frame, double-hasp lock and side catches, English handle with ring attachments). Huge, central hornback cuts on both sides. Lined in quality leather in British tan. (W 16 ½ -inch by H 14-inch (with handle) by D 7 ½ -inch). The bottom is protected by five huge feet. Blind-stamped: 16 848. Unsigned. Ca 1897-1898. In 1897, a similar style cost $5.20.

The emerging middle class represented by business owners, merchants, bankers, lawyers and other professionals began to show its developing wealth through luxury possessions. Alligator *travel satchels* became an ultimate expression of their success and rising social status.

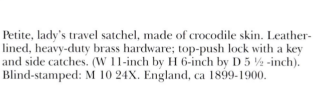

Petite, lady's travel satchel, made of crocodile skin. Leather-lined, heavy-duty brass hardware; top-push lock with a key and side catches. (W 11-inch by H 6-inch by D 5 ½ -inch). Blind-stamped: M 10 24X. England, ca 1899-1900.

Luxurious English alligator *travel cases*, dating back to the second half of the 19th century, represented the top of the line. Commissioned for important clients, aristocracy and royalty to travel in comfort and style, they were properly monogrammed and outfitted with full sets of vanity items and toiletries made of gilt sterling and natural tortoise. Crafted with utmost care from splendidly pliable skins and linings of velvet, silk moiré or leather, these remarkable antiques in excellent condition are extremely rare today and can sell at auctions for up to $3,000.

Amazing, Victorian daytime purse made of hornback crocodile skin and appointed with a heavy German silver Repoussé frame (W 6 ¼ -inch by H 4 ¾ -inch by D 3-inch). Hallmarked: Pat. Feb 27, 1900. American.

Ultra rare, Victorian karung lady's pocketbook, with lavishly articulated sterling silver corners. Kidskin-lined, coin pocket (4 ½ -inch by 3 ¼ -inch). Hallmarked (on sterling corners): Tiffany & Co. Sterling Silver. Blind-stamped (on the skin): Tiffany & Co. New York, Snake. American, ca 1890s.

As women's lives and activities became more diverse in both Europe and America, demand for handbags suited to particular occasions spawned a new industry: handbag manufacturing. Bulky, luggage-type satchels were transformed into portable, attractive, daytime handbags and *châtelaine* purses with belt fasteners.

Dainty, genuine alligator châtelaine purse. Metal frame with fancy embossing, ball-catch, chain, and belt-attachment. Front handkerchief pocket, fully suede-lined. (W 6 ½ -inch by H 7 ¼ -inch). American, 1896-1897. In 1897, a smaller style (4 ½ -inch by 4 ¾ -inch) cost $1.25.

Above: Museum-quality, Victorian opera-pouch made of alligator skin, with heavily embossed sterling silver frame in Repoussé design. Leather-lined. (W 8 ½ -inch by H 9-inch by D 2 ½ -inch). Hallmarked: 800 (European, possibly German); ca 1890s.

Those early handbags, made from expensive, durable crocodile skins, were fitted with multiple compartments for a fan, money, eye glasses, and later on a lighter and cigarettes. Alligator purses for afternoon sported ornate frames in elaborate repoussé designs featuring cupids, flowers, birds, or serpents. Those with sterling silver frames were hallmarked to confirm their production date and maker. Carved cameos, garnets, coral, and seed pearls were often used in their ornamentation.

Scarce, Victorian java-lizard opera-pouch, with a beautifully appointed Repoussé silver frame. Suede-lined. (W 8 ½ -inch by H 8 ½ -inch). American, ca 1890s.

The most astounding among them were leather-lined *opera pouches* with lavishly articulated sterling silver frames. Absolutely unique and handmade in black alligator or Java lizard, these are very hard to find today.

By the turn of the 20th century, alligator daytime handbags were sold in small specialty shops throughout America.

Montgomery Ward and Sears catalogs offered a good selection of alligator and "alligator grained" leather lady's purses and Gladstone bags, for 48-hour delivery anywhere in the country.

A new material, keratol, was introduced in 1902 as a substitute for leather and was widely used for embossing.

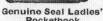

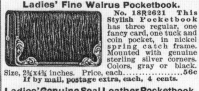

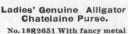

Sears, Roebuck & Co. Catalog handbags ad, 1897.

EDWARDIAN EARLY 20TH CENTURY

The Edwardian period, 1902 to the early 1920s, began when Queen Victoria's son was crowned King Edward VII of England. He brought cosmopolitan flair to the arts and fashion following restraints of the Victorian era. *"Appearances are never unimportant,"* advertised Mark Cross in 1902.

Sears, Roebuck & Co. Merchandise Catalog ads. **Top left and bottom:** Fall/Winter 1914-1915. **Top right:** Kraus McKeever & Adams handbags ad, *The Jewelers' Circular* November 30, 1921.

King Edward's love of elegance and his appreciation of quality translated into a new trend for gentlemen's accessories. Crocodile wallets, flasks, document portfolios, cigar cases, desktop accessories, and other small articles trimmed with silver and decorated with sporting and golf motifs were popular at the time and have become collectible today.

Edwardian gentleman set.
Left: Sterling silver and crocodile skin hip spirit-flask (5 ½ -inch high). Hallmarked: Mappin & Webb 2 Queen Victoria Street. Birmingham, England, 1902.
Right: Crocodile skin desk-top set (ink-well and vesta), measure W 1 ¾ -inch by H 1 ¾ -inch; England, ca 1903.

Edwardian gentleman ring-lizard wallet or card case, trimmed with sterling silver, lined in chamois leather. (W 5 ½ -inch by H 3 ½ -inch). Hallmarked: Chester, England, ca 1900.

The growth of domestic and trans-Atlantic travel by the turn of the 20th century created high demand for traveling accessories. Mark Cross, B. Altman & Co., Macy's, Bergdorf Goodman, and Bloomingdale's, among other retail stores, started to offer a great assortment of brass-trimmed, leather-lined alligator *carryalls* and Gladstone *valises*. Other accessories made from exotic skins included carriage bags, medicine cases, fitted traveler's cases, jewel boxes, and flasks in all sizes and colors.

Outstanding, expertly-crafted, Nile crocodile Gladstone, lined in green moire. Pliable skins, polished solid-brass hardware. The expandable pouch on the front (two pull-closures, special slots and compartments). A monogram under the luggage-type handle. (W 14 ½ -inch by H 13-inch with handle by D 10-inch). England, ca 1904-1905.

Popular English Gladstone bags for gentlemen, as well as a wide selection of travel satchels, club bags, trunks and ladies' vanity boxes were made from horn-back or smooth crocodile skins. They came in a great array of sizes: from massive, 22-inch monsters to petite, 8-inch boxes. Often branded with a serial number on the bottom, they were distributed in America by L.E. Morrison & Co. Trunk Factory of Indianapolis. In 1902, you could also buy them from mail-order catalogs.

A prototype of the indispensable tote—an Edwardian leather *shopper* of innovative construction—emerged about 1908. It was a true engineering marvel and became one of the most popular multi-functional styles. Mounted on a new-style, overlapping frame, with solid locks and safe latches, it was fitted with a single or double handle.

Above: Set of early genuine crocodile club-bags, in different sizes. Very tough, large-scaled skins. Both are leather lined, with brass trim, multiple locks, fasteners, and latches. Strong, luggage-type handles. The smaller piece is blind-stamped on the bottom: 12 135. Late 1890-early 1900.

Left: Monumental, daytime handbag made of Nile crocodile (smooth and hornback cuts), with sliding solid-brass fasteners and locking top-clasp. Fully leather lined (attached framed coin-purse). (W 13 ½ -inch by H 8-inch by 2 ¾ -inch D). England, ca 1910-1915.

A new *broken bottom bag* (an accordion bottom, as we know it today) by Simpson Crawford Co. could fold inward when un-loaded and expand fully when loaded. It was beautifully lined in fine calf and made from high-grade crocodile—in costume colors including tan, navy and green. To follow the trend in 1909, Saks & Co. sold similarly fancy shoppers fitted with a coin purse and mirror, powder box, puff, smelling salts, perfume bottle, and card compartments.

Remarkable, forest-green crocodile châtelaine pocketbook, elaborately articulated with etched sterling silver. Leather gussets open wide to 2 ¾ -inch. Open pouch for handkerchief on the top; back pocket, for small knick-knacks. Sterling push-clasp, and metal belt-fastener. Fully leather-lined, with a spacious interior. (W 4 ¾ -inch by H 5-inch) Hallmarked: Birmingham, England, 1901.

Romantic Art Nouveau was one of the styles during this period that, in opposition to Victorian conservatism, exploded with the new aesthetics in art and fashion. It celebrated expressive feminine forms, subtle colors, and sensual, flowing lines depicting flora and fauna. Fine materials—such as tortoise-shell, ivory, carved glass, and gemstone cabochons— became widely used to accessorize at that time.

This was an era of the revival of old styles as well as the creation of new, multi-functional styles suited for travel. Durable-yet-attractive lady's handbags in a variety of leathers and skins, with sterling or enamel adornments, replaced fragile beaded reticules. Crafted by skillful artisans and jewelers, the new handbags had transformed from a utility object into a fashion statement. By 1903, a vast assortment of such daytime and afternoon bags were sold nationwide by the largest retailers, such as Gimbel Brothers, Bonwit Teller, and Mark Cross. Especially popular were marvelous, fashionable *châtelaine purses* in various costume colors.

Above: Highly collectible, genuine alligator music-sheet portfolio, trimmed with sterling silver. Structured top handle; moire-lined. Beautiful workmanship! (W 14 ¾ -inch by H 10 ½ -inch by D 1-inch). Hallmarked: Birmingham, England, 1901 (LK).

Some *châtelaine purses* were made of textured leathers imprinted with alligator, seal, Morocco, or walrus patterns. Genuine alligator and sealskin handbags were by far the most expensive. Special occasion handbags were sometimes trimmed in sterling silver, such as an amazing alligator sheet-music briefcase featured above.

Spectacular, purple crocodile sterling silver pocketbook. Leather gussets, outside pocket and multiple inside compartments, including a coin-purse with a snap; chamois leather-lined. (4 ¾ -inch W by 2 ¼ -inch H). Hallmarked: Birmingham, England, maker Albert Cohen & Co., 1903.

The favorites with the ladies of means were tiny (only 4 ½ by 3 inches) and supple, alligator *pocketbooks*, trimmed with sterling silver. They had calf bottoms and gussets, and were fully lined in soft leather. Priced at $3.19 over a hundred years ago, today the best pieces in stylish forest-green, adorned by sterling silver details, could bring up to $1,000.

The demand for high-quality skins, as well as the new opportunity to deliver them quickly from overseas by steamboats, expanded the industry from Europe to America. Ostrich, lizard, snake and especially quality skins of African crocodiles or American Alligator started being used more frequently in accessories, alone or in combination with smooth, patent leather.

As reported in 1905, leather became very important for making accessories. It was used to make boots and shoes, lady's pocketbooks and handbags, dress suitcases and trunks, traveling bags, belts, gloves, and caps. Specially prepared leathers were also used for millinery and clothing, as well as to accent furniture, carriages, automobiles, and automobile garments.

This perfect, Edwardian Bakelite frame-bag was updated with a newer matte-cobra body – most likely in the late 1960s – when elite New York designers, such as Jacomo, were inspired by Victorian and Edwardian fashion. Lined in luxurious lambskin; brass ball-link strap; glass beads along the frame. Superb quality! (W 13 ½ -inch by H 8-inch by D 3-inch). Frame: ca 1915-1919.

The *envelope* in various sizes and materials was the other newest style. So very modish and exceptionally popular in America, they were made of plush fabrics or leathers, to express the favor for soft textures. When the oyster-color envelopes—embroidered with real pearls—were shown in Paris in 1913, a small sign was placed next to them that read, "For Americans and Duchesses Only." Some of them had a new frame made of *faux tortoiseshell*, which became widely popular for years to come.

By 1914, handbags were viewed as an expression of individual fancy. Makers exhibited no limit of imagination. Many of the new daytime purses looked like miniature satchels. They were mounted on stiff frameworks so that they could stand at the base and hold a great number of things in their little, yet capacious interiors. Others were fitted with a mirror and a powder puff, a pencil and a memorandum pad, a coin purse, tiny scissors, pins, and other little necessities. In the summer of 1914, the leather *vanity box* was launched and received so enthusiastically by New York women.

Manufactures had requisitioned every conceivable kind of material—from monkey fur to Chantilly lace—as well as the time-honored leather. It was represented in a myriad of kinds, such as crocodile and seal, alligator and the newest rhinoceros, walrus and elephant, lizard and pigskin.

Unfortunately, the prosperity of the Edwardian era did not last long and was interrupted by the realities of World War I from 1914 to 1919.

Sears, Roebuck & Co. Catalog handbags ad, 1913-1914.

FLAPPER TWENTIES

The end of the First World War in 1919 brought a breath of fresh air to people's lives—and changed attitudes. Visual arts prevailed in all aspects of life in the 1920s. Chic Art Deco style became the quintessence look of the Roaring Twenties. Almost an entirely American phenomenon, it was, however, born in France and derived its name from the Exposition of Decorative Arts and Modern Manufacturers in Paris in 1925.

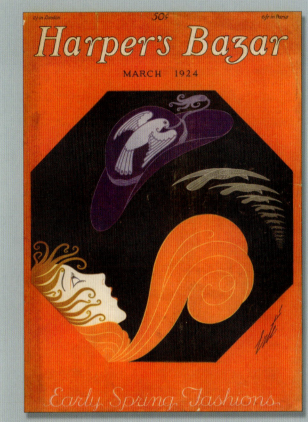

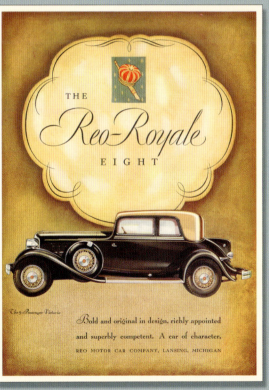

Art Deco merchandise ads. **Top left:** *Harper's Bazaar* cover March 24, 1924. **Top right:** *Montgomery Wards Merchandise Catalog* merchandise ad, 1928-1929. **Bottom left:** Accessories ad, *Vogue* October 1, 1926. **Bottom right:** *Vogue* ad, 1924

One-of-a-kind, olive alligator purse with pleated leather top and stunning, heavily beaded frame decorated with cloisonné accents, in rainbow colors. Leather interior, snake-chain strap. (W 7 ¼ – inch by H 7 ½ – inch by D 1 ½ -inch). France, ca 1920s.

In this age of decadence, prohibition, jazz, and the Charleston, it was crucial for society women to be flapper-fashionable: short hair, red lips, flat figures, oceans of fringe and swinging pearls, and huge dark eyes sparkling from under low brims. For the first time, French designers showed the clothes with shorter hemlines. Easy and comfortable to wear, they were loose and sexy. Dresses had fullness around the hips; coats were wrapped low. The fluidity of the silhouette was achieved by manipulation of adaptable, textured fabrics, such as silk, velvet, moiré, and brocade.

Upscale, sterling silver mesh purse, accented by a jeweled clasp, etched frame, and fringe. The stripe pattern is achieved by interchanging silver sterling with gold-plated sterling. (W 5 ½ -inch by H 6 ½ -inch). Stamped: Whiting & Davis Mesh Bags Reg U.S., Pat'd Sterling. American, ca 1922.

Delicate, moon-shaped clutch made of classy olive lizard. Polished chrome hardware. Satin interior trimmed with skin, attached coin-purse and mirror. (W 9 ¾ -inch by H 5 ¼ -inch). France, ca 1924.

The color combinations in rich earth colors were legion. Fashion definitely favored red, but the most important and especially striking was black; it dominated to appear alone or in color combinations.

Superb, black crocodile Art Deco clutch! Tailored gussets; sterling silver clasp articulated with black enamel and marcasites; satin-lined. (W 10-inch by H 6-inch). Unsigned. France, ca 1925-1927.

Edwardian platinum and diamonds had become the base for Art Deco accents. Rubies, emeralds, sapphires, coral, lapis, and jade were often added to achieve a bold color palette. Imitation gems—combined with *marcasite* and rhinestones—decorated the enameled or silver frames on evening purses. Gold-toned frames demonstrated a strong Egyptian influence, in the forms of falcons and sphinxes.

Art Deco Jewelry Mode ad (*Vogue*, October 1, 1926).

The uncluttered, top-handled pouch from Paris evolved into a new model, with no handle—an innovative *underarm clutch*. Although the handbag had been launched as a style item earlier, by 1925 it steadily grew in importance as a fashion necessity.

Sleek, genuine crocodile clutch trimmed with sterling silver. Leather gussets, moire lining; attached coin purse; adjustable back-handle. (W 9-inch by H 8-inch). Hallmarked: Frankfurt, Germany, 800. Labeled: Dr. Albersheim Frankfurt AM. Germany, ca 1924-1925.

The ravishing mode of the 1920s demanded a different bag for every occasion and every costume. A tailored 'gator envelope—for sports, a spacious croc' swagger for shopping, an antelope pouch on a gleaming frame jeweled with marcasite or gems to take to a luncheon or tea, a lovely Aubusson needlepoint bag for a theater date or a fun night out.

Montgomery Ward & Co.'s Fall/Winter Merchandise Catalog handbags ad, 1928-1929.

Casual daytime handbags were created from sturdy, durable leathers intended for long service. Afternoon styles were fashioned from chic skins. Department stores promoted vast collections of high-quality handbags—imported or domestic—made from genuine alligator and crocodile, ostrich, reptile grain, seal, calf, and antelope. Amazing imports, reflecting the fashions of the world, were delivered from Europe by boat several times a year.

Exquisite, genuine iguana-lizard pouch, with braided leather handle; silver clasp; suede-lined. (W 8 ½ – inch by H 7-inch). Matching faux-lizard notebook, with sterling silver trim (W 8 ½ – inch by H 6 ½ - inch). Hallmarked: 900 Gertrude. Labeled: Gristav Gruber, Wien I., Rotenturm str.22. Austria, 1928.

Special, genuine ostrich suitcase made of two whole cuts of full-quill skins. Brass locks (original key); hand-stitched; moire-lined. (W 15 ¾ -inch by H 10-inch by D 5-inch). Unused solid-brass monogram included: RB. Labeled: Genuine Ostrich. England, ca 1920s.

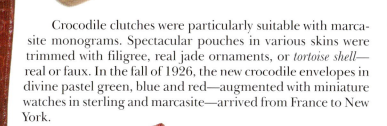

Crocodile clutches were particularly suitable with marcasite monograms. Spectacular pouches in various skins were trimmed with filigree, real jade ornaments, or *tortoise shell*—real or faux. In the fall of 1926, the new crocodile envelopes in divine pastel green, blue and red—augmented with miniature watches in sterling and marcasite—arrived from France to New York.

Elite, crocodile Porosus, Art Deco clutch. Crafted from a single, whole, central belly-cut of superb symmetry. Tailored gussets, flap closure. No hardware! Satin-lined, fitted coin-purse with attached mirror. Complete with a leather note-book (gilded paper edges, gold-plated pencil, still in working order!), hallmarked 'Cassegrain-Paris'. (W 10 ¼ -inch by H 6 ¼ – inch). France, ca 1925-1926.

In 1925, the first French marvels by Coco Chanel were brought to America by Saks Fifth Avenue stores, and were replicated for mass production. Among them, there were beautifully fitted underarm bags of lizard-calf and antelope, with a huge knob of snakeskin—"so in accord with modernity!" Opulent French under-the-arm styles in saffian or boa-snake on gilt frames were finished in a meticulous manner, with sterling silver, 14-karat gold, pearl, or amber-inlaid accents.

Art Deco handbags ads. **Top left:** February 1926 (Chanel's New Bag at Saks Fifth Avenue). **Bottom left:** December 1926 (Genuine Aubusson, Beauvais or Petit Point Handbags at Saks – Gerald Square). **Center:** May 1930 (Bags with Prystal at Russeks Fifth Avenue). **Right:** October 1926 (The New Umbrella Handbags at Saks Fifth Avenue).

The unbreakable *Prystal*—a new, hard plastic that resembled crystal—revolutionized Art Deco handbag fashion in 1930, when over 10,000 leather styles by Lanvin, Patou and Chanel, all trimmed with plain or carved Prystal, were offered at the largest handbag event of the decade. Another hard plastic material, Galalith, was widely used to adorn a greatest variety of leather and skin clutches and envelopes.

Alligator-grain pouch, with a faux-shell frame and fixtures. Fabric-lined interior, attached coin-purse, and encased beveled mirror. (W 7 ¾ -inch by H 7-inch). Provenance: Similar pouches were advertised by Saks – Gerald Square in December 1925.

Soft, leather pouch accented by a carved French Galalith clasp, and Elephant plaque. Moire lining; flat back-handle. (W 8 ¾ – inch by H 7-inch). Labeled: Made in France. France, ca 1929.

The American debut of the new European imports exhibited fabulous *matching sets* of skin handbags and silk umbrellas, with handles articulated in carved ivory, tortoise, stone, or Galalith—like the featured Parisian set in coffee brown. It was truly a phenomenal example of Art Deco's practical luxury, indeed!

Museum quality, genuine alligator clutch-set, complete with original silk umbrella. Elegantly articulated by carved Bakelite trim. Built-in mirror and coin purse; fabric lining. (Unfolded W 9 ½ -inch by H 17 ½ -inch by D 2-inch; folded W 9-inch by H 6 ½ -inch). France. Provenance: Similar sets were advertised by Saks Fifth Avenue in October 1926.

In 1928, the majority of women were buying more handbags than ever, about four a season. To satisfy the increasing demand, a remarkable assortment was produced domestically and imported from France, Italy, and England.

Petite, genuine alligator clutch with a brass monogram and leather gussets. Moire-lined, with an attached mirror. (W 8 ¼ -inch by 4 ½ -inch by D 1-inch). American, ca 1927.

Astounding, micro-beaded, Art Deco style cocktail pouch. Enameled frame studded with sparkling rhinestones. Glass and cut-metal (gold and silver) beads. Satin-lined. (W 9-inch by H 8 ½ -inch). Labeled: Freddy 10 Rue Auber – Paris tel. Ric. 78 08 Made in France. Possibly 1950s reproduction.

Lovely, pony-skin vanity. Gold-plated scroll trim. Built-in mirror; pleated pig-skin interior. (W 8-inch by H 4-inch by D 1 ¾ -inch). Ca late 1920s.

In addition, skillful replicas of popular designs by celebrated French couturiers—Chanel, Lanvin, Patou, Molyneux, and Vionnet— were copied in the United States for sale in various department stores, such as Bonwit Teller, Saks Fifth Avenue, Saks-Herald Square, Lord & Taylor, Gimbel Brothers, Russeks, B. Altman & Co., Stern Brothers, John, Koch & Co., Arnold Constable, and RH Macy's & Co. They were also offering domestically produced, affordable horn-back crocodile and alligator handbags, as well as a variety of crocodile-grain leather pouches.

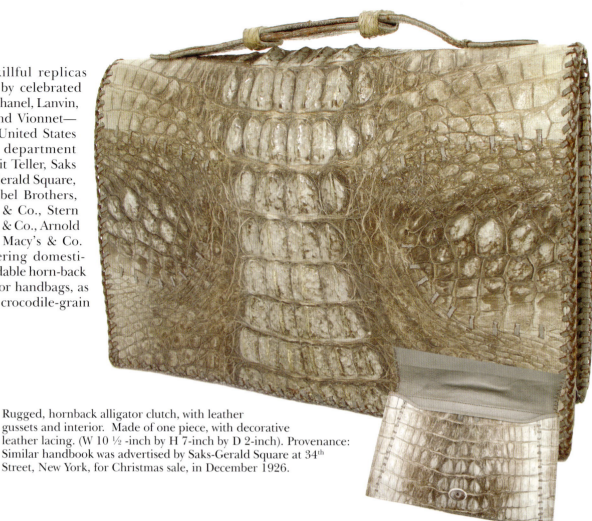

Rugged, hornback alligator clutch, with leather gussets and interior. Made of one piece, with decorative leather lacing. (W 10 ½ -inch by H 7-inch by D 2-inch). Provenance: Similar handbook was advertised by Saks-Gerald Square at 34th Street, New York, for Christmas sale, in December 1926.

The importance of furs—as a part of the trend for texture diversity—was tremendous, representing about thirty animals, including ermine, mink, fox, broadtail, lynx, blue hare, bear, leopard, zebra, squirrel, nutria, chinchilla, and many others.

Compact, genuine hornback baby-alligator shopper. Leather lining; swivel coin-purse; leather braided strap; welted seams; brass Inner-Grip frame. (W 9 ½ -inch by H 6 ½ -inch). Stamped (frame): Jemco U.S.A. Pat 1915.313. American.

Art Deco handbags, ca 1925-1929, France. **Top left:** Petite, needlepoint vanity, satin-lined. Brass filigree frame encrusted with carved, semi-precious jade and carnelian. (W 9 ½ -inch by H 6 ½ – inch). **Top right:** Silk evening pouch, intricately embroidered with silk-cord. Brass-filigree frame with faux pearls and garnet cabochons. (W 9-inch by H 6-inch). **Center:** Brown suede wristlet, trimmed with sterling silver (marcasites and white cloisonné). Purple moire lining. (W 5 ½ – inch by H 4-inch, 5 ¾ -inch loop-handle). **Bottom left**: Brown morocco-leather clutch, with brightly polished silver trim, moire lining, swivel coin-purse, back handle. Bold, French Galalith detail imitating ivory. (W 7-inch by H 5 ¼ -inch). **Bottom right:** Evening brocade purse, with a beautifully etched frame. Elaborate pull-clasp, with brass-filigree and carved carnelian. Satin interior. (W 9 ¼ – inch by H 5-inch).

In the center of the formal Art Deco ensemble was a divine evening purse painstakingly beaded, embroidered, woven, or studded—by hand—in a head-spinning variety of styles. Lined in scrumptious silks or decadent kid, and fitted with new coin purses and mirrors, they created the most intimate personal space for a night out. By the end of the 1920s, the crisp symmetry of the early Art Deco style had been gradually transformed into a flow of curvy lines of the feminine 1930s.

L'adylike Thirties

The self-indulgent Art Deco period ruled for almost a decade. However, when the Great Depression occurred in 1929, very few people could afford to be fashionable anymore. Most women were happy with a simple, warm dress and a practical, low-priced handbag.

1930s fashion and merchandise ads. **Top left:** *Vogue* cover September 1, 1934. **Top right:** *Vogue* ad, September 1, 1934. **Bottom left:** Chanel, Schiaparelli Jewelry ad, *Vogue* March 15, 1938. **Bottom right:** Azka handbag with Prystal strap-anchors ad, *Vogue* September 1, 1934.

Unique, genuine alligator clutch, with softly pleated front. Moire lining. Ornamented by rarely-found-today carved Prystal frame accents. (W 11 ½ -inch by H 7 ½ -inch by D 2-inch). American, ca 1934.

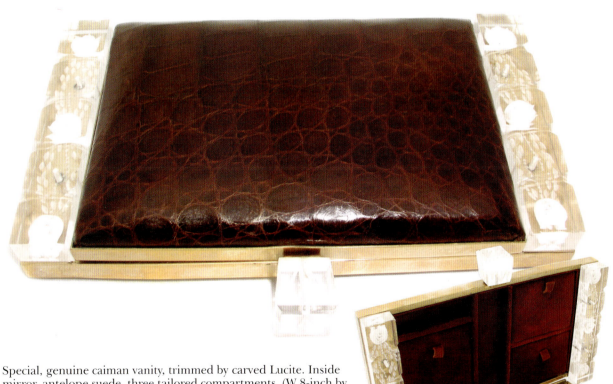

Special, genuine caiman vanity, trimmed by carved Lucite. Inside mirror, antelope suede, three tailored compartments. (W 8-inch by H 4 ¼ -inch by D 1-inch). Labeled: E 8151 Art 57 Caiman Cabra Antilopada Industria Argentina. Argentina, ca late 1930s.

Expensive leather bags were out of reach for most people, which motivated manufacturers to experiment with composition materials to lower their costs. *Vinyl, Bakelite, French Galalith* and *Prystal* were widely used during this period of economic despair—a time that became one of the most creative decades in the history of fashion, so rich in amazing designer talent.

The 1930s mode was marked by the transformation of the boyish style of the Flapper era into dramatic femininity and romanticism. It was strongly influenced by a group of talented French couturiers and led by an especially prolific Parisian designer, Madame Elsa Schiaparelli. Her extravagant vision literally defined the dramatic mode of the late 1930s and the practicality of the 1940s. During those hard times, in collaboration with artist Salvador Dali, she created amazing handbags. *"In difficult times,"* Elsa remarked, *"fashion is always outrageous."*

Exceptionally rare–museum-quality–The Lanterne Bag made of genuine crocodile. It was created by Elsa Schiaparelli in collaboration with Salvador Dali, in 1938. Feminine lines, shiny skins, 24K-gilt trim, leather interior, with a coin purse. It features a flash-light mechanism, installed under the frame, which also serves as a little vanity featuring a mirror, and lipstick case. Incredible imagination! Push the button to turn on the lantern – and you can see the insides of the purse even in the dark. Convenient! The mechanism (with a battery) is 24K-plated, and beautifully engraved with the Dali's sketch picturing a lounging Goddess. Amazing! (W 9 ½ -inch by H 7-inch by D 3 ½ -inch). Signed (interior): Made in France. Labeled (lantern): Straeter Lite-On Guaranteed 24 carat gold finish.

"I Dream about an Evening Dress," by Dali

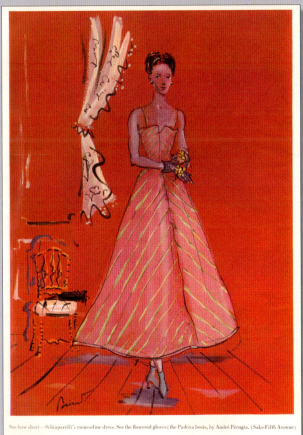

See how short—Schiaparelli's mousseline dress. See the flowered gloves; the Padova boots, by André Pérugia. (Saks-Fifth Avenue)

1930s fashion and merchandise ads. **Top left:** Schiaparelli designs ad, *Vogue* January 15, 1937. **Top right:** "I dream about an evening dress" ad by Dali, *Vogue* March 15, 1937. **Bottom left:** Schiaparelli dress ad, *Vogue* March 15, 1937. **Bottom right:** Chanel dress ad, Vogue March 15, 1938.

The Art Deco style of the 1930s became a pinnacle of ingenuity. A vast variety of handbag shapes, sizes and handles were invented: a top handle, a back handle, a drawstring, or no handle at all. *Double-deckers, bracelet bags* and *boudoir bags*—outfitted with full sets of makeup accessories—made up a kaleidoscope of choices to complement sweet and tidy fashion by day and real glamor by night.

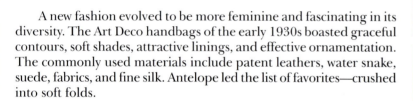

Impressive, genuine alligator double-decker vanity, with folding zig-zag hinges. Leather-lined. (W 6 ½ -inch by H 3 ¼ -inch by d 3 ½ -inch). Signed: Genuine Alligator Made in Cuba. Ca late 1930s. Featured with a genuine turquoise set (brooch and earrings), by Grosse, Germany, 1968.

A new fashion evolved to be more feminine and fascinating in its diversity. The Art Deco handbags of the early 1930s boasted graceful contours, soft shades, attractive linings, and effective ornamentation. The commonly used materials include patent leathers, water snake, suede, fabrics, and fine silk. Antelope led the list of favorites—crushed into soft folds.

A group of lovely exotic skin handbags from the 1930s, in different skins and styles. **Top left:** Petite, alligator-skin clutch, with a hornback inlay. Welted seams; flat back-handle; solid-brass frame stamped Jemco (U.S.A. Pat 1.915.313); Inner-Grip clasp; suede interior, attached wallet. (W 9 ½ -inch by H 6 ¾ -inch). Unsigned. Ca 1932. **Top right:** Adorable, bell-shaped, ring-lizard wristlet. Pleated and padded sides; satin-lined. (W 9-inch by H 6 ½ -inch without handle by D 4-inch). Unsigned. Ca 1930s. **Bottom left:** Shapely, genuine crocodile wristlet, suede-lined. Tightly-scaled skins. Unique, solid-brass lever clasp. (W 9 ½ -inch by H 9-inch without handle by D 2 ¾ -inch). Labeled: Belle Handbag New York. American, ca 1939. **Bottom right:** Lovely, genuine lizard bracelet-purse. Severely tailored, tapered body; rounded gussets; circle-handles; belt-closure. (W 12-inch by H 10 ½ -inch by D 4-inch). Signed: Styles by California Alligator Co. American, ca 1937.

Dashing, red alligator-skin vanity purse, with 24K-gilt trim. Magnificent, etched filigree lift-clasp. Interior mirror, suede lining, tailored compartments, individual covers and pulls. (W 7-inch by H 5-inch by D 1-inch). Argentina, ca 1934.

Fashion still dictated an appropriate handbag for each costume. Street clothes were sharply distinguished from the formal ones – hence the same bag for both occasions was out of the question. The greatest array of envelopes and pouches accompanied street clothes. They were softly gathered or stiff, with massive frames or no frames, with back-straps or top-handles. There was also a considerable difference in proper size. The satchels for street wear were large enough for shopping, whereas the afternoon purses were usually small, barely able to fit a compact, a change purse, and a handkerchief.

Glossy, genuine alligator satchel, with woven-brass handles. Self-covered frame; leather-lined; attached coin-purse. (W 9 ½ -inch by H 7 ½ -inch by D 2-inch). Stamped (mirror case): I. Magnin Inc. & Co. Signed: Koret Made of Genuine Alligator. American, 1935. Provenance: Similar bag is shown in the 1935 Lewis handbags ad (page 40).

Pretty, genuine cobra arm-purse, with an innovative closure– a chained pin. Leather-lined, Talon-zipper. (W 7 ½ -inch by H 6-inch without handle by D 3 ½ -inch). Signed: Viki Original. Ca 1939.

Cute, pleated tegu-lizard wristlet (central-belly cut). Lucite button-closure, bracelet handle. Fabric-lined, with a mirror. (W 9-inch by H 6 ½ -inch by D 2 ½ -inch). American, ca 1934.

The significant change in the daytime handbag design can be traced back to the fall of 1930. There were so many innovations and improvements! Size was no longer an obstacle in the carrying of cigarettes, engagement books, or letters. Generous proportions of the new shoppers, together with the preservation of their slim outlines and flat profile, became possible due to the latest innovation—the widening of side gussets.

Stylish, genuine alligator arm-purse. Domed, solid-brass frame, front push-clasp. Lined in luxurious suede, with a cased round mirror. (W 9 ¾ -inch by H 8 ½ -inch by D 3 ½ -inch). Brazil, ca 1936.

In the spring of 1930, the nation was preoccupied with the Great Depression that led to a great deal of unemployment. The handbag industry was no exception. To solve this problem, manufacturers offered affordable replicas of the best couturier creations.

Genuine hornback alligator clutch, made on 1-piece cut. Welted seams, faille interior, skin-trimmed interior pockets. (W 9-inch by H 8-inch by D 1 ½ -inch). American or English, ca early 1930s.

However, not everybody was pinching pennies during the Depression. The discreet luxury of a deceivingly simple purse accented with precious metal or gemstones was also characteristic of that decade. Such elite purses were custom-made by the renowned houses of Hermes, Cartier, Koret, and Lewis and became the first designer *It* bags. The notion of a status handbag was brought to light.

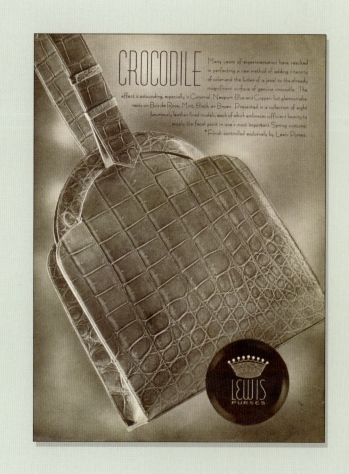

Lewis crocodile handbag ad, *Vogue* 1938.

It was also the time when a whimsical figural purse was born. In addition to a fashion statement, a handbag became a pop-art object to display or wear.

Unique, snakeskin arm-purse, shaped as a bird-house. Quite a complex construction, and great attention to detail! Lid-cover, with a snap-closure; roomy interior neatly lined in quality leather. Very well made! (5 ½ -inch in diameter by H 8-inch). Unsigned. Ca 1936.

A trend toward formality was reflected in the tendency to glorify frames for formal wear. Made of heavy gilt metal, curved or square, the new elite styles were set with huge—real or faux—pearls, corals, turquoise and crystal, or delicate patterns of marcasite. Lift-locks were fashioned from carved Prystal, Galalith, or jade. Real tortoise shell often adorned the frames. The image of elegance—with its long, slender lines—was a keynote for formal afternoons. The decorations distinguished small, formal pocketbooks from larger, casual satchels made of leather or skin.

Lavish, embroidered velvet bracelet-purse, accented by a magnificent gold-plated frame, with huge, semi-precious cabochons. Burgundy leather interior. (W 11-inch by H 10-inch by D 3-inch). Signed: Koret. Ca late 1930s.

Alligator skins of smooth, perfectly matched grains were polished to present a mirror-like surface, and then they were severely tailored. Delightfully soft skin pouches of a completely round shape—with a calm, matte finish—were presented as the latest craze, equipped with a peculiar innovation: *a talon fastener* (a zipper, as we know it today). Smooth in operation, it guaranteed full security that the contents would stay inside.

Playful, pliable java lizard canteen-purse, with a newly fashionable, Talon-fastener, prominently displayed right on the top. Black moire interior, red leather trim. (8 ½ -inch in diameter, W 2 ½ -inch). Labeled: Saks Fifth Avenue. Provenance: Advertised in March 1, 1938 issue of *Vogue*.

By 1934, gracious curves and rounded silhouettes were seen prominently in all fashion designs, contrasting the clean geometry of 1920s Art Deco styles. Leather purses were tailored in a newly feminine manner—with oblong shapes, softened edges, and an abundance of ruffles and pleats.

Fantastic, genuine cobra-skin clutch, with a large brass clasp; back handle; and satin-lined interior. (W 14-inch by H 8 ½ -inch by D 3 ½ -inch). Labeled: Wilshire Original. American, ca 1934.

Different, triangle shoulder pouch made of python skin, with antiqued brass frame, and a fancy brass chain-strap; suede-lined. (W 12-inch in widest part by H 11-inch by D 3-inch). Unsigned. Ca 1937.

In 1935, Coco Chanel, Jean Patou and Elsa Schiaparelli led the fashion trend toward slightly shorter skirts to make the softer sex even more innocent. Immediately, the trend was reflected in handbag designs.

Handbags Ad, *Vogue* 1937.

The 1935 mode was marked by the peaceful co-existence of the vanishing Art Deco and the emerging Retro styles that were defined by a wealth of softer lines. So important in its aesthetic impact, the Retro style of the late 1930s emerged as a treasure box of new fashion ideas. Beautiful, unusually shaped handbags by Corde, constructed from silk cord sewn together in attractive motifs, became a hit with younger ladies.

Picturesque, silk-corded clutch, with a pair of twisted, clear Lucite bracelet handles. Lined in faille. (W 11 ¾ -inch by 7-inch by D 1 ¾ -inch). Signed: Genuine Corde. Ca 1936-1937.

Luxurious alligator clutch, with tailored, pleated front. Curved, silver-tone frame; flat top-handle can be expanded to be used as an arm-purse. Welted seams. Lined in quality leather, with an original mirror in a leather sleeve. (W 14-inch by H 9-inch by D 3-inch). Brazil, ca late 1930s – early 1940s.

The period from 1936 to 1938 saw a true "reptile galore," when skin bags were primarily imported from France and England. Many one-of-a-kind styles featured extravagant shell frames and braided handles. Luxurious, easy-to-drape Mexican alligator was considered the aristocrat of genuine skins. Certain popular styles, sold exclusively at specialty stores, started to be recognized by the names of their makers.

Awesome, top-quality shopper made of whole, hornback, baby-alligator skin. Intact feet; massive, Bakelite duplet-frame. Suede-lined, attached coin-purse, zippered compartment. Truly amazing! (W 12-inch by H 8 ½ -inch by D 3-inch). Braided strap is possibly a replacement. European, ca 1938.

Smart,
English Kit Bag made
of patched crocodile skin. Riveted leather frame; heavy-duty brass side-fasteners; front push-lock; folding leather gussets; suede interior; and attached coin purse. First introduced in the Edwardian era, this particular model was in demand for decades and sold all across America. (W 11 ½ -inch by H 7 ½ -inch by D 5-inch). English import. Provenance: Advertised by Macy's in September 1936.

1930s handbags ads. **Top left:** Advertisement of the Talon Fastener in Handbags, Vogue March 1, 1938. **Top right:** Lewis handbag ad, Harper's Bazaar, 1935. **Bottom left:** Lewis handbag ad, Harper's Bazaar, 1934. **Bottom right:** Talon fastener ad, Vogue March 15, 1939.

Restrictions of metals decreased its use in handbags, and manufacturers substituted it with plastics and wood. As a result, the first wartime restrictions and shortages dictated a more practical approach to fashion. As a result, the first wartime collection in Paris in October 1939 demonstrated a complete change in style. In an interview during a brief visit to New York in 1939, Elsa Schiaparelli predicted that *"the simple, practical mode would eventually replace the fussiness, which no longer belonged with the spirit of the time."*

A hat was no longer regarded as an "elaborate piece of nonsense", but became a functional covering for the head. Handbags, suppressed for several years in Europe, exploded in legions of new, practical, hand-free styles for the sensible 1940s.

Among travel bags, a smart, graceful English Kit Bag was popular. Long familiar throughout the world as a "boon companion," it came equipped with end latches and a tiny lock and a key.

During the productive period of 1936 to 1939, the high-fashion styles—French originals and their replicas—were sold side by side with domestically made "utility values." The familiar styles of pouch, envelope, back-strap, and swagger remained, all equipped with the new interior slide-fastener (zipper) made of metal. In 1939, women across the world fell in love with finely patterned wool tweed garments. The favorite Paris hat style was definitely the beret.

The growing shortage of leather and strategic metals during the war prompted technological experimentation with plastics, resulting in the creation of two important innovations: a plastic zipper and a new composition material, *Lucite*. A patented mixture of several ingredients, this hard, clear, plastic became broadly used for handbags and other accessories, along with Art Deco Prystal, faux tortoise shell, and Bakelite.

PRACTICAL FORTIES

In the 1940s, as the world was preoccupied with World War II, the dynamics of society had changed, once again. Women became more actively engaged in social causes and represented a growing part of the workforce. There was not much room for over-the-top femininity, long skirts, or petite purses with sparkling gems.

1940s fashion and merchandise ad. **Top left:** *Vogue* cover March 1, 1940. **Top right:** Holzer handbag ad, *Town & Country* 1946. **Bottom left**: Coro Craft jewelry ad, *Vogue* October 1944. **Bottom right:** *Vogue* ad, June 1949.

To-die-for, genuine alligator satchel with massive, scalloped Bakelite frame, studded with brass rivets. The softest, pleated skins. Rolled, twisted handles. Kidskin interior (comb, coin-purse, leather-backed mirror). Outrageously gorgeous and desirable! (W 12-inch by H 8 ½ -inch by D 5-inch). Ca 1946-1948.

Left: Ample, caiman-skin travel bag, with gilt trim, side latches, and top sliding clasp. Floating hinges. Lined in black leather; gray leather trim (belted slots for small items). Coin purse, mirror, and a pair of gloves. (W 12-inch by H 12 ½ -inch by D 5 ½ -inch). Marked: IRV (logo). Switzerland, ca 1948-1949.

The broad-shouldered Retro fashions and shorter hemlines replaced the graceful look of the 1930s. It did not take long for handbag designs to catch up with the general trend. From stylish and whimsical, decorative and elite, they became bold, large and useful. They highlighted practicality and a noticeable lack of ornamentation.

The dominant silhouette was slender, yet slightly boxy, with padded shoulders and almost-knee-length skirt – a new American look in development since 1941. It started from the head—ideally small—sharply outlined by either short, shingled hair or smooth, long hair. In the early 1940s, the fashion palette was brilliantly spotted with color, with the prints still prevailing. Later on, darker, more sophisticated shades of solid, earthy colors prevailed.

Vogue handbags ads, from the 1940s. **Top left:** September 15, 1940. **Top right:** October 15, 1940. **Bottom left:** May 1944. Bottom right: 1945.

Bold, genuine caiman clutch, with a snap-closure; leather-lined interior trimmed with skin. (W 14 ½ -inch by H 7-inch by D 2-inch). Signed: Industria Argentina Made in Argentina. Provenance: Similar style was advertised by Gimbels in their March 16, 1947 advertisement.

Simplicity and durability were the highlights of hand-bag styles in the 1940s. The emphasis was on casual bags for daywear, with a growing trend toward dressy, oversized, tuck-under-the-arm types or smaller, Bakelite-trimmed, double-handled shoppers with double handles.

Lady-like, roomy lizard purse, with a bold, curvy Bakelite frame trimmed with brass. Fabric interior. (W 11 ½ -inch by H 9-inch by D 4-inch). Labeled: Genuine Lizard by Bass. American, ca 1946.

Ironically, despite the restrictions on leather during the war, both in Europe and the United States, the handbags grew five times larger, sometimes over 13-inch long! Manufacturers argued that the gigantic size was a necessity, rather than a fashion trend, which had emerged from France. Parisian ladies—presumably because of a lack of cars and taxis—needed a larger bag to fit the number of papers they carried that did not exist before the war.

Marvelous, quilted genuine alligator clutch. Lined in black rayon faille, with red-leather trim. (W 14-inch by H 9-inch by D 2 ½ -inch). Unsigned Deitsch. American, ca 1940-1943.

Hands-free styles became indispensable,
such as the *shoulder bag* and a *wrist bag*.

Cute, pear-shaped genuine cobra wristlet, lined in rayon taffeta.
(W 8-inch by H 10-inch by D 3-inch). Unsigned. American.
Provenance: Similar styles, in alligator and snakeskin, were
advertised by Macy's in October 1948 (Columbus Day Sale).

Shiny, caiman shoulder bag, with an adjustable strap.
Welted seams; accordion gussets and bottom; huge,
beautifully tailored lambskin interior. So plush! Practical,
yet elegant and classy. (W 13 ½ -inch by H 10 ½ -inch by
D 4-inch). Dual signature: Pisk Buenos Aires (stamped on
the underfold); and Caiman Industria Argentina (fabric
label sewn into the interior). Brazil/Argentina, ca 1944.

When leather was restricted, American makers switched their attention to suitable fabrics.
The most popular became *broadcloth*, 100% wool
that closely resembled the finest suede in finish,
softness and luster. It was perfect for shirring,
tucking and quilting. Embellished with jeweled
clips and Lucite zipper pulls, capacious broadcloth clutches became a luxury—to rival precious
skins—that went so well with their newly flat
footwear.

Set of handbags from 1944-1946, trimmed with
various types of plastic (Bakelite, Lucite, Prystal, and
Celanese plastic). Top left: Beaded vanity-box, with
a twisted handle, and marvelous, Bakelite lid. Possibly by Magid. Top right: Classy, suede satchel with a
substantial Prystal clasp (L 3 ¾ -inch by W 1 ½ -inch
by ½ -inch). Labeled: Rosenfeld Original. Bottom
left: Petal-soft, broadcloth daytime purse, with a huge
flower-clasp made of clear-n-ruby Lucite (W 4 ¼ -inch
by H 2 ½ -inch). Labeled: Rosenfeld Original. Bottom
right: Amazing, silk-corde purse, with an impressive,
riveted, arch-handle made of two-tone Celanese plastic. (W11-inch by H 10-inch by D 4 ½ -inch). Labeled:
Genuine Corde.

A major fascination with alligator and crocodile had begun in the late 1940s. Because European imports were halted during World War II, French originals—so predominant since the 1920s—were completely replaced by domestic American production by the mid-1940s, and later by *South American imports.*

Examples of the 1940s import from South America. **Top right:** Slim, alligator portfolio-bag, with an unusual lift-plate clasp; wide, gathered arm-handle; tailored kidskin interior, with multi-layered pouches and pockets. (W 11-inch by H 8 ½ -inch by D 1 ½ -inch) Signed: Industria Argentina Made in Argentina. **Bottom right:** Practical alligator satchel, with rolled handles. Wood frame and clasp wrapped in skin. Leather-lined, trimmed with gold-n-red cord. Coin-purse and mirror. (W 9 ¼ -inch by H 10-inch by D 4-inch). Signed: Genuine Alligator Made in Cuba. Provenance: Similar model was advertised by Macy's in October 10, 1948 (Columbus Day Sale).

Consequently, the change resulted in the rapid growth of existing domestic makers, such as Mark Cross, Deitsch Brothers, Koret, Harry Rosenfeld, Coblentz, Evans, and Nettie Rosenstein, as well as the development of new brands, including Menihan, Jana, Josef, Chandler's, and others. A number of American department stores and specialty shops, among them Bonwit Teller, B. Altman & Co., Saks Fifth Avenue, Jay Thorpe, Bloomingdale's, Lord & Taylor, Gimbel Brothers, Tailored Woman, John Wanamaker, Macy's, and Stern Brothers, started selling quality products under their own labels.

1940s handbags ads. **Top left:** Chandler's alligator handbags ad, Vogue 1946. **Top right:** Menihan alligator handbag ad, Town & Country 1946. **Bottom left:** Josef handbag ad, Vogue 1943. **Bottom right:** Jana alligator handbag ad, Harper's Bazaar 1948.

Most desirable were the supple underarm handbag styles in glowing Mexican baby alligator, with generous pleating and handsome faux-amber clasps, created by Rosenfeld for Bergdorf Goodman in 1943. Any woman fortunate enough to own one in those days ranked it among her most-prized possessions, right up with her jewels and furs. Today, they cost a fortune!

One-of-a-kind, alligator clutch in high-fashion style. Generously pleated, supple skins. Enormous size and tons of personality! Unusual, square gussets; thick, welted seams. Astounding, huge Bakelite bullet-clasp, with hammered-brass trim. Spacious, moire-lined interior, accented with tan leather, and a newly-fashionable plastic zipper. (W 16 ½ -inch by H 8-inch by D 4-inch). Signed (authenticity card): Rosenfeld. Ca 1943-1944.

As a result of metal shortages during wartime, the frames, straps and clasps were made of wood or various plastics, such as Lucite, Bakelite, or faux tortoise. The handbags were large and bold, presumably because a trend for extravagance had emerged as a form of escapism. The arguments were purely psychological in nature—women simply wanted more beauty in their lives during those gruesome times.

Impressive, crocodile Porosus frame-bag, with a unique wood frame, lined in sublime, royal-purple leather. (W 12-inch by H 8 ¼ -inch by D 4-inch). Possibly West Germany (American zone), ca 1948.

Oversize, genuine alligator satchel, with a massive mock tortoise-shell frame, and neat leather interior. (W 13 ½ -inch by H 7 ½ -inch by D 4 ½ -inch). Signed (mirror): Richere. Provenance: Very similar styles were offered by Saks-34th – the specialty shop at Herald Square in New York – in October 1946, for $69.50-$39.95.

Later, in the mid- to late 1940s, the rage for grotesquely oversized bags cooled down a bit. Softer, reasonably sized models started to emerge. The clutch returned, but in a more practical, mid-sized version, with softly curved lines to offset the uniform-like silhouette of the clothes. Wide wrist-handles and sturdy top-handles became very popular.

Below: Really cool trio of wrist-bags by De Lumur, Florida – in smart, geometric shapes – made of skin squares encased in plastic. Shaped as baskets, in green lizard, brown alligator and red alligator. Felt bottom, rayon taffeta interior, zippered tops with pulls. Plus, a wallet with matching lining. (W 10-inch to 11-inch by H 5 to 6-inch by D 1 ½ -inch to 4-inch). American. Provenance: Exactly the same styles were presented for the first time by Saks-34th in September 1949, "Real alligator handbags squared off (like handsome mosaic) with simulated tortoise shell". At that time, they cost only $7.98!

Above: Distinctive, faille boat-purse, adorned by an oversize, solid, two-tone Lucite clasp (2 ½ -inch in diameter, H 2-inch). Amazing, carved detail inside. The purse opens by splitting in half, literally, with the interior pocket on the bottom. How unusual! (W 9-inch when closed and 12-inch when opened by H 8-inch by D 7-inch). Labeled on the bottom (inside): Rosenfeld Original. American, ca 1945-1946.

A more generous use of materials allotted by government regulations soon became apparent. The fashion silhouette had changed to a tiny waist, rounded shoulders and puffy hemlines.

In 1946, the attention of the fashion world had eventually shifted from Paris to New York, and American-style handbags grew in importance. They became smaller, with suit-bags, neatly tailored shoulder bags and barrel bags still prevailing.

Unique, folding cobra-skin arm-bag, lined with rayon faille. (W 8 ½ -inch by H 4 ¼ -inch by D 4 ¼ -inch; 13-inch long handle). Labeled: A Wilshire's Original. American. Provenance: A similar twister was advertised as the best Christmas gift by B. Altman & Co. in December 1944.

Capacious alligator wristlet lined in loud-red leather, with original accessories. Pliable, thick skins; impressive details; unexpectedly roomy interior; coin purse. (W 6 ¼ -inch by H 8-inch by D 4-inch). Unsigned. American, ca 1946-1949.

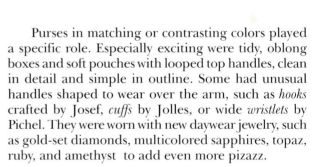

Purses in matching or contrasting colors played a specific role. Especially exciting were tidy, oblong boxes and soft pouches with looped top handles, clean in detail and simple in outline. Some had unusual handles shaped to wear over the arm, such as *hooks* crafted by Josef, *cuffs* by Jolles, or wide *wristlets* by Pichel. They were worn with new daywear jewelry, such as gold-set diamonds, multicolored sapphires, topaz, ruby, and amethyst to add even more pizazz.

Jolles alligator handbag ad, *Vogue* November 1945.

Refined, genuine caiman triplet, with contrast stitching; wood clasp; folding gussets; and luxurious suede interior. No metal parts. (W 10 ½-inch by H 10-inch). Singed: Industria Argentina. Ca 1948.

Practical, genuine caiman travel-box. Luggage-type clasp, with a key; vinyl-lined interior; vanity mirror, and slots for knick-knacks. Gold-tone hardware, protective feet. (W 10 ¾-inch by H 6-inch by D 8-inch). Signed (on the lock): M.R. Canda Argentina Industria. Ca 1946-1948.

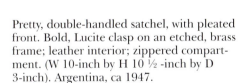

Pretty, double-handled satchel, with pleated front. Bold, Lucite clasp on an etched, brass frame; leather interior; zippered compartment. (W 10-inch by H 10 ½-inch by D 3-inch). Argentina, ca 1947.

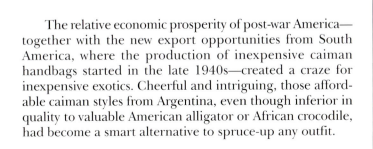

The relative economic prosperity of post-war America—together with the new export opportunities from South America, where the production of inexpensive caiman handbags started in the late 1940s—created a craze for inexpensive exotics. Cheerful and intriguing, those affordable caiman styles from Argentina, even though inferior in quality to valuable American alligator or African crocodile, had become a smart alternative to spruce-up any outfit.

In addition to South American imports, *Vogue* and *Harper's Bazaar* magazines featured the greatest variety of matching sets—a purse and a pair of sturdy platform sling-back shoes—crafted from exotic skins in brilliant colors by premium domestic makers, such as Koret, Deitsch and Lesco. Genuine skin bags clearly went mainstream and rapidly became the trademark of a distinct American look.

Matching set: a double-handled satchel and a pair of sling-platform, both made of supple crocodile. Handbag: Self-covered frame; faille-lined; multiple compartments. Polished, gold-plated accents. (W 9 ½ -inch by H 8-inch by D 4 ½ -inch). Stamped (erroneously): Genuine Alligator. Signed: Pichel. American, ca 1946. Platforms: Palter DeLiso Inc. New York.

The post-war trend revealed a revived interest in high glamor. Inspired by ideals of femininity of the early 1900s, the corseted silhouette, introduced by Christian Dior's "New Look" in 1947, defined the upcoming decade. This dramatic new look was based on a superbly fitted jacket with a tiny "wasp-waist" and a full, calf-length skirt. To complement the look, a slim handbag emerged as the new style star.

Lovely, genuine alligator jewelry box, with a removable tray, lined in luxurious suede. (W 6 ½ -inch by H 3 ½ -inch by D 3 ½ -inch). Ca 1945-1947.

GLAMOROUS FIFTIES

Vibrant, fun and diverse, the "New Look" was an impressive mix of high glamor and casual practicality. An abundance of accessories—worn properly with every outfit for any occasion—was an integral part of the style.

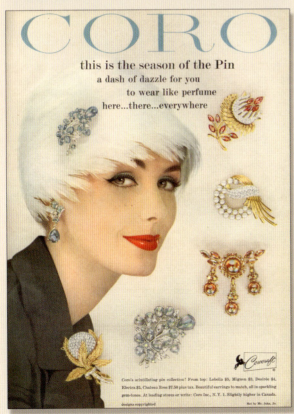

1950s fashion and merchandise ads. **Top left:** Koret alligator saddle-bag ad, *Harper's Bazaar* cover, March 1956. **Top right:** Lucille de Paris crocodile handbag, *Vogue* October 1, 1958. **Bottom left:** Corocraft jewelry, *Vogue* October 1, 1958. **Bottom right:** *Vogue* November 1, 1950.

Softness was a key element in the designs of the early 1950s. A wide variety of purses complemented luscious minks, sexy stilettos, pretty hats with mysterious mesh, glittering artistic faux jewelry, and chandelier earrings.

Elaborate neck scarves, parasols, gloves and fans added a touch of razzle-dazzle to evening outfits made with embroidered organdy and shantung. Illustrating the trend were designs by Hattie Carnegie, Oleg Cassini and Nettie Rosenstein. The slim silhouette and shapely profile was achieved by special undergarments designed by specialists, including Lily of France.

In 1950, special attention was paid to clever styles for larger women. The arsenal of slenderizing tricks to create a younger, slimmer look included vertical stripes, horizontal pleats across the bodice, boleros, elbow-length sleeves to cover the upper arm, and capacious carry-alls.

Smart, genuine crocodile bucket-duffel, with unusual folding closure. Quality! Soft construction: ellipse-shaped body and bottom. Leather-lined. (W 10-inch by H 12-inch when unfolded by D 4 ¾ -inch). Unsigned. European, ca 1950-1951.

Handbag and fashion ad (*Vogue* 1953).

Travel bags in durable alligator and ostrich were elegantly detailed and fitted with huge outside pockets to accommodate passports and tickets.

A set of awesome travel handbags made of genuine alligator skin and lined with red leather. Both have a removable folder with three slots, marked "Passport Papers", "Tickets", and "Money". The interiors feature a roomy swivel wallet, separated in three small compartments. (Small: W 11-inch by H 8 ½ -inch by D 3-inch. Large: W 13-inch by H 9 ½ -inch by 2 ½ -inch). Provenance: These Passport-and-Travel satchels were advertised by Saks Fifth Avenue in their November 30, 1954 ad, for $185.

Exclusive, crocodile Portemonnaie – for town and travel – with a removable watch (marked: Regnal Jeweled, Antimagnetic, Swissmade). Roomy, leather interior with multiple compartments. Complete with a coin-purse, comb, and monogrammed replacement tab. Snap closure. Folding crocodile skin gussets. Protective bottom-feet. (W 11 ¾ -inch by H 7 ¼ -inch by D 3-inch). Labeled: Wilcof Original. Provenance: This style–called "T'N'T"–was advertised by Bergdorf Goodman in November 1955.

Nettie Rosenstein offered a collection of handbags and jewelry to match her clothing lines. Smaller, curving, boat-like purses with double straps emphasized her A-line clothing designs, whereas sleek clutches went well with her streamlined H-silhouette.

Luxurious, full-quill ostrich skin lunch-box. Leather-lined, with a brass clasp. (Measures W 9 ½ -inch by H 5 ¼ -inch by D 4 ¼ -inch). Signed: Nadelle. American, ca 1950.

Impressive, crescent-shaped genuine python arm-purse, quilted from nine cuts of skin. Brass bracelet handles. Zippered top, and faille interior. (W 16 ½ -inch by H 10-inch by D 3-inch). Labeled: Original by Caprice. Zip pull stamped: Caprice. American, ca 1954.

The "New Look" displayed its unique personality in numer-ous boxes, satchels, barrels and pouches. Two distinct shapes—a small box-bag and a large tailored satchel with inside zippers and double compartments—dominated daywear in 1950.

Premium, genuine crocodile satchel, with self-covered frame; suede-lined. Gold-plated clasp. Semi-rigid construction; tailored, 4-piece gussets, and welted seams. Top-notch quality and attention to detail! (W 10 ½ -inch by H 8 ½ -inch by D 3 ½ -inch). Signed: Koret. Ca 1956.

Clever, genuine alligator frame-bag, with unusual front opening. Interesting, triangular shape; brass trim; leather interior, with an attached coin purse, and authenticity card. (W 10-inch by H 6-inch by D 4-inch). Unsigned. Authenticity card states: "Jay Koppel & Co. 48 East 21st Street, New York 10, N.Y. Approved by National Authority for the Ladies' Handbag Industry. Copyright 1956 NALHI."

A change toward softness and femininity also was reflected in handbag styling, featuring elegant shapes and fluid draping in fabric, leather and skins.

1950s fashion and handbags ads. **Top left**: *Vogue* cover October 15, 1950. Top right: *Vogue* fashion ad, March 15, 1952.
Bottom left: Nettie Rosenstein fashion ad, *Harper's Bazaar* Mar 1956. Bottom right: Schiaparelli fashion ad, *Vogue* January 1953.

The revival of long gloves, in lace or soft pastel suede, was also noted. Classic shoulder bags and trim boxes were created to enhance the beauty of a gloved hand. An evident comeback of the luxuriously long clutch bag in the 1950s was a reaction to the modest, pre-war style.

Right: Curvy, alligator lunch-box vanity, trimmed with brass and lined with suede, with an interior mirror. (W 8 ½ -inch by H 6-inch by D 3 ½ -inch). Labeled: Wilcof Original. Ca 1952-1956.

Left: Spacious – so very supple – genuine alligator clutch. Zippered, front compartment under the flap, with a large pull. Faille interior. (W 15-inch by H 9-inch by D 3 ½ -inch). Unsigned. American, ca 1952.

Dressy looks prevailed for town and evening, accented by diminutive, tailored purses in leather and skin.

Group of classic clutches from the 1950s. **Top left:** Coral leather, with gold-plated corners; faille-lined; flat back-handle. (W 10 ½ -inch by H 6 ¼ -inch by D 1 ¾ -inch). Signed: Bienen-Davis. **Top right:** White genuine ostrich, adorned by a gold-plated, etched filigree frame, with foiled, blue cabochons. Aqua-satin interior. (W 8 ½ -inch by H 5 ½ -inch by D 1 1/2-inch). **Center:** Elegant silk, lined with satin, adorned by the bejeweled time-piece. (W 9 ½ -inch by H 7 ½ -inch by D 2-inch). Signed: Holzer. **Bottom right:** Genuine python, with two large outside pockets, zippered top, and black leather interior. (W 12 ½ -inch by H 9 ½ -inch). Signed: MM Morris Moskowitz Genuine Reptile.

Group of handbags from the 1950s, in different styles and materials. **Top left:** Elegant, faux-crocodile clutch; silver-tone frame; faux marcasite ornaments. Flat back-handle; satin-lined, coin purse. (W 9-inch by H 6-inch by D 1 ½ -inch). Signed: MM (Morris Moskowitz). **Top right:** Sexy, bias-cut python clutch, with a large pleated bow on the side. Shiny, smooth skins! Zippered top; leather-lined. (W 11-inch by H 7-inch by D 1 ½ -inch). Signed: MM Morris Moskowitz (gilt plaque); and MM (zipper-pulls). **Bottom left:** Artistic, woven-straw purse, decorated by a bunch of grapes made of wood. Moire-lined. (W 10-inch by H 6-inch by D 4 ½ -inch). Labeled: Bags by Josef Made in Italy. **Bottom right:** Magnificent, Kelly-style handbag of crocodile Porosus. Leather-lined; mirror encased in faux tortoiseshell. Clochette with keys, and a lock. (W 13-inch by H 10-inch by D 5-inch deep). Signed: Lane Crowford's Made in France, Genuine Crocodile. The mirror is signed: Signature by Marcel.

By 1949, the fashion industry expressed concern for the increasing volume of foreign imports. Low retail prices of products manufactured in the American zone of West Germany could not be matched in the United States because of America's high production costs. By the 1950s, skin bags were imported from all over the world, including France, Italy, Argentina, Holland, India, Belgium, England, and Spain.

One-of-a-kind, two-tone crocodile Porosus bracelet-bag. Unique, enameled frame; structured handle. The front, bottom and right gusset – tan skin. The back, handle and left gusset – taupe skin. Very special! Leather-lined. (W 11 ¼ -inch by H 14 ½ -inch by D 3 ½ -inch). Unsigned. France or Germany, ca 1953. In the 1950s, both countries were known for their production of fancy, enameled frames.

In the late 1950s, a new silhouette, as well as the shorter skirts prompted a change in handbag and shoe designs. Shoes became more covered and handbags followed softer lines. The new, exciting styles included town satchels with twisted handles and a variety of novelty boxes.

Vogue fashion and handbags ads, from the 1950s. **Top left:** October 15, 1950. **Top right:** February 15, 1958. **Bottom left**: Ronay handbag, September15, 1952. **Bottom right:** 1952.

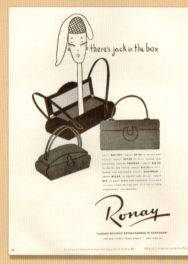

Enormous travel bags in alligator created a real craze in 1957! Some models for travel were specially equipped with timepieces and hidden jewelry compartments, and giant gate-frame bags measured about 13 ½-inch wide and 11-inch deep.

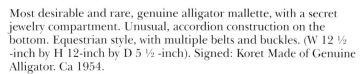

Most desirable and rare, genuine alligator mallette, with a secret jewelry compartment. Unusual, accordion construction on the bottom. Equestrian style, with multiple belts and buckles. (W 12 ½ -inch by H 12-inch by D 5 ½ -inch). Signed: Koret Made of Genuine Alligator. Ca 1954.

Sizable, genuine caiman travel bag in unique pastel color, lined in scrumptious black suede. Secure, gilt side-locks. Strong, structured handles. Self-covered frame. (W 14-inch in the widest parts by H 15 ½ -inch by D 6-inch). Unsigned. Switzerland, ca 1950.

The casual chic of Lucille de Paris handbags became the quintessence of 1950s glamour. Koret introduced fun styles for outdoors, including a huge saddlebag. Even tiny lunchbox handbags became especially desirable.

Fabulous duo of timeless, exotic-skin purses by popular Lucille de Paris. Brown alligator is W 10-inch by H 6 ½ -inch by D 2 ¾ -inch. Taupe crocodile is W 9 ¼ -inch by H 11-inch. Both signed: Lucille de Paris Made in U.S.A. Ca 1956-1957.

Fantastic, water-snake box – shaped as a heart – with an arching handle, and black leatherette trim. Lined in quilted satin. (W 7-inch by H 9 ½ -inch by D 7-inch). Unsigned. Japan, ca 1953.

Luxurious evening exotic skin bags sparkled with rhinestones, colorful glass beads and glitzy faux jewels in the Cartier style.

Darling, baby-crocodile Porosus cocktail-clutch, with a jeweled flip-frame, encrusted with clear rhinestones and genuine turquoise. Accordion gussets and bottom. Moire lining. (W 7 ½ -inch by H 5 ¾ -inch by D 1 ½ -inch). Unsigned. France, ca 1955-1957.

Delicate, genuine baby-crocodile Porosus cocktail-purse. Intricate, filigree frame made of brass, encrusted with green semi-precious cabochons. Leather-lined. (W 8 ¼ -inch by H 5 ¼ -inch by D 2-inch). Unsigned. France, ca 1952-1954.

Exotic skins in a variety of finishes were also very popular in innumerable versions of clutch bags. They varied from small ones—easily held in the hand—to elongated ones, clutched high under the arm. Frequently, a handle lay flat along the back so a woman could carry it either way.

Pair of vinyl evening clutches printed with lizard pattern (satin-lined). Made in the U.S.A. in the mid-1950s under the influence of revival of the Art Deco style, which is reflected in their streamline design, flat back-handles, and faux-gem details. **Black:** Faux java-lizard; green, poured-glass gems to imitate emerald. (W 8 ¼ -inch by H 7-inch by D 1 ½ -inch). Signed: Mondaine. **White:** Faux tegu-lizard; imitation cloisonné frame. (W 8-inch by H 6-inch by D 3-inch). Signed: Meyer's Made in U.S.A.

Fantastic, scalloped genuine python and leather clutch, lined in rayon, with metal shoulder strap. (W 13 1/2- inch by H 6 ¾ -inch). Labeled: Original by Caprice Made in USA. American, ca 1954-1955.

In 1952, leading department stores became fashion trendsetters, as they commissioned more than two hundred foremost designers from France, Italy, Belgium, and the United States to design lines especially for them. The stores included Saks Fifth Avenue, B. Altman & Co., Franklin Simon, Jay Torpe, De Pinna, Tiffany & Co., Tailored Woman, Stern's, Bergdorf Goodman, Bonwit Teller, Oppenheim Collins, Best & Co., Peck & Peck, Bloomingdale, Lord & Taylor, Arnold Constable, Black, Star & Gorham, Gimble Brothers, Henry Bendel, and Macy.

A great variety of fur novelties overtook the fashion scene. Fox totes, broadtail cosmetic cases, zebra billfolds, mink cigarette cases, and African leopard satchels became especially fashionable.

Splendid, top-quality crocodile satchel – in vertical shape – with accordion leather gussets, and suede interior. Unusual, side belt-closures. (W 11-inch by H 9 ¾ -inch by D 3 ¾ -inch). England, ca 1956.

Above: Handsome, spacious genuine leather and fur satchel, with accordion gussets, and very roomy leather-lined interior. Beautiful styling! (W 11 ¼ -inch by H 10-inch by D 3-inch). England, ca 1952.

In 1955, as soon as Lanvin and Balmain showed their new, disciplined lines of garments (a tube, a bell, and a ball), similar geometric shapes appeared in handbag designs, including oblongs, squares, and tall rectangles. Prices for fine alligator handbags at that time grew considerably, from about $125 to over $225 apiece.

Lady-like, upscale genuine crocodile frame-purse, in a distinct, elongated, oval shape. Lined with leather, and featured with its original box. Signed: Revitz Exact match. France, ca 1955.

Sleek, genuine alligator bell-purse, lined in saddle leather, with very wide gussets. Rocking bottom; welted seams. (W 10-inch by H 10-inch by D 2-inch). Signed: Sydney of California. Ca 1955.

The extravagant fashions of 1957 established the size as the ultimate chic feature in handbags. While flipping through fashion magazines of that period, I could not help but notice how overwhelming the trend for over-sized alligator bags had become. In 1948, they were advertised as "big, yet simple and styled in fine taste." In the early 1950s, they became "generously sized," and later, in 1954, "giant", over 13-inches wide! Capacious diplomats and attaché cases were popular in a jumbo, 14-inch size. The trend reached its pinnacle in 1958, when some alligator models for travel, sold for $252, measured an enormous 12-by-18 inches!

Above: Luxurious, genuine crocodile Porosus frame-bag – in a square shape – with a self-covered frame, semi-structured top handles, and a simple squeeze clasp. Kidskin lined. Unsigned. Switzerland, ca 1956.

Above: Striking crocodile frame-bag – in rare yellow – with unique, white enameled frame. Two-tone, leather-lined interior. (W 11-inch by H 10-inch by D 3-inch). Signed: Rosenfeld Genuine Alligator. Ca 1956.

Breathtaking, crocodile Porosus shopper, with crocodile heels adorned by lavishly bejeweled Musi shoe-clips. (W 15-inch by H 9 ¼ -inch by D 4 ¼ -inch). Signed: Coblentz Made in France. Ca 1958.

Starting in the mid-1950s, a smaller alligator satchel was introduced to establish a distinction between casual and evening wear. The general theme of evening fashion was simplicity, with casual restraint. Representing the influence were trim alligator boxes by Nettie Rosenstein, as well as fabulous and affordable faux alligator double-deckers.

Equestrian, genuine alligator box-purse. Beautiful quality! Structured brass handle draped with skin. Faille interior. (W 8-inch by H 6 ½ -inch by D 4-inch). Unsigned. American, ca 1952-1958.

By 1959, a change in the direction of fashion was apparent. Trend-setting television stars appeared with upswept hairdos and fashion designer Yves St. Laurent was taking the hem above the knee. His new daytime fashions for the young were in opposition to everything shown before. It was quite obvious that a very young, girlish look grabbed his attention and that of other fashion designers.

Swanky, alligator-print leather double-decker, with two clasps and top handle. Moire-lined. (W 6 ½ -inch by H 7 ½ -inch by D 4 ¾ -inch). Signed: Supreme Originals. American, ca 1954-1955.

YOUTHFUL SIXTIES

    The feminine, sporty look of the early 1960s was reflected in clean lines of the accessories. Visual simplicity of their forms, achieved by spare use of textural details and vibrant colors, was in the center of 1960s design, which replaced the "razzle-dazzle" of the 1950s. Martin Van Schaak, among other designers of that time, interpreted its logical geometry in his marvelous evening wear collection.

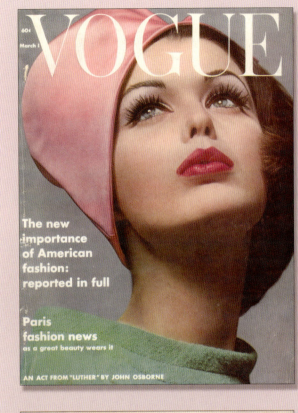
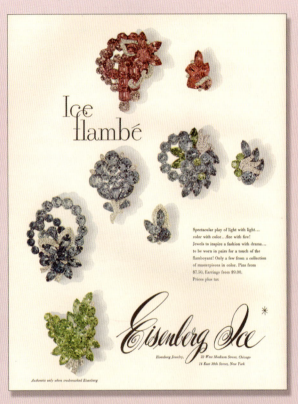

1960s fashion and merchandise ads. **Top left:** *Vogue* cover March 1, 1962. **Top right:** Eisenberg Ice jewelry ad, *Vogue* March 15, 1960. **Bottom left:** *Harper's Bazaar* ad 1961. **Bottom right**: *Vogue* fashion ad, March 1, 1960.

1960s collection of breathtaking cocktail purses by incomparable Martin Van Schaak. All satin-lined. **Top:** Sapphire velvet; pineapple clasp, encrusted with rhinestones and sapphire cabochons. (W 8 ½ -inch by H 7 ½ -inch). **Center left:** Navy silk; jeweled bar-handle. (W 9-inch by H 9 ¼ -inch). **Center right:** Emerald satin; stunning clear Lucite bar-clasp, bejeweled by dozens of sparkling rhinestones; split handle. (W 9-inch by 7-inch). **Bottom left:** Shimmering, gold brocade; bracelet handles; Chanel-style, poured-glass accent. (W 7 ½ -inch by H 10-inch). **Bottom right:** Colorful raw silk; fabulous ornament: a heron (W 1 ¾ -inch by H 3-inch). Amazing attention to detail! Burgundy cloisonné, 24K-gilt, dozens of gleaming pave-rhinestones. (W 8-inch by H 6 ½ -inch).

Daytime handbags proved to be as big and bold as hats, in classic black or deep jewel-tones, to accent rather than to blend.

Pair of chic crocodile frame-bags from France, ca 1960-1964. **Left:** Sleek black; concealed frame. Amazing symmetry of the central belly-cut! Prominent display of the umbilical cord right in the center. Leather-lined. (W 13-inch by H 11-inch by D 3 ½ -inch). Signed: Made in France Expressly for Macy's Associates. **Right:** Dramatic burgundy; kidskin-lined. (W 10 ¼ -inch by H 12 ¼ -inch by D 3-inch).

Newly fashionable evening bags were often
made of alligator, lizard and snakeskin.

Glamorous alligator evening bag, with a bar-frame,
heavily bejeweled with faux and semi-precious gems,
in rainbow colors. Leather-lined. (W 8-inch by H 6
½ -inch by D 2 ¼ -inch). Signed: Created by Original Handbag Co. American, ca 1962-1963.

For the affluent, alligator and crocodile were
still the most prized handbags.

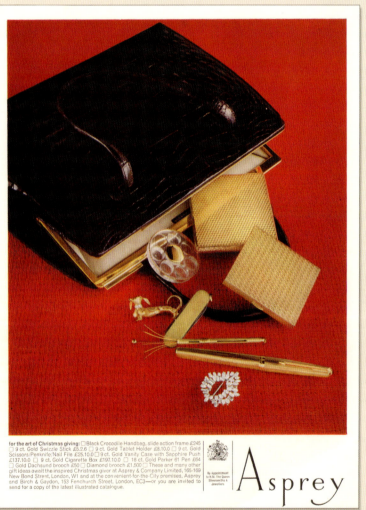

for the art of Christmas giving: □Black Crocodile Handbag, slide action frame £245
□ 9 ct. Gold Swizzle Stick £5.2.6 □ 9 ct. Gold Tablet Holder £8.10.0 □ 9 ct. Gold
Scissors/Penknife/Nail File £25.10.0 □ 9 ct. Gold Vanity Case with Sapphire Push
£137.10.0 □ 9 ct. Gold Cigarette Box £197.10.0 □ 18 ct. Gold Parker 61 Pen £64
□ Gold Dachsund brooch £50 □ Diamond brooch £1,500 □ These and many other
gift ideas await the inspired Christmas giver at Asprey & Company Limited, 165-169
New Bond Street, London, W1 and at the convenient-for-the-City premises, Asprey
and Birch & Gaydon, 153 Fenchurch Street, London, EC3—or you are invited to
send for a copy of the latest illustrated catalogue.

Asprey

Asprey crocodile handbag ad, *Vogue* Nov 1966.

Right: Elite, crocodile Porosus pocketbook. High style
and panache! Perfectly symmetrical, whole, central belly-
cut envelopes the front and back. Accordion gussets and
bottom; stitched-and-sealed seams; 24K-gilt. Three-
compartment, leather-lined interior. (W 8 ½ -inch by H
11-inch by D 3-inch). Signed: G (Grimaldi) Paris Made in
France. France/Monaco, ca 1964-1967.

Affordable lizard was best used to mix, not to match other accessories.

Streamline, java-lizard clutch, in impressive duo-combination of brown and white. Optional shoulder strap; deep back pocket; leather-lined; 24K-gilt fixtures. (W 11 ¾ -inch by H 7 ½ -inch by w 2 ¼ -inch). Signed: Andrea Pfister Made in Italy Leather Lined. Ca 1963-1965. In 1963, Andrea designed collections for Lanvin, in Paris. Later, in 1965, he showed the first collection under his own label, and, in 1968, started his production line. His collections of handmade handbags and shoes are on display in the Metropolitan Museum, New York. His followers include Elizabeth Taylor and Madonna. He respects the client who is "the woman who mixes different pieces – an Armani top, for instance, with a Donna Karan skirt, and a jacket by Ferre. My shoes work best on the woman who's sure enough of herself to create her own combination."

Peacock and pheasant feather purses became a rush in the 1960s.

Cute, genuine peacock feather purse, trimmed with solid brass and lined in taffeta. (W 5-inch by H 4 ½ -inch). American, ca 1963-1964.

Jacqueline Kennedy fashion ad, *Vogue* August 1, 1961.

The 1960s were defined by the reign of an American icon, First Lady Jacqueline Kennedy. Fresh, young and elegant, her classic style captivated the world. Millions of women across the globe copied her preferences in fashion through the 1960s, and some of their influence lives on to this day.

Jackie Kennedy loved jewels and accessories; she wore subtle alligator handbags with almost every outfit created for her by fashion designer Oleg Cassini. A French man of Russian aristocratic heritage, he designed clothes for Hollywood stars in the 1950s and 1960s. Together, they revolutionized fashion by bringing it forward as an important part of international affairs.

Couple of marvelous vintage exotics by upscale Christian Dior, ca 1960s. **Left:** Classy water-snake shoulder bag, with leather gussets, suede interior, floating hinges, and removable shoulder strap (W 9 ¼ -inch by H 6 ¼ -inch by D 2-inch). **Right:** Simple, black crocodile saddle-bag, lined in lambskin, with adjustable shoulder strap (W 10-inch by H 9 ¾ -inch by D 2-inch).

The general look of the early 1960s was young and fresh.

Pair of trendy, exotic-skin shoulder bags from the late 1960s. **Left:** Turquoise caiman; softly-pleated skins; leather-lined; welted leather seams; complex construction of the gussets, with multiple decorative accents. Signed: Creazioni Paparini for Antonio da Pesarra Made in Italy. Original tags: erroneously marked as "Genuine crocodile." **Right:** Spacious, genuine baby-python; adjustable leather shoulder strap; 3-piece, leather-and-python gussets and bottom. (10 ½ -inch by H 8-inch by D 4 ½ -inch). Labeled: Ingledew's For the Greatest Names in Fashion.

Structured, genuine python clutch, with architectural accents. Leather-lined; chain-strap. (W 13-inch by H 7-inch by D 1 ½ -inch). Labeled: Original by Caprice U.S.A. American, ca 1959-1961.

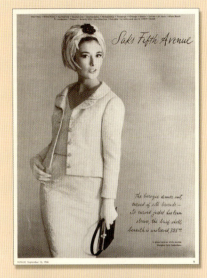

A dramatic note was struck in the accessories. Bold hats complemented clean, uncluttered clothes. No woman dared to go out without one. Towering turbans and high-crowned slouches were among the most theatrical styles.

1960s handbags ads. **Top left:** Saks Fifth Avenue fashion and handbag ad, *Vogue* September 15, 1964. **Top right:** Coblentz crocodile handbag and fashion ad, *Harper's Bazaar* 1963. **Bottom left:** Lucille de Paris alligator handbag ad, *Vogue* March 1, 1960. **Bottom right:** Lucille de Paris for Saks Fifth Avenue handbag ad, *Vogue* March 1, 1960.

Still important, gloves were produced in various lengths, from two-button, wrist-long to the formal ones ending close to the shoulder. Shorter ones were worn with a longer sleeve, and vice-versa. The etiquette required removing short gloves while eating, drinking, smoking, putting makeup on, or handling merchandise in a shop. Formal gloves could be left on. Bracelets were allowed over the gloves, but not finger rings. The handbag silhouette echoed the trend to present the gloved hand in the best light.

Pair of fabulous handbags, from the 1960s, created to be worn with gloves of different length. **Top:** Dramatic, burnt velvet frame-bag, with a pair of black, elbow-length gloves – for an evening out. (W 11 ¼ -inch by 9 ½ -inch by D 3-inch). **Bottom:** Spectacular, feminine, needlepoint day-time purse – with a lavishly embossed metal frame, lined in marvelous pink leather – shown with a pair of wrist-length gloves, in pale-pink – for a special afternoon. (W 13 ¼ -inch by H 8 ¾ -inch by D 2 ¼ -inch).

In the meantime, the status of crocodile was at its highest ever. A daytime shopper with double handles remained roomy. A Spanish import, represented by Tano of Madrid among other makers, established the crocodile handbag's reputation of top quality and style.

Group of stylish, exotic-skin handbag from the 1960s, by a premium Spanish design house, Tano of Madrid. **Top left:** Unique, two-tone satchel, made of six baby-alligator skins – hornback inlays – with structured handles. Accented by gray leather; optional strap; zippered top; suede-lined. (W 14 ½ -inch by H 9-inch by 3 ½ -inch). **Center right:** Ample, genuine crocodile pocketbook, with no metal parts. Leather-lined interior; folding gussets and bottom. (W 12-inch by H 8-inch by D 2 ½ -inch). Ca 1964. **Bottom left:** Impressive, striped cobra-skin hobo, with a drawstring-type belted closure. Unique construction; very roomy: beautiful quality throughout. Suede-lined, with a large, chained interior purse, and zippered top. (W 12-inch by H 12-inch by D 2 ¾ -inch). Ca 1965-1966.

While hats grew larger in proportion, with time handbags gradually diminished in size. Several styles were devoted strictly to teenagers, such as the featured tiny satchel made of faux black alligator.

Sleek, miniature satchel made of genuine leather printed with alligator pattern. Jeweled ram clasp, accented by pave rhinestones, and colored enamel. Molded gussets, welted seams; satin-lined. (W 6 ½ -inch by H 5 ½ -inch by D 3 ½ -inch). Signed: MM Genuine Leather. American, ca 1967-1968.

Thick, low shoe heels prevailed. Handbags were selling especially well in stores with shoe departments, enabling a thorough coordination of accessories in style and color. The newly fashionable turtle skin became an affordable substitute for expensive crocodile.

Matching set of genuine turtle purse and shoes, from 1967. **Left:** Flat heels, with a stylish metal detail. Signed: Joseph Larose Exquisite Footwear. **Right:** Sweet, genuine turtle satchel, accented by bold Bakelite handle and turn-clasp. Leather-lined, expandable front compartment. Sealed, contrast seams. (W 7 ¾ -inch by H 8 ½ -inch by D 2 ½ -inch). Signed: Imported from Italy by Hudson's Detroit.

While handbags diminished visibly in size, they held the same load due to a new construction of accordion gussets and pleats.

Left: Pretty, genuine turtle shoulder bag, with an unusual, belted bottom; very wide, expandable leather gussets; long rolled shoulder strap; gilt trim; leather-lined. (W 8 ½ -inch by H 6-inch by D 3-inch). Signed: Made in France for B. Altman & Co. New York. France, ca 1968.

Imported from Asia by French tanning companies, anteater skin grew to a status symbol in Paris couture. The House of Hermes showed it in their traditional handbags, and the upscale boutique Jacomo—located in New York at 25 East 61st Street—widely used it in their fabulous evening purses. In fact, it was James Kaplan and Heidener Laurenz, the Jacomo owners, who set a trend of using exotic skins and rugged textures, traditionally associated with daytime, for evening wear. Their one-of-a-kind, handmade pieces with original antique gold or sterling frames—in Victorian, Florentine, or Art Deco styles—were imported from France and Italy. Mostly, they were crafted of Calcutta lizard, exotic python, fine crocodile or classic alligator. The featured styles include a luscious, red crocodile envelope accented by a graceful Florentine gold handle and a genuine coral rosebud catch, a soft pouch of pastel python with a Victorian sterling frame, and a true "killer": a black anteater pouch on a filigree frame with genuine and faux jade cabochons. In the 1960s, these cost $110 to $225. Today, these outstanding, museum-quality objects are valued in the thousands.

Below: Close-up details of the superb, exotic skin evening-purses by Jacomo.

Ultra rare pieces of fashion distinction imported from France, by Jacomo, 1961-1964. **Top left:** Splendid, crimson crocodile pocketbook, adorned by a genuine coral rose-bud clasp; arched, gilt handle. (W 10-inch by H 10-inch by D 2-inch). **Center right:** Enchanting, genuine baby-python evening bag, on an antique, Victorian frame (German silver), lined in platinum satin (W 8-inch by H 7-inch). **Bottom left:** Stunning – made in 1964 – black anteater skin evening purse, crowned by an antique, Victorian frame (brass filigree), encrusted with jade-cabochons, and amethyst gems. Lined in pink moire (W 9 ½ - inch by H 7-inch). All labeled: Made in Paris France, by Jacomo.

Earrings and pins with imitation gems reached extreme sizes. The popularity of pearls, genuine or faux, was endless. Pillbox hats and knitted swimsuits were must-haves. And the handbags accented by various plastic ornaments came into the spotlight once again.

Set of 1960s handbags with plastic trim and handles. **Left:** Olive-leather pocketbook: wide, dark-brown plastic handle; accordion gussets; rayon interior. (W 9-inch by H 8 ½-inch by D 3 ½-inch). Signed: Susan Gail Original. **Right:** Black-patent leather pocketbook; brass rivets; faille-lined. (W 11-inch by H 11-inch by D 3-inch).

1960s fashion and handbags ads. **Top left:** *Harper's Bazaar* fashion and handbag ad, 1965. **Top/bottom right:** *Vogue* fashion ads, March 15, 1967. **Bottom left:** Hermes maroon bucket bag, $70, at Bonwit Teller; Judith Leiber dark maroon patent bag, $85, at Henry Bendel; Walter Kateen burgundy turtle bag, $96, at Henry Bendel – all *Vogue* March 15, 1967.

In 1968, Mary Quant—a kinky fashion designer from England—brought attention to the unorthodox London fashion scene by creating her signature "Chelsea Look": a shift dress with very short skirt, high boots, colored stockings, brightly colored flannel, and shiny plastic bags. In America, she distributed her merchandise through the J.C. Penney chain of retail stores.

The same year, Andre Courreges introduced his most seductive collection: dresses with defined waists and scalloped edges, as well as signature handbags in the shape of round pots with curvy flaps. They were sold at his "Couture Future" boutique as well as Bonwit Teller stores in New York City. Those legendary handbags created in embossed croc' leather are impossible to find today.

By the late 1960s, gloves and hats were on the way out, while sunglasses moved in. Modern glasses were quite different from their prototypes. Sunglasses emerged as a style item, as equally important as jewelry, cosmetics or purses. Young and old wore them year round, during the day or night, in the sun or shade, often coordinating with handbags in shape and color.

This genuine alligator satchel by Coblentz goes beautifully with faux leopard gloves and a pair of cool shades, by Dior – a popular trend since the late 1960s.

In 1969, the whole fashion world, including Paris, looked to Rome. Deterioration of the French haute couture and the unification of the fashion industries of Milan, Florence and Rome led Italy into the leadership role for the handbag industry. The Italian fashion was for everybody, young or old, and relied on talented designers, superb materials and skillful craftsmanship. The fashion houses of Gucci and Pucci became international status symbols.

Exquisite, silk purse by remarkable Pucci is accented and lined with black leather. (W 9-inch by H 5 ½ -inch by 1 ¾ -inch). Signed: Emilio Pucci. Made in Italy, ca 1969.

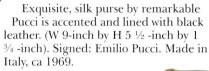

In the spring of 1967, it was clear that as long as short skirts were here to stay, pint-sized handbags would swing along with them. There were very few frame handbags. Instead, the envelopes, swaggers and shoulder bags with very little hardware became extraordinarily popular.

Tiny, bamboo-crowned suede evening purse, by legendary Gucci. Suede and satin interior. (W 7-inch wide by H 8-inch high with handle). Labeled: Gucci Made in Italy. Ca 1968-1969.

The trend in fashion was moving toward commercialism. Most prominent designers, including Chanel, Yves Saint Laurent, Pierre Cardin, Givenchy, and Emanuel Ungaro—whose private clientèle was noticeably shrinking—started opening boutiques in order to reach a mass market of young customers. A trend for individuality was being established for the years to come.

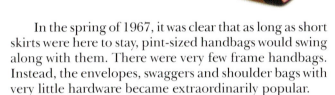

Classic crocodile pocketbook in a famed piano-bag style introduced by Hermes. Leather-lined. (W 9 ¾ -inch by H 7-inch without handle by D 2-inch). Signed: Lederer de Paris Made in France. Ca 1964.

From the late 1960s to the 1980s, the production and sale of some skin handbags was temporarily halted in the United States, due to a ban on a few alligator and crocodile species. Most of the American department stores started to dump their expensive stock. The "sale" lasted for several years—with no supply contracts being renewed for several decades—until the population of the American Alligator recovered in the 1980s. A profitable farming industry enabled the return of the glorious supremacy of this exquisite leather.

Today, the alligator and crocodile leather trade has reached new success heights worldwide. The largest brands sell their offerings for thousands of dollars. A demand for a more affordable alternative to expensive, brand-new handbags has created a market for the almost-forgotten treasures of the past: classic, vintage, alligator handbags!

CHAPTER THREE
LEADING MAKERS

"You Can Never Have Too Much of a Good Thing"

Imagine you came across an older genuine alligator purse somewhere in an antique shop or a flea market. A lot of questions may start popping up in your head. Is it valuable? Is it a good bargain? Will it hold and not fall apart on me if I use it every day?

Unfortunately, not every old bag is original vintage. Even fewer are considered valuable collectibles. Very rarely they are made of top quality skins. Frequently, they are dreadful and not worth the investment. Remember that their value always depends on the quality and condition; that is why some of them are worth thousands, and others—only pennies.

That is the reason why it is so important to know the difference and invest only in the best quality you can afford. And, it is my hope that this book will help you understand what a valuable collectible is; how to recognize a good buy and take advantage of it; and how to avoid costly mistakes while shopping for fine vintage.

After years of dealing with thousands of customers and handling about ten thousand handbags, I learned that people buy for different reasons. Some acquire vintage to use and wear; others—for investment and collection.

Have you ever wondered why some well-to-do women who can afford pretty much anything prefer vintage to new designer stuff? Well, it is because a discriminating customer appreciates its versatility, timeless quality, handmade workmanship, and, above all, the opportunity to create a unique, personal look.

Those savvy collectors are after the best status bags to mix with their up-to-date, designer's wardrobes. They know the quality and craftsmanship, and do not mind paying fairly for the exclusive right to own a superb piece of fashion history. A prestigious brand is the most important factor influencing their buying decision. They understand the uniqueness of vintage. And, its great original condition is of crucial importance to them.

In the late 1990s, the Sotheby's fashion department set forth guidelines of collecting fine vintage. At their very successful standing-room-only auctions—where hip New Yorkers learned how to mix and match the styles of different decades—the best brands of the past specializing in alligator handbags were offered up for bid: Hermes, Mark Cross, Gucci, Chanel, Lucille de Paris, Nettie Rosenstein, Lederer, Saks Fifth Avenue, Rosenfeld, Roberta di Camerino, Martin Van Schaak, Koret, and others.

Besides the mentioned makers, there are also several other recognizable vintage brands to choose from—including Deitsch, Coblentz, Rendl, Lesco, Vassar, and Bellestone— which are somewhat more affordable and accessible.

The next group of buyers is represented by budget-conscious women with a good sense of style. Some of them are always on the look out for a magnificent, rare piece in an outrageous designer color, with unusual details. Something really extravagant that nobody else owns!

Others settle for more affordable, mass-produced pieces or unsigned high-end purses. Their reasons for purchasing vintage are both aesthetic and economic: to save on luxury! They are always interested in a good bargain, because their approach to beauty is practical and hands-on. They collect to wear and usually look effortlessly stylish in a modern wardrobe adorned by vintage finds, as one of my valued customers, Dr. Monica Arnold from West Hartford, Connecticut, attests:

"I got addicted to owning a fashion item with a bit of history. I love the workmanship of the older bags. I like that in contrast to other vintage clothing they can be found in great condition, and I love imagining who may have owned them. I'm not going for a completely vintage look, but mix my vintage bags and shoes (unworn only) with my wardrobe. I enjoy having accessories that no one else has. Now when I go to the mall I wouldn't consider buying a new bag—how boring! Plus, with nearly fifty bags, I need to change my

Exceptionally valuable, crocodile Porosus satchel by Martin Van Schaak, ornamented by a fabulous, gold-plated shell-clasp. Two outside compartments lined in moire; leather-lined interior. (W 10-inch by H 13-inch high w/handles by D 3-inch). Signed: Martin Van Schaak New York. American, ca 1964. Acquired in 2004 from the Doyle Auction House, New York.

purse almost every day to show them off. I learned that I should only buy from trusted dealers. But...the lure of a bargain or better yet a bag with an unusual shape, color or clasp will sometimes get me. I have the heart of a collector and also collect vintage costume jewelry, but that's a whole other story."

There is also a group of collectors who specialize in vintage novelties. They are very particular about makers, brands and condition, and extremely knowledgeable about the historic value of vintage. They appreciate its rarity and invest in its preservation. Those collectors comprise the most experienced, well-informed group with independent opinions. They do not need to see a signature to know the bag's market value. Some of them own dozens and dozens of spectacular, extremely valuable collectibles that they display in their homes. They hardly ever use them and consider preservation of their original condition as one of the most important aspects of collecting.

For several years, some young talented designers have been drawing inspiration from vintage, in order to utilize the cool ideas of the past in their modern vision. They collect unique handbags in unusual materials, bizarre shapes and off-the-wall colors. Sometimes, they would literally dissect a bag to see how it was made. Usually, they are not worried about the condition, because they collect ideas, but not objects.

In addition, the use of vintage exotics as decor accents has recently emerged as one of the coolest trends in home decorating. People mix-and-match their vintage novelties with various modern articles to create elegant arrangements and discreet storage spaces in their homes or offices. Stacks of distressed crocodile luggage could provide an ample, highly decorative storage space in rustic bedrooms. An exquisite evening alligator bag sparkling with jewels looks absolutely fabulous displayed in a well-lit curio cabinet of a traditional dining room.

Whether you are looking for vintage status pieces or unique decor accents for your home—climb into a comfortable armchair with your favorite snack and get prepared for an exciting journey. You'll travel through eras and decades, styles and designs, brands and trademarks, and hundreds of pictures of absolutely lovely, precious vintage gems that will satisfy your cravings for beauty—and inspire you in your search for new treasures to add to your collection or wardrobe.

"Nothing to Wear" Auction Catalog, Sotheby's (April 8, 1998).

COBL'ENTZ
NEW YORK CHIC WITH A FRENCH ACCENT!

Coblentz Bag Company, Inc., a member of the National Authority for the Ladies' Handbag Industry (NALHI), which was located in New York at 30 East 33rd Street, was founded by Louis J. Coblentz in the 1930s. The company operated until the late 1970s. It specialized in exquisite, top-quality genuine reptile and ostrich handbags that were sold at high-end boutiques and department stores.

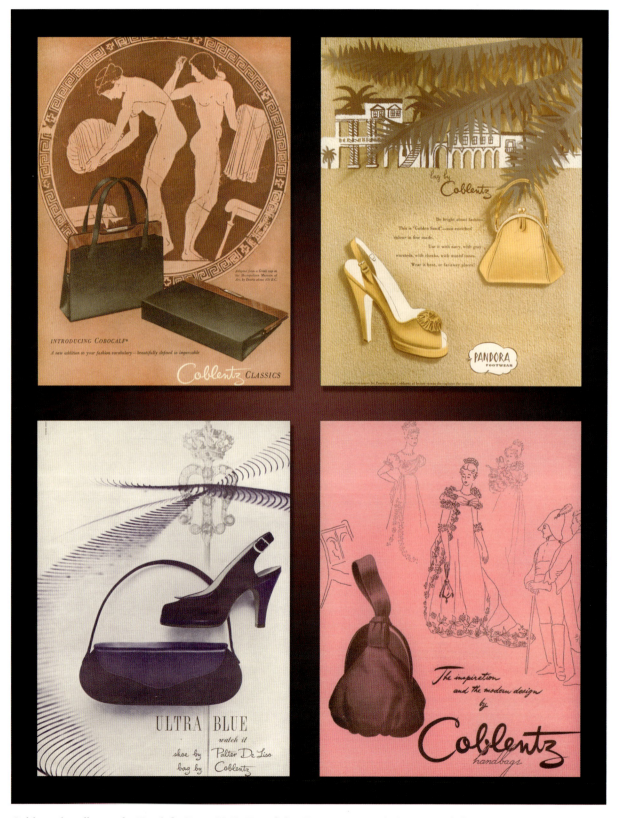

Coblentz handbags ads. **Top left**: *Vogue* 1945. **Top right**: *Harper Bazaar* 1949. **Bottom left**: *Vogue* August 1950. **Bottom right**: *Vogue* 1946.

Adorable alligator purse shaped as a petite doctor's bag. Upscale features: molded gussets; unique handle attachment; self-covered frame; freely attached pouches for a coin purse and mirror; protected bottom. (W 8 ½ -inch by H 11-inch w/handles by D 5-inch). Signed (mirror): Coblentz. Provenance: Similar style was advertised at Bergdorf Goodman in 1951 for $49.50.

The peak of the company's success came with its line of high-fashion alligator and crocodile handbags in 1949 that sold at Bonwit Teller stores. Praised for their impeccable style, finest skins and superb craftsmanship, they were a smart interpretation of French style from the perspective of a New Yorker.

Above: Exquisite alligator frame-bag, of elegant proportions. Beautifully matched, central belly-cuts feature utmost symmetry. Effortless style throughout! (W 10-inch by H 11-inch w/handle by H 3 ¾ -inch). Signed: Coblentz Original. Provenance: Advertised by B. Altman & Co. in December 1955.

Often inspired by celebrated French designers and craftsmen, Coblentz handbags were the epitome of high class. They fit the New York lifestyle perfectly: a generous size, a streamlined design, balanced lines, and plenty of interior room for one's possessions. These handbags represented quality at its best—the ultimate New York chic with a French accent!

Superb crocodile Porosus satchel. Upscale features: padded skins; contrast stitching; self-covered frame; unusually tall handle mounts. Leather lined interior features a famous Coblentz frame wallet. (W 12 ¼ -inch by H 8 ¾ -inch by H 3 ¾ -inch). Signed: Coblentz Made in France. Ca 1962.

The style of the brand reflected the personality of its founder, Louis Coblentz, a respected executive who was an active member of New York society. As an ambassador of good will, he represented the American business community at several European trade fairs. Starting from the early 1930s, he took numerous trips to Europe to build his enterprise by merging the skills and resources of both worlds.

On February 21, 1944, the federal Office of Price Administration appointed Mr. Coblentz as a special consultant to work with the industry on regulations for women's handbags. After the war, the Coblentz family led an active social life. They maintained residences on the Upper East Side of New York City and in Paris, and spent their leisure time with prominent New Yorkers at the Montauk Manor.

In 1948, Coblentz hired Deglin-Wood, Inc., a promoter who also represented the American League Baseball Club of N.Y.C., Inc. (also known as the New York Yankees) to advertise his brand in fashion magazines and on the radio. This fascinating fact demonstrates the brand's popularity.

In the 1950s, Louis Coblentz was actively involved in the promotion of economic ties between Britain and the United States. He participated at the British Industries Fair, in May of 1952, as part of the American delegation of executives.

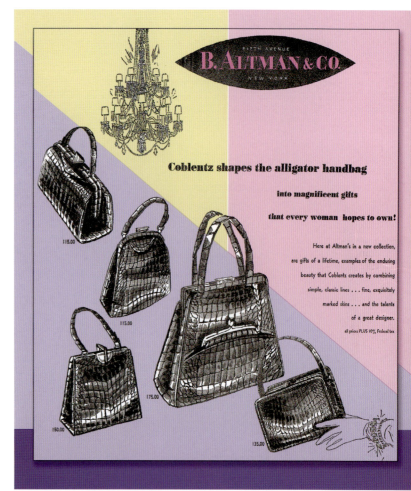

Coblentz alligator handbags ad by B. Altman & Co., 1954.

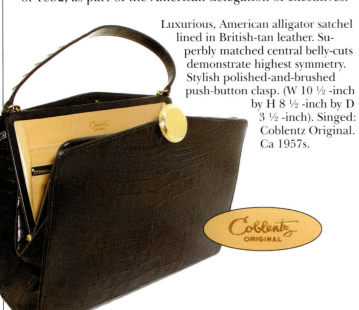

Luxurious, American alligator satchel lined in British-tan leather. Superbly matched central belly-cuts demonstrate highest symmetry. Stylish polished-and-brushed push-button clasp. (W 10 ½ -inch by H 8 ½ -inch by D 3 ½ -inch). Singed: Coblentz Original. Ca 1957s.

Right: This alligator piece is so gorgeous and so valuable that I decided to provide numerous pictures to feature it in detail. Superb quality of skins and workmanship! Very wide, sculptured gussets; finely polished, gilt-brass trim; welted seams; protective bottom feet; and a tall, self-covered frame. The ample interior is neatly lined in contract tan leather, with finely tailored, multiple compartments. It features a full set of accessories, including a coin purse, a mirror in a leather sleeve stamped "Saks Fifth Avenue", and a comb. Ultimate luxury, indeed! Signed: Coblentz Original. Ca 1950s.

For several decades, elegant Coblentz skin handbags—a must-have for ladies of means—were sold across the country by B. Altman & Co., Saks Fifth Avenue, Bonwit Teller, and Lord & Taylor stores. Their important styles included a satchel, a barrel, a bar-belle, a trapeze, and a classic envelope that were often custom-made in France for exclusive Saks Fifth Avenue collections. In the 1930s, their specialty was a variety of suede pouches, and in the 1940s—luscious cashmere and Permasuede purses. A concealed frame was their signature feature used in large, trendy crocodile styles of the 1950s and the early 1960s.

Superlative, crocodile Porosus satchel of enormous size! Outstanding, huge, highly symmetrical belly-cuts. Top-notch craftsmanship: strong stitching; sealed seams; gilt trim; structured handles; floating hinges; leather-lined; huge, framed wallet. (W 15-inch by H 9 ¼ -inch by D 4 ¼ -inch). Signed: Coblentz Made in France. Ca 1960.

Louis J. Coblentz died in February of 1963, but his company remained in operation until 1978. It survived the ban on alligator skins and developed several new lines of leather and vinyl handbags for Bergdorf Goodman, including the attractive Perma Plastic handbags that were awarded the Leather Industries of American Handbag Designer Award in 1974.

Prestigious alligator skin satchel. Remarkable quality and style! (W 11-inch by H 6 ½ -inch by D 4 ¼ -inch). Signed: Made in France for Coblentz Genuine Alligator. Ca 1964.

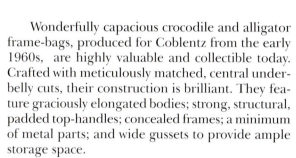

Wonderfully capacious crocodile and alligator frame-bags, produced for Coblentz from the early 1960s, are highly valuable and collectible today. Crafted with meticulously matched, central under-belly cuts, their construction is brilliant. They feature graciously elongated bodies; strong, structural, padded top-handles; concealed frames; a minimum of metal parts; and wide gussets to provide ample storage space.

Only whole skins of valuable species were used on each side of a bag—silky-soft and pliable! The kid-lined interior is usually outfitted with multiple compartments for an encased mirror, a comb, and a coin purse.

Most Coblentz handbags dating from the 1950s and 1960s are stamped with the company's signature *Coblentz* or *Coblentz Original*. The French-made bags are clearly marked *Made in France*. Very few are stamped *Genuine Alligator*.

Today, stylish Coblentz crocodile handbags are indisputably among most coveted of collectibles—and remain the vintage of choice to mix with modern couture. Absolutely timeless in style and generous in size, they are amazingly relevant today. You can save thousands of dollars by buying a vintage masterpieces for a fraction of its original cost. You can treat yourself to a luxury that only the most wealthy clients would own fifty years ago!

Fashionable python-skin brief. Leather accordion-gussets; gilt lever-clasp; leather-lined. A removable, beaded shoulder-strap is a replacement. (W 12 ½ -inch by H 7-inch by D 2 ¾ -inch). Signed: Coblentz.

DEITSCH

AMERICAN SPECIALIST IN REPTILE HANDBAGS SINCE 1873

"Look for the Deitsch dragon—a symbol of America's specialist in reptile handbags."

This appealing marketing slogan was found on printed ads in fashion magazines starting from the 1930s, when one of the oldest American handbag companies, Deitsch Brothers, actively promoted their fine exotic-skin handbags. The cute Deitsch dragon did not just promise the highest expertise in reptile bags—it really delivered!

Deitsch handbag ads. **Top left**: *Vogue* 1962. **Top right**: *Harper's Bazaar* 1944. **Bottom left**: *Harper Bazaar* 1945. **Bottom right**: *Harper's Bazaar* 1944.

Supple, tegu-lizard shoulder bag in desirable red. Quality features: pleated front; adjustable, leather-backed shoulder strap; huge button-clasp. No metal parts whatsoever! Fabric interior. (W 11-inch by H 7 1/2-inch by D 4-inch). Labeled: Deitsch. American, ca 1944. Provenance: Very similar style was featured in the Harper's Bazaar 1944 ad (opposing page, bottom right advertisement).

Deitsch Brothers had a history of success and prosperity going back to the 19th century. In 1873, Deitsch & Bros. Proprietors formed an enterprise trading in hats and clothing, boots and shoes, furnishings, dry goods, and groceries. One of their first locations in New York City was at the corner of F and Larimer Streets. The business grew rapidly and in 1897 they moved to Seventeenth Street.

Ownership of the company changed on March 17, 1909, when Deitsch Brothers Leather Goods Corporation was established and Edward J. Deitsch was appointed president. In October of 1927, the company leased a 25,000-square-foot production facility for manufacturing women's handbags and luggage at 317–323 East Thirty-Fourth Street in New York City.

Impressive, soft-sided, quilted alligator-skin clutch, with leather gussets and welted edges. Quality features: an amazing, Celanese plastic pin-closure; a bias-cut front flap. Outstanding and quite rare! Spacious, rayon interior. (W 17-inch by H 8 ½ -inch by D 2-inch). Labeled: Deitsch. Ca 1946.

Very pretty, yellow java-lizard shoulder bag. Replaced shoulder strap. Faille lining. Original coin-purse attached by a gold-tone chain. (W 8-inch by H 5-inch by D 5-inch). Marked: Deitsch. Ca 1940s.

Since the late 1920s, for almost four decades until the late 1960s, Edward and Alan Deitsch, together with their families, were actively involved in the development of the well-respected Deitsch brand. The company moved to a new location in the 1930s at 185 Madison Avenue, where they produced a wide array of fine alligator, crocodile and lizard-skin goods. They regularly participated in various trade shows and fairs, and became a member of the National Authority for the Ladies' Handbag Industry (NALHI).

Impressive alligator frame-bag. Quality features: brass trim; wide, rounded gussets; protective bottom-feet; leather interior, with coin purse. (W 12-inch by H 7 ½ -inch by D 2 ½ -inch). Signed: Deitsch. Ca 1950s. The authenticity card states: "This bag is made of quality reptile skins. The workmanship reflects the skill and experience of the oldest established firm in the industry. If given proper care, it should give years of service. To clean, use only a high grade of paste wax, such as Simoniz or Neutral Kiwi Boot Polish. Apply sparingly to avoid caking in the grain of the leather. Never use saddle soap. Water or other liquids will permanently spot the surface of this bag. We cannot guarantee these products against rainspotting. A small plastic bag carried in the bag, and wrapped around the bag if you are caught in the rain, will prevent this spotting. DEITSCH – The Leader in Reptiles Since 1873."

Beside managing their domestic production, along with wholesale and retail operations, Deitsch Brothers also imported fine leather goods from Belgium.

Collection of quality handbags by Deitsch. **Top left:** Lady-like alligator shopper. Quality features: folding, rolled handle; brass trim; relief accents; trapunto stitching; leather-lined, coin purse. (W 11 ½ -inch by H 7 ½ -inch). Signed: Deitsch. Ca 1954. **Top right: (a)** Boxy, brown alligator lunch-box, with brass clasp, and leather interior. (W 9 ¾ -inch by H 4-inch by D 4 ½ -inch). Signed: Deitsch. Ca 1947. **(b)** Tremendous, black alligator frame-bag. Leather-lined, with multiple compartments. (W 15-inch by H 10-inch by D 5-inch). Marked: Deitsch. Ca 1958. **Center right:** Slim alligator shopper. Quality features: rounded brass frame; leather interior, with accessories (coin purse, plastic comb and mirror), zippered interior pouch. (W 14-inch by H 9 ½ -inch by D 2 ½ -inch). Marked: Deitsch. Ca 1957. **Bottom left:** Classic, top-handled frame bag in black crocodile. Quality features: size; self-covered frame; brass trim; leather interior with multiple pouches. (W 11 ½ -inch by 8-inch). Signed: Deitsch. Ca 1956. **Bottom right:** Curvy, barrel-style red tegu-lizard arm purse. (W 8 ¼ -inch by H 5 ¼ -inch). Signed: Deitsch. Ca 1948.

The 1940s became a prosperous time for handbag makers, when women were anxious to slip-on something more feminine than a shoulder bag that looked like a mailbox. They were happy to put a curvy alligator bag over their arm with a new frivolous outfit. The Deitsch Brothers brand was ready to offer a new assortment of charming exotics.

Precious, java-lizard clutch, in unusual metallic-pink, accented by a Bakelite kiss-clasp. Brass trim; rayon faille interior. (W 9 ¾ -inch at widest points x H 5 ¼ -inch). Signed: Deitsch. Ca 1950s-1960s.

In March of 1945, the Morton Freund Advertising Agency was hired to conduct an aggressive marketing campaign to advance the brand and bring it mainstream. At that time, Deitsch reptile bags were sold all over the country in fine department stores and through the mail from their headquarters at 36 E. 31st Street in New York.

The variety of their models was astounding: lovely bracelet and wrist bags, novelty lunch boxes, sleek clutches, simple square-shaped pocketbooks, and large single-handled totes in different styles, shapes, and sizes.

Unique alligator bucket arm-purse. Unusual features: soft-sided; wide strap; collapsible frame; wide, triangle-platform bottom. (W 10-inch by H 5 ½ -inch by D 4 ½ -inch). Labeled: Deitsch. Ca 1937.

Utilitarian alligator mail-box bag. Quality features: flat back; expanding, pleated front; no-metal closure; adjustable strap. (W 10 ½ -inch by H 10 ½ -inch by D 3 ½ -inch). Signed: Deitsch. Ca 1944.

The Deitsch company was not short on eye-catching designs and attractive accents made from Lucite, enamel, wood, and other materials. Most of their handbags were fitted with a set of accessories consisting of a leather coin purse to match the bag's interior, a comb, and a mirror. Some fancy clutches even had a compact and a lipstick encased in matching skin—so very enchanting!

Elegant and quite rare, crocodile vanity-clutch lined in delicious, red leather; with accessories (crocodile-covered lipstick case and compact). Stamped (on the gilt-brass trim): Made in Belgium. Superb quality! (W 9-inch by H 4-inch by D 2-inch). Signed: Deitsch. Belgium, ca 1950s.

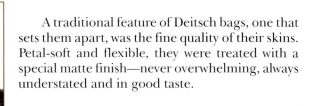

A traditional feature of Deitsch bags, one that sets them apart, was the fine quality of their skins. Petal-soft and flexible, they were treated with a special matte finish—never overwhelming, always understated and in good taste.

Wonderful, amazingly artistic piece! Buttery-soft, pleated baby-crocodile Porosus skin. Unique features: domed, self-covered frame; stunning, highly-polished brass clasp with silver filigree. Marvelous quality! (W 10 ¼-inch by H 9-inch). Signed: Deitsch. Belgium, ca 1950-1952.

Besides typical black and brown, the brand also produced styles in elegant, earthtone colors enhanced by kidskin lining in contrasting colors. Forest green, navy blue, burgundy, or luscious brandy was used with panache to bring forward the traditionally simple, clean silhouette of the brand.

Slim, ellipse-shaped alligator clutch. Top quality features: architectural, brass handle wrapped with skin; leather gussets and interior; coin purse attached by a gold-tone chain. (W 13 ½-inch by H 7-inch high w/handle by D 1 ½-inch). Signed: Deitsch. American, ca 1953.

The company imported their finest and most expensive styles from Belgium, where skilled artisans were contracted by Deitsch Bros. to create exclusive alligator styles for distribution in the United States. Today, these marvelous pieces are highly regarded as valuable collectibles by avid collectors.

Right: Exotic, python-skin satchel, lined in faille. Front flap; structured, folding handle; baby skins of beautiful, tight texture. (W 10 ¼ -inch by H 6-inch by D 2 ¾ -inch). Signed: Deitsch. Ca 1950s.

Unique, alligator arm-purse in desirable red. Top quality features: folding, triangle gussets; swivel top handle. Leather-lined. (W 11 ½ -inch by H 5-inch high by D 5-inch deep). Stamped: Deitsch. Ca 1948.

The high demand for Deitsch bags and their wide popularity was not an accident. They were due to a century-long tradition of dedication and excellence from the family. One who was a key to the company's success was Alan B. Deitsch, the company president.

Only 56 years old when he died in 1957, Alan Deitsch lived an exceptional life. Besides running the family business, he was also an amateur steamboat historian. A member of the Steamship Historical Society and the Belgian Nautical Research Association, he was credited with owning one of the largest collections of steamship photographs in the country. During World War II, he served as a civilian expert with the U. S. Navy. A native New Yorker, Deitsch graduated from Columbia University in 1921. He was survived by three sons.

Ralph Henry Noveck and Lawrence Noveck headed the Deitsch Brothers Leather Goods Corporation in the 1950s and 1960s. The company was still active in the industry after almost a hundred years of prosperous business. Today, the brand occupies a well-deserved place in the history of American fashion as one of the most prolific makers of fine reptile handbags.

Right: Very fine, double-handled, alligator lunch box. Features: brass clasp; leather lining with a coin purse. (W 10-inch by H 4-inch by D 4-inch). Signed: Deitsch. American, ca 1952.

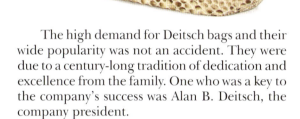

Substantial, tegu-lizard satchel. Quality features: polished, solid-brass trim and clasp; platform gussets; leather-lined. (W 11-inch by H 7 ½ -inch by D 4-inch). Signed: Deitsch. Ca 1961.

DEPARTMENT STORE BRANDS

"A department store is one of the centers of modern life."—Isaac Gimbel, 1931

Among the nation's oldest retailers, B. Altman & Co., R.H. Macy & Co., and Bloomingdale's started selling fancy alligator goods in the 19th century. In the early days, horse straps were sold right next to the ladies' walking boots, colored silks, and precious alligator. In 1883, the assortment of real alligator products was represented by club satchels and travel cases that cost in the range of 20 cents to 75 cents apiece. Large steamer trunks, tourist bags and dressing cases sold for about $3 apiece. The selection was surprisingly wide. In July of 1895, Bloomingdale's announced a two-million-dollar Realization Sale of twenty thousand, $2, real alligator bags for a mere 98¢ apiece.

Department store handbag ads, *Vogue* 1940s-1960s. **Top left:** Long, beige alligator handbag by Lucille at Bergdorf Goodman, $255. Black crocodile shopper, with bamboo handles, at Jacomo, $355. Orange lizard handbags, with front jewel, at Jacomo, $138 (1962). **Bottom right:** Green snakeskin by Deitsch, at Lord & Taylor, $36. Shrimp-pink sueded snakeskin envelope with jade clasp, by Deitsch, at Lord & Taylor, $25. Top-handled, green alligator handbag, at Lederer, $150 (1962). **Top right:** I. Magnin & Co., California – Seattle. Alligator handbag by Koret, and jewelry by Hattie Carnegie and Nettie Rosenstein (1942). **Bottom left:** Gimbels Philadelphia (March 1, 1940).

The history of American alligator cannot be told without mentioning Saks Fifth Avenue, one of the most popular American department stores with long-standing traditions. Behind it lies a remarkable story of the oldest national retail operation, Gimbel Brothers, Inc. An archived issue of the *New York Times* reported that in 1923 Gimbel Brothers, Inc. acquired the entire capital stock of Saks & Co., as well as the title to the Saks's Herald Square store and the Saks Fifth Avenue chain.

Impressive, Victorian crocodile club-bag. Quality features: front hornback inlay; luggage-type handle; slide-fasteners; top, sliding locking-clasp; leather-lined interior, with spacious compartments. Thick skins, with large-scaled texture. The bottom is constructed of two bias-cut pieces, and blind-stamped: 12 135. (W 13-inch by H 9-inch by D 6 ½ -inch). Ca late 1890 - early 1900.

Adam Gimbel, founder of the store, came to the United States from Bavaria, Germany, almost a century and a half prior to the Saks acquisition. He arrived with $25 in his pocket and a determination to build a solid business, which later grew into a multi-billion-dollar investment. The story of his life is an American dream-come-true.

Adam Gimbel landed in New Orleans, Louisiana, in 1835. For the next several years, he traveled up and down the Mississippi River with a pack over his shoulder selling "notions" to ladies. In 1842, he opened a little store in Vincennes, Indiana. Honest and just dealing with people, Adam Gimbel made friends quickly. Money was short, so he bartered furs for various goods. Adam read daily commerce newspapers, studied his customers' needs, and earned a reputation for fair dealing. His famous store sign read: *"We are not satisfied unless customers are."*

As Vincennes prospered, so did Gimbel's business. Year by year, the store grew and expanded, first branching out in Milwaukee, Philadelphia, and finally New York City, in 1910, where he opened with 27 acres of floor space. In 1922, the domestic net profit was over four million dollars. The company also operated overseas in Paris, London, and other major European cities. Additionally, several purchasing departments were opened in China, Japan, and the Philippines.

In April 1923, Gimbel Brothers, Inc. merged with Saks & Co. to form the largest retail enterprise of its kind in the world. Isaac Gimbel, one of Adam Gimbel's sons, was one of the company's visionaries. In the 1930s he envisioned the department store of the future as an establishment engaged in various activities, with intelligent management as its basis.

Shapely, java-lizard wristlet, adorned by a massive, Bakelite frame trimmed with riveted brass. Quality features: pliable, thick skins; ample, chamois-leather lined interior. (W 10-inch at widest points by H 8 ½ -inch by D 2 ½ -inch). Labeled: Saks Fifth Avenue. Ca 1945.

Pair of popular Bellestone frame-bags. Quality features: cushioned skins; intense gloss; famous rolled handles, reinforced from inside by rubber inserts; roomy, leather interiors with accessories. Sold in Saks Fifth Avenue. Signed: Bellestone. Stamped on the brass frame: Made in Belgium. Ca 1950s.

Above: Enormous, alligator frame-bag in classic design. Top quality features: ample size; self-covered frame; spacious leather interior with multiple open and zippered compartments. (W 15-inch by H 10-inch by D 5-inch). Signed: Deitsch (sold in Saks Fifth Avenue). Ca 1958.

Premium crocodile satchel, with gilt accents and riveted frame. Top quality features: supple skins, with neat scale-pattern; wide, tailored gussets; trapunto stitching; self-covered frame; leather-lined. Light in weight! (W 9 ½ -inch by H 6-inch by D 4-inch). Signed: Saks Fifth Avenue Made in France. Ca 1950s.

Affluent crocodile doctor's bag, with riveted gilt trim. Top quality details: molded gussets and accents, plenty of intricate stitching; ample, kidskin interior, with expandable compartment. (W 10 ½-inch by H 7-inch by D 6 ½-inch). Signed: Saks Fifth Avenue Made in France. Ca 1950s.

Such innovative management style created a new formula for success—the distribution of quality products under the store's exclusive label. In the 1930s, their inventory of alligator and crocodile handbags was primarily imported from France, but some collections were manufactured by leading American brands, such as Deitsch Brothers, Lederer, Mark Cross, Coblentz, Bellestone, and Lucille de Paris—all under the exclusive Saks Fifth Avenue trademark.

Luxurious alligator shoulder bag, in equestrian style. Expandable leather gussets and bottom; three-compartment leather interior. Unique features: chain-and-skin shoulder straps; protective bottom-belts; snap-closure. (W 7 ½-inch by H 5 ½-inch by D 3 ¾-inch). Signed: Rosenfeld Genuine Alligator. Created for Bonwit Teller in late 1960s.

Fabulous, baby-alligator clutch, with delicate, gilt-filigree clasp. Top quality features: rounded shape; expandable gussets; kidskin interior. Impeccable symmetry of the single, whole, central belly-cut on front and back! The umbilical scar is prominently displayed above the clasp. (W 8 ½-inch by H 4 ¾-inch by D 4-inch). Signed: Saks Fifth Avenue Made in France. Ca 1960s.

Their merchandise sold primarily in their stores were marked with the cursive *Saks Fifth Avenue* name, with no maker's signature. Thus, for example, when collecting strictly Lucille de Paris handbags, do not exclude their handbags made for Saks Fifth Avenue, but not marked *Lucille de Paris*.

Pair of elite, platform-bottom satchels, in different skins and sizes. Striking quality! No metal parts; wonderful, supple skins; deep flaps, with belted closures; trapunto stitching; leather interiors. High end! Black crocodile Porosus bag: W 11-inch by H 13-inch by D 5 ½-inch. Python bag: W 9 ½-inch by H 7-inch by D 4-inch. Both signed: Saks Fifth Avenue Made in France. Ca 1960.

Below: Very expensive, baby-crocodile Porosus satchel. High-end features: superb, underbelly skins of impeccable symmetry; complex, 4-piece gussets; welted seams; tailored interior, with multi-dimensional pockets, trimmed with matching skin. Original price tag for $145.55 – a fortune in the 1950s. (W 12-inch by H 7-inch by D 2 ½-inch). Signed: Exactmatch by Revitz. Ca 1956-1957.

This is a fine French Handbag.

To keep it looking its best do not allow it to get wet, because it may rainspot. If it does get wet, wipe it immediately.

To preserve its lustre, polish it regularly with a neutral shoe paste wax.

Ceci est un sac français de qualité.

Pour lui conserver sa plus belle apparence ne le laissez pas se mouiller; ou, dans ce cas, essuyez-le immédiatement.

Cirez le régulièrement avec un cirage neutre.

Triomphe
MADE IN FRANCE
EXPRESSLY FOR
MACY'S NEW-YORK

Set of chic, French-made crocodile bags by Triomphe, ca 1964-1968.
Top right: Large-scaled pocketbook, with deep flap; structured handle; leather-lined. (W 9 ½-inch by H 12-inch w/handles by D 2 ½-inch). Signed: Triomphe Made in France Expressly for Macy's New York.
Bottom left: Shiny satchel, with 24K-gilt trim; leather-lined. (D 10-inch by H 7 ½-inch by D 3 ¼-inch). Signed: Triomphe Made in France Expressly for Bamberger's N.J.

Some of the brand-name handbags, produced domestically or in Europe through the 1960s for Saks Fifth Avenue stores, bore two identification marks— one of the maker and the other of the store. The maker's mark, usually in gold, can be found stamped on the bag's interior, under the clasp. The store mark can usually be found either stamped on the other side of the interior or on a fabric label. Original Saks Fifth Avenue handbags had fabric labels sewn to the interior seam. They were never glued on.

Most French-made handbags sold by Saks Fifth Avenue were marked with the store logo and the signature of the maker.

Luscious, crocodile Porosus satchel, with folding handles. High-end features: outside compartments; complex, tailored gussets; neat, contrast stitching; secret, side-pull closure. (W 13 ¼ -inch by H 8 ½ -inch by D 2 ¼ -inch). Signed: Made in France Expressly for Gimbel Brothers. Ca late 1950s.

Absolutely fabulous, navy-blue crocodile briefcase, adorned by bold, 24K-gilt equestrian accents. High-end features: tailored from a single, whole belly-cut (front and back); sizable, tile-like scales; exceptionally pliable skins, with bombe finish; leather bottom and gussets; thick leather edge-welting; capacious leather interior. The structured handle is reinforced by two inserts, and leather tips – for added strength. (W 12-inch by H 13-inch w/handle by D 5-inch). Signed: Sacha Genuine Alligator France. This is an example of erroneous identification of crocodile as alligator, due to confusing export requirements existing in the 1960s. Provenance: Similar style was advertised in the September 1968 issue of *Harper's Bazaar*.

Luxurious, supple alligator wristlet, with a zippered closure, and rolled bracelet handles. Fine leather interior, mirror backed with leather, marked: Monsac. (W 9 ½ -inch by H 7-inch by D 4-inch). Labeled: Bergdorf Goodman. Provenance: Similar style was advertised by B. Altman & Co. in their Christmas 1941 collection.

Striking, convertible alligator clutch adorned by unusual, gilt-wire handles. I call this model The Victory purse, because of the two V-catches, on both sides, which hold the wire handles in place. You can easily transform it into a fashionable arm-purse by using a different arrangement of the handles, as shown. You can also play with the flap, which can be tucked inside or taken out, in order to create many different looks. Smart! Petal-soft skins, with bold scale-pattern. Expensive, intensely shiny, bombe finish. Roomy leather interior. (W 12-inch by H 6 ½-inch). Signed: Sacha Genuine Alligator France. Provenance: Sacha's custom handbags were created for Saks Fifth Avenue in Paris under the personal supervision of the unsurpassed artist-designer, Madame Sacha (Saks Fifth Avenue ad, November 1965).

Among other popular department store brands were Bonwit Teller & Co., B. Altman & Co., Lord & Taylor, Bergdorf Goodman, I. Magnin, Henry Bendel, Neiman Marcus, and Macy's. Their handbags were usually branded by the store's mark and may also have an additional stamp of exclusivity indicating they were made specifically for the store; for example, *Made in France for I. Magnin.*

Top-quality, exotic-skin handbags sold by leading department stores in the 1950s-1960s. **Top left:** Delightful, baby-crocodile Porosus cocktail purse, adorned by a decorative flip-frame: 24K-gilt, rows of genuine turquoise cabochons. (W 8-inch by H 5 ¾-inch by D 1 ¼-inch). Signed: Saks Fifth Avenue Made in France. **Top right:** Pretty, genuine turtle shoulder bag, with expandable leather gussets. Unique, gold-plated handle holders. Signed: Made in France for B. Altman & Co. New York. **Bottom left:** Timeless, crocodile frame-bag, with elegant, simple details: gilt trim; beautifully structured handle; kidskin interior. (W 12 ½-inch by H 14-inch by D 3 ½-inch). Signed: Made in France by Marshall Fields & Company. Ca 1964. **Bottom right:** Understated crocodile pocketbook, with fashionable accents and features: square flap; lever-closure; perfect top handle; gilt trim; fine belly-skins. (W 10 ¾-inch by H 12 ½-inch by D 2 ½-inch). Signed: I. Magnin & Co. France. Ca 1965.

DOFAN
IT'S IN THE BAG—LUXURY, THAT IS.

"If you're hunting for the smart, the new, the exquisite in handbags, you'll find them all at Crouch & Fitzgerald."

The 1949 *New York Times* advertisement quoted above lured buyers into the Crouch & Fitzgerald store at 48th Street & Madison Avenue in New York City. There you could find exotic skin handbags by the best names in the industry: Koret, Harry Rosenfeld, Lucille de Paris, Deitsch Brothers, Theo Rendl, and Dofan. The Dofan Handbag Co. was a distinguished manufacturer with large factories in Paris and Grenoble, France, and New York City.

Dofan handbag ad, *Vogue*, November 15, 1948.

Premium alligator frame-bag, with a deep, swagger-pocket, and impressive, enameled clasp. First-class workmanship! (W 12 ¾ -inch by H 7 ½ -inch by D 3 ½ -inch). Signed: Dofan Made in France. Ca 1956.

Represented by a cute Taurus logo, the Dofan brand was registered in 1944. At that time, America's fashion industry was booming and new players came into the marketplace to satisfy the growing demand for luxury.

Softly-pleated cobra-skin purse, with a substantial, curved Bakelite frame. Great presence! Moire-lined. (W 10 ¾ -inch by H 7 ½ -inch by D 4 ½ -inch). Signed: Dofan. Ca late 1950s.

Tall, slim alligator pouch, with self-covered frame and top handle. Unique features: only two whole cuts used to create the body, with no bottom. Leather interior. (W 9 ½ -inch by H 11-inch by D 1 ¾ – inch). Signed: Dofan Made in France. Ca 1957.

Dofan Handbag Company announced its first fall collection in June, 1948; it became a raving success. The next spring, Robert E. Sommers, president of Deauville Bags for more than seventeen years, was appointed director of sales for Dofan, located at 14 East 33rd Street in New York City. Their 1949 Christmas Collection of fine leather bags was exceptional. It flew off the racks, as did each collection of beautiful French imports they released during the 1950s and 1960s.

Starting in 1951, the Dofan brand collaborated with Best & Co. stores supplying fashionable merchandise. Artfully shaped in butter-soft alligator skins, beautifully detailed with enamel clasps, and accented with Bakelite frames or 24-karat gold-plated trim, they projected quiet elegance at excellent value.

As the magazine *Handbags and Fashion Accessories* reported, in February of 1950, Jack Kiernan, an industry veteran of twenty-five years and previously associated with Harry Rosenfeld and Josef, was appointed general sales manager for Dofan Handbag Company. In the mid-1950s, the company joined the National Authority for the Ladies' Handbag Industry (NALHI).

Classy, genuine leather pocketbook imprinted with crocodile pattern, in an original box (stamped Joseph Magnin, copyright 1963 Marget Larsen). Fine workmanship: contrast stitching; satin-lined underflap; gilt trim; leather interior; coin purse, encased mirror stamped "Dofan". (W 11-inch by H 6 ½ -inch by D 2-inch). Signed: Dofan.

Petite, crocodile-grain chain-purse. Features: gilt-filigree strap and lever-clasp; satin-lined. (W 7-inch by H 4 ½ -inch by D 3-inch). Signed: Dofan. Ca 1960s.

By the early 1960s, Dofan had changed locations and in 1961 settled at 30 East 33rd Street in New York. Besides their specialty—fine calf and alligator—the company broadened their market by developing an economy class collection of leather and vinyl handbags embossed with alligator patterns. Very affordable, they did not compromise the quality and styles of the brand. Neat and compact, the economy bags looked so real! By the 1970s, Dofan sold fine leather "instant import-ants" and vinyl "dofanettes" at Tailored Woman and Franklin Simon stores.

The Dofan genuine skin handbags are branded with the Dofan logo. Their alligator-embossed leather bags, lined in fabric, are usually marked "Genuine Leather." Their alligator-pressed vinyl bags are marked "Made in France by Dofan." Although cute, imitation bags by Dofan are not as collectible as their splendid genuine skin styles.

EVANS
THE GIFT OF TRUE ELEGANCE

Collectors look for spectacular skin purses marked Evans Elegance that were handmade by Evans Case Co., of Massachusetts, starting in the late 1930s. Evans accessorized their leather bags with sets of novelties, such as cigarette lighters, combs, coin purses, mirrors, and even perfume atomizers.

THE GIFT OF TRUE *elegance* IS AN EVANS

In all the world, no Christmas inspiration like an Evans. The luxury of an incomparably styled Evans handbag…the elegance of an Evans original lighter…gifts to make the giving memorable…and to enrich so many occasions of her life.

Shown: EVANS SYMPHONY, in genuine alligator with baby calf lining and fittings to match, including powder box, lipstick holder, Evans automatic lighter and comb, $150. Genuine alligator with faille lining, $130; or in calf… black, brown or navy…$58. Other elegant Evans bags from $15.

TABLE LIGHTER…an Evans original, in bone china encrusted with gold and French Enamel Topaz, $20. Other Evans Table Lighters from $5.

® *Evans*

EVANS CASE CO., NORTH ATTLEBORO, MASS.

Evans Elegance handbag ad, *Harper's Bazaar* December 1953.

Dramatic satin vanity-pouch, with a lid-cover jeweled with bold, ruby-glass cabochons. Masterpiece! An early example of glamorous Evans handbags, which are always in demand with collectors. (W 9 ½ -inch by H 5 ¾ -inch by 2 ¾ -inch). Signed: Evans. Ca late 1930s.

They made elegant handbags that conveyed prestige at its best! When a high-end alligator purse became a must-have accessory and the domestic market was exploding with dozens of new companies, this brand stood apart. It commanded the highest prices, comparable only to Mark Cross.

Pair of identical, high-end, superlative frame-bags, in genuine alligator, fully lined in leather, with pockets and slot for their complete kits of original accessories. Signed: Evans. American, 1953.

Most notable were their alligator bags fitted with a watch, cigarette case, lighter, lipstick, comb, and compact. Those were the hallmarks of the superb Evans brand, sold in New York at Dale Fifth Avenue in 1948 and Saks Fifth Avenue in the 1950s.

Delightful crocodile satchel, with a time-piece, and plastic handle (replacement). Faille interior. Very different! (W 8 ¾ -inch by H 15-inch by D 4 ½ -inch). Signed: Evans Elegance. Ca 1950s.

Relatively scarce on the market today (because nobody ever wants to let them go!), they are highly valued for their distinctive character and outstanding craftsmanship. Evans bags were styled in two basic designs: a refined, top-handled daytime bag and a simple, elongated afternoon clutch with exquisite hardware. Quality crocodile, alligator, ostrich, and Morocco skins, in shades of black, brown, navy, red, and emerald, were often used in those terrific creations.

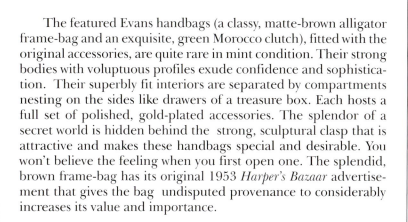

Charming Morocco leather book-clutch, with solid-brass trim. Top quality features: flat black-handle; complete set of original accessories. Practical and glamorous! (W 9-inch by H 6 ¾ -inch by D 2-inch). Provenance: Similar Evans styles were advertised by Saks Fifth Avenue in December 1951.

The featured Evans handbags (a classy, matte-brown alligator frame-bag and an exquisite, green Morocco clutch), fitted with the original accessories, are quite rare in mint condition. Their strong bodies with voluptuous profiles exude confidence and sophistication. Their superbly fit interiors are separated by compartments nesting on the sides like drawers of a treasure box. Each hosts a full set of polished, gold-plated accessories. The splendor of a secret world is hidden behind the strong, sculptural clasp that is attractive and makes these handbags special and desirable. You won't believe the feeling when you first open one. The splendid, brown frame-bag has its original 1953 *Harper's Bazaar* advertisement that gives the bag undisputed provenance to considerably increases its value and importance.

Museum-quality, genuine alligator frame-bag, complete with the kit of accessories. Ultimate luxury! Impeccable quality throughout! A rare find in mint condition, with proper provenance (*Harper's Bazaar* 1953 ad, page 95). (W9 ½ -inch by H 9 ¼ -inch by D 3 ¼ -inch). Signed: Evans Elegance.

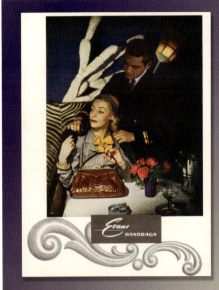 

Evan handbags ad. **Top left:** *Town & Country* 1947. **Top right:** *Vogue* 1947. **Bottom left:** *Town & Country* 1944. **Bottom right:** *Harper's Bazaar* 1947.

Behind the exceptional Evans brand is a remarkable story that author Larry Clayton shares in his book, *The Evans Book*. Alfred F. Reilly, Samuel Haslan and Fred Burden founded the Evans Novelty Company about 1918. Reilly was a man of various talents: a creative and experienced jeweler and a determined and smart businessman. The company started by making picture frames and neck chains for the United States Army. Later, energetic Reilly secured a large contract from United Drug Company to manufacture compacts for face powders.

In the 1920s, with 75 employees and a 3,500-square-foot production facility, Evans grew and was incorporated in 1922 as Evans Case Co. Alfred Reilly became its chairman and appointed his three sons as officers. Reilly spent considerable time traveling to promote their products. Their lines included an array of products, such as cigarette lighters and cases, compacts, vanities, pocket flasks, costume jewelry, as well as mesh bags and various handbags.

During World War II, due to restrictions on the uses of metal, their production of compacts and jewelry was temporarily halted. But Evans continued to manufacture cigarette lighters and handbags accented with hand-finished wood frames.

Below: Impeccable alligator purse, with rare matte finish. Mind-bending quality! Hard-sided construction; brass frame; immaculate, leather interior; complete set of accessories. A rare find in mint, unused condition! (W 10 ¾ -inch by H 14-inch by D 3 ½ -inch). Signed: Evans Elegance. Ca 1950s.

The period 1946–1950 was the most prosperous for Evans Case Company, as they opened sales offices in New York, Los Angeles, Chicago, Boston, Cleveland, and Dallas. They advertised in the magazines *Vogue, Harper's Bazaar, Town & Country, House Beautiful,* and *House & Garden*. Radio and television shows promoted their brand and leading department stores clamored for Evans products. Very few makers of fashion accessories of that time received as much window display and counter space as Evans did. Their design specialists carefully analyzed fashion trends and created product lines to be anxiously anticipated by the public, at least three years ahead of the industry trends.

Reportedly at the peak of the company's success in 1955, Reilly's spouse ran the handbag department, but her unpopular decisions and management style caused two senior managers to leave their positions. The handbag department closed and the company was sold. The Reillys retired to Florida.

Beautiful Evans handbags have withstood the test of time and become prized possessions today.

GUCCI

SYMBOL OF HIGH-PROFILE CREDIBILITY

"Gucci's style is strong but not overpowering. Not show-offy. Softly elegant." —Maurizio Gucci

The name Gucci has been associated with high fashion, fine leather goods and wealth. The company began as a saddlery, in 1906 in Florence, Italy, by Guccio Gucci. His linked initials have adorned the company's products ever since. His son, Aldo, together with his brothers, Adolfo and Vasco, took the company to America and, ultimately, to the world.

They crossed the ocean in 1953 and opened their first shop in the United States at 7 East Fifty-eighth Street in New York City. In the 1958, their new collection was sold right next to Hermes and included many exquisite handbags carefully "plotted" to hold a carload of necessities without bulging. Among the first was a huge, rectangular crocodile bag in classic black, measuring 18-by-12 inches. Originally selling for $252, it was a treasure of a bag!

Breathtaking, genuine alligator vanity, treated with the shiniest bombe finish. Awesome, 24K-gold plated details. Exceptional quality of skins and craftsmanship! Fixtures are stamped: Gucci (in three places). Interior vanity-mirror under the lid. Kidskin interior with accessories (wallet, clochette with keys, original dustbag). Authenticity card, price tags. Sold at Neiman-Marcus. (W 8 ¾ -inch by H 9 ¾ -inch by D 5 ¼ -inch). Signed: Gucci Made in Italy (serial number). Italy, ca late 1990s.

By the 1980s, Gucci's popularity became multinational, with sales balanced among Europe, America and Japan. Twenty-five shops were opened in the United States alone. In 1985, Aldo's nephew, Maurizio Gucci, assumed the dual titles of president of Guccio Gucci, the Italian parent company, and chairman of Gucci Shops Inc., the American subsidiary.

Born in Florence, Maurizio Gucci studied law and economics at Catholic University in Milan. After working for seven years in the United States, he returned to Milan to work from an office overlooking the Via Montenapoleone, Milan's most fashionable shopping street. The 36-year-old executive laid out an ambitious plan to transform the family company into a modern corporation. His goal was to preserve the classic Gucci style that was the center of the company's philosophy.

Elite, crocodile Porosus pocketbook in classic style. Soft, folding gussets and bottom. Gold-plated clasp. Leather-lined. (W 12-inch by H 13-inch w/handle by H 3 ½ -inch). Signed: Made in Italy by Gucci. Italy, ca 1959. Shown with a pair of vintage black crocodile pumps, ca 1950s.

Luxurious, java-lizard pocketbook. Quality features: beautifully textured skins; gilt fixtures; accordion gussets; leather-lined; lizard coin-purse. (W 9-inch by H 11-inch w/handle by D 2-inch). Signed: Made in Italy by Gucci. Ca 1960s. Shown with a thermoset (plastic-n-metal) necklace by Trifari (ca 1950s).

The rapid growth of the brand resulted in an astounding increase in its annual production, from 10,000 handbags annually to 700,000 by the end of the 1980s. "They have been extremely successful in an extraordinarily short time," once noticed the Florentine fashion designer Emilio Pucci. Smart advertising campaigns promoted the diversity of their styles and targeted a relaxed, casual market in America. Gucci captured the hearts of American consumers, and also strengthened their position worldwide.

Trendy java-lizard saddle-bag, trimmed with polished, silver-tone metal. Quality features: adjustable strap; expandable bottom and gussets; tailored leather interior; coin-purse. (W 9 ¾ -inch by H 9-inch by D 3-inch). Stamped: Gucci (double Gs logo). Signed: Gucci Made in Italy (metal plaque and zipper pull). Ca 1970s. Shown with an amazing, woven metal cuff-bracelet, by Boucher No.78238, ca 1950s.

By the end of the 1980s, Gucci's incredible success spawned a proliferation of imitations that took two distinctive forms: blatant counterfeits and unlawful registration of the Gucci brand name as a trademark by local entrepreneurs in several third-world countries. Unfortunately, the problem continues to this day. Still, there is only one real Gucci brand.

Sultry python clutch, with a removable bamboo handle. Polished, silver trim. Zippered top; hidden, zippered compartment on the front. Lined in Gucci-signature satin. (W 11-inch by H 14-inch by D 3 ½ -inch). Labeled: Gucci Made in Italy (blind stamp, serial number). Italy, ca 1980s.

In the late 1990s, designer Tom Ford introduced some changes by incorporating modern features and elements. This helped to elevate the brand to the status of a modern icon.

Sublime, sizable alligator hobo-bag, with exquisite matte finish, accented by bold equestrian details – in brushed gold. Stunning size and style! Snap-closure; suede interior; authenticity card, and price tags. Sold at Neiman-Marcus. (W 12 ½ -inch by H 13-inch w/handles by D 3 ½ -inch). Signed: Gucci Made in Italy (serial number). Italy, ca late 1990.

Today, every Gucci purse is regarded as a treasured possession, even more so their vintage alligator and crocodile handbags are regarded as important collectibles at leading auction houses. Especially collectible are their classic styles from the 1950s, such as an iconic satchel crowned by a bamboo handle and a top-handled treasure box. At auctions they fetch solid prices in thousands of dollars.

Because of the continued demand for classics, Gucci replicated their most popular styles from the 1950s and 1960s in recent, limited-edition collections. Made with very expensive black crocodile and matte cognac alligator, and lined with decadent suede and kidskin, the featured examples are destined for immortality. Investment pieces surely, they satisfy the most discriminating taste and craving for luxury, and enhance any wardrobe. Today, Gucci successfully maintains a reputation as one of the most prestigious international design houses in the world.

Sleek, genuine alligator saddle-bag, with bamboo clasp. Upscale features: deep back pouch; long strap, buckle-closure (24K-gilt) stamped "Gucci"; lambskin interior; leather coin-purse, gilt, round mirror; authenticity card, price tags. Sold at Neiman-Marcus. (W 9 ½ -inch by H 7 ½ -inch by D 3-inch). Signed: Gucci Made in Italy (serial number). Italy, ca late 1990.

HERMES
ULTIMATE STATUS SYMBOL IN LEATHER ACCESSORIES

"Hermes successfully adapted and refined the saddle maker's skills to create a range of sturdy, voluminous bags that marry classic style and function."—Claire Wilcox, fashion consultant at London's Victoria and Albert Museum

Leather craftsmen Thierry Hermes and Emile-Charles Hermes founded the House of Hermes in France in 1837. They began by making bridles and saddles for small shops, which were as numerous in the 19th century as gas stations today. Among their customers were the great stables of France and carriage makers on the Champs-Elysees in Paris.

The family business grew rapidly and steadily. By 1865, it had moved from the outskirts of Paris to its present location in the heart of the city, at 24 Rue du Faubourg, Saint-Honore. With the move, the company entered the retail business and sold equestrian equipment to private customers.

The invention of the motorcar in the late 19th century adversely affected demand for equestrian articles, so the company created new motor-travel supplies. Travel bags, mallettes with hidden bottoms for carrying jewels and valuables, handbags, wallets, and other small goods became the new cornerstones of the company's production.

In order to utilize their contingent of highly skilled leather craftsmen, Hermes transferred the traditional techniques used in saddle making—saddle stitching by hand—to their new handbag line. This ancient technique, mastered by Hermes to perfection, became the company's trademark and propelled it into the stratosphere of stardom. Hermes became one of the most prestigious leather goods brands in the world, and their handbags became ultimate investment articles to pass from one generation to the next.

During World War I, the company made another radical change in its production by introducing a zipper. It happened almost by accident. In a 1968 interview, Jean R. Guerrand-Hermes, a son-in-law of Emile Hermes, recalled that in 1917 Emile Hermes was commissioned to buy harnesses for the French artillery in Canada. Upon arrival there, he noticed that the military car assigned to him had a canvas top closed with a new device called a zipper. In fact, he pointed out, the first zipper was invented about 2,000 years before Christ, made with the teeth of the hawk.

Since then, it had been reinvented many times, but no one was successful in registering the invention, until Hermes did. When the war was over, the Canadian company that supplied the army with zippered tops lost its business. Emile Hermes bought out their stock and managed to secure an exclusive patent when he returned to France. As soon as the legal papers were in order, the company launched its first bag with a zippered fastener. It was known as the Bugatti bag and was a version of their traditional jockey bag. The new, zippered closure, known as the "Hermes closure," was born to become one of the most radical inventions in the history of fashion.

Besides using a zipper in handbags, the company ventured into the clothing business by introducing their first leather jacket with the zippered front in 1920. *"Fortunately, our first customer was the Prince of Wales (now the Duke of Windsor), and we sold 10,000 after that,"* Guerrand reminisced in the late 1960s.

Since the 1930s, the Hermes company has been producing a series of classic models that became status symbols. Today, the popularity of the brand is astounding, despite hefty price tags that accompany their creations. They say the *H* in the word "Hermes" should be pronounced in a whisper—and so should the price! Most of their styles are sold for thousands of dollars. Their handbags and their silk products are truly handmade phenomena in the mass-

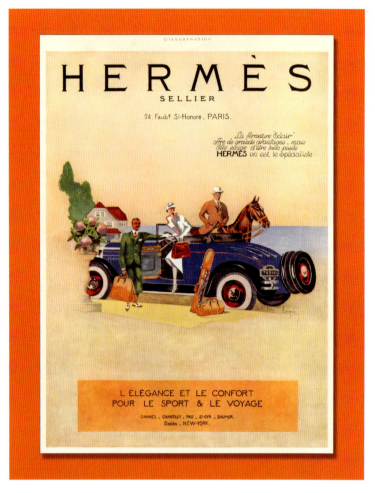

Hermes handbags ad, September 13, 1924, France (*L'Illustration*, 13 Septembre 1924).

production world, highly appreciated by quality-conscious consumers who pay a hefty price for the privilege of owning them.

In 1968, during a trip to Bonwit Teller and the Hermes Boutique, Jean R. Guerrand-Hermes commented that the Hermes prices were high, yet cheap considering the amount of time invested in the production of one handbag. It took a cobbler on average sixty hours to create one perfect handbag. That meant only four handbags could be created per month per cobbler. In 1968, a Hermes' crocodile purse cost $895, a lizard bag cost $295, a silk blouse cost $110, and a silk scarf cost $25.

Despite prices and long waiting lists, Hermes customers are not all rich and famous. Housewives worldwide might have saved for several years to buy one status bag. For example, the Kelly bag—a sturdy, all-leather or linen-and-leather handbag with a front flap and a top handle—was named for Princess Grace of Monaco, the former Grace Kelly, in appreciation of her support of the brand. In the 1950s, she was among the first buyers of this model, which, according to Mr. Guerrand, was based on a large handbag the company had been producing for almost eighty years for jockeys to store their saddles.

Regardless the model, design or material, every handbag by Hermes combines utter functionality and exquisite classic style. The result of such a fortunate marriage is the name that is associated with the finest quality and highest collectibility. Hermes has maintained a philosophy of top craftsmanship by closely controlling the entire production and refusing to license their lines. For over 150 years, the Hermes headquarters have remained in Paris, France, where their extensive collection of equestrian art and paintings, as well as the articles produced for their outstanding label, are housed at the Hermes Museum of the Faubourg Saint-Honore. It was lovingly put together by Emile-Charles Hermes.

Avoid the disappointment of buying a reproduction by acquiring Hermes products only from authorized dealers, and vintage Hermes articles from experts in vintage designer handbags.

Highly desired – astronomically expensive! – handbags by one of the most prestigious makers in the world – Hermes – in different skins, colors, and styles, from the 1940-1970s. All treated with famous saddle hand-stitching, and lined with supple goatskin. **Olive-brown**: Elegant, box-leather Pullman. Outside compartments; solid-brass sliding locks, and a key-lock. (W 11 ¾ -inch by H 13-inch by D 3-inch). The lock is stamped (inside): Hermes-Paris. Signed (interior): Hermes Paris. Ca late 1940s-early 1950s. **Gray**: Sporty ostrich shoulder bag, with fabulous, gun-metal hardware. (W 8 ¾ -inch by H 6 ¾ -inch by D 2-inch). Stamped (hardware): H carriage logo. Signed: Hermes Paris Made in France. Ca 1980s. **Red**: Sleek java-lizard clutch, with a removable shoulder strap, and 24K-gilt accent. (W 9 ¼ -inch by H 6 ½ -inch by D 2-inch). Signed: Hermes Paris Made in France. Ca 1970s. **Black**: Sublime, baby-crocodile Porosus satchel, with 24K-gilt brass accents. Outrageously valuable and expensive, central belly-cuts of superb symmetry and texture. The whole, single cut was used to tailor the back and the scalloped front. Folding bottom and gussets. Ample interior, composed on two separate compartments, with a famous Hermes wallet with a snap, and a deep outside pocket – neatly lined with Hermes-signature goatskin. (W 10 ¼ -inch by H 12-inch w/handle by D 3-inch). Stamped (lock interior): Hermes Paris. Signed: Hermes Paris. Ca 1960s.

Judith Leiber
Luxurious Whimsical Collectible Novelties

Judith Leiber was born Judith Peto in Budapest, Hungary. In 1939, she became an apprentice at the Hungarian Handbag Guild and the first woman Meister (master) to be recognized by the Guild for her skill and workmanship. She once commented that she learned how to make the handbag from start to finish: *"I used to make handbags for the Americans in exchange for dollars. After the Germans and the Russians, there was very little left in Hungary."*

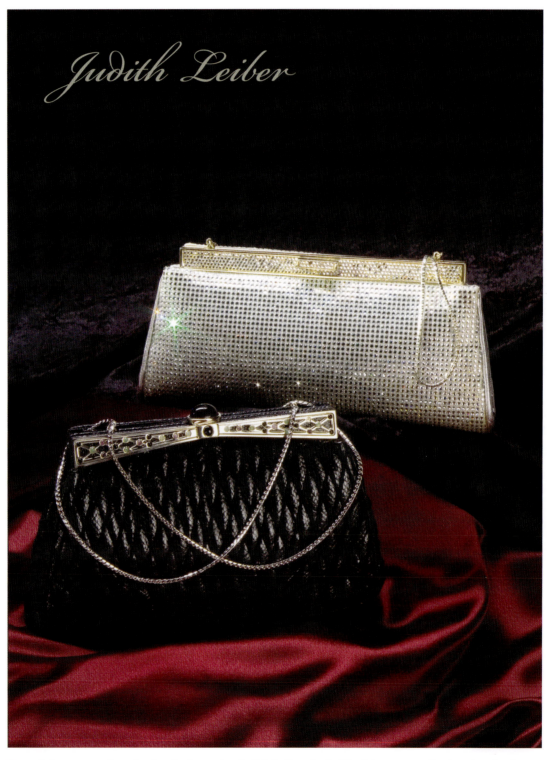

Duo of elegant evening clutches by inventive Judith Leiber. **Left:** Black karung, quilted and embroidered with silk cord. Filigree frame,with onyx cabochon-clasp; silver trim; satin-lined. (W 10-inch by H 6-inch by D 2-inch). Labeled: Neiman-Marcus by Judith Leiber, 1978. **Right:** Sparkling rhinestone encrusted frame clutch, with silver-leather gussets; silver trim, drop-in shoulder strap, satin interior. (W 10-inch by H 7-inch by D 2 -inch), 1967.

Spectacular, genuine alligator evening-bag, in fabulous turquoise. Semi-precious clasp (green chrysoprase and lapis lazuli). Doubled straps; accessories; lambskin interior. (W 7-inch by H 5-inch by D 3-inch). Signed: Judith Leiber (gilt plaque). Judith Leiber LLC design, ca 1990s.

Striking, baby-alligator clutch in desirable ivory. Gem-studded, 24K-plate frame, with twenty-six semi-precious cabochons (garnet, jade, tiger-eye, onyx, amethyst, ruby, lapis, rose quartz). Pleated, matte skins; unique, side-pull clasp; kidskin lining. (W 10-inch by H 6-inch by D 3-inch), 1990.

After World War II, Judith immigrated to the Unites States with her husband, Gerson Leiber. They met in Budapest when he was a sergeant in the US Army. By then, she was an experienced handbag designer. In New York, she started her career by working for several well-known labels, such as Richard Koret, Morris Moskowitz and leading American fashion designer Nettie Rosenstein. *"I learned there how to make a diversified collection,"* Ms. Leiber mentioned. *"In Europe at the time there were only about six handbag styles."*

Adorable, genuine alligator gift-box, with attractive, gilt-wire details. Fully leather lined. (W 7-inch by H 4-inch without handle by D 3-inch); 1974.

Monumental alligator tote, with unique, yet practical details: drawstring, tassel and shoulder strap. Impeccable! Whopping, 6 1/2-inch wide gussets. Leather-lined; complete with accessories. (W 11-inch by H 9-inch). Labeled: Judith Leiber; 1983.

In 1963, together with her husband, Judith Leiber launched her own business, and it became one of the most successful in American fashion. She has been awarded numerous accolades, including the Handbag Designer of the Year Award in 1992, and the Council of Fashion Designers of America Lifetime Achievement Award in 1994.

Sultry, genuine karung shoulder bag, with a semi-precious clasp (African tourmaline). Identical to the turquoise alligator purse, page 105. (W 7-inch by H 5-inch by D 3-inch). Signed: Judith Leiber (gilt plaque). Judith Leiber LLC design, ca 1990s.

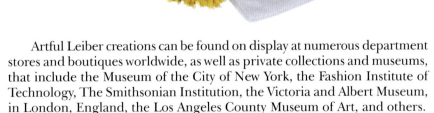

Fuchsia karung shoulder bag, in its original dustbag, with the set of original accessories and tags.

Darling, baby-alligator châtelaine frame bag, with a gold ball clasp, and silk-cord strap with tassels. Kidskin-lined. Tailored. (W 5-inch by H 6-inch by D 3-inch). Labeled: Judith Leiber; 1978.

Artful Leiber creations can be found on display at numerous department stores and boutiques worldwide, as well as private collections and museums, that include the Museum of the City of New York, the Fashion Institute of Technology, The Smithsonian Institution, the Victoria and Albert Museum, in London, England, the Los Angeles County Museum of Art, and others.

Elegant and practical, natural python zipper-bag, with self-frame, and long double shoulder straps. So soft and capacious, it is a perfect choice for everyday use. Leather lining, and a jeweled pull. (W 14-inch by H 9-inch by D 6-inch). Singed: Judith Leiber. Ca 1985.

For over forty years, her distinctive and recognizable style—a smart mix of humor, artistry and function—has attracted an enormous following. One of her signature pieces is a tiny, jeweled minaudiere (evening bag). Its figural shape is lavishly encrusted with thousands of Swarovski crystals and it is outfitted with a set of gold-plated accessories: a comb with a tassel, a swivel mirror, and a coin purse.

Luxurious, genuine ostrich skin bag, with a frame shaped in an attractive pagoda-style, accompanied by a removable shoulder strap, and accented by a tiger-eye cabochon clasp. Faille-lined, with accessories. (W 10-inch by H 7-inch by D 3-inch). Labeled: Judith Leiber (plaque); 1979.

Delightful, genuine frog-skin frame bag, with gold trim, drop chain, and self details, lined in satin. (W 8-inch by H 5-inch by D 2-inch). Labeled: Neiman-Marcus by Judith Leiber. Ca 1980.

Right: Absolutely spectacular alligator pleated pouch, with ribbed, gold frame, accented by a sizable tiger-eye cabochon. Outstanding quality and style! Generously pleated skins on both sides. Leather-lined. (W 10-inch by H 7-inch by D 4-inch). Labeled: Judith Leiber (golden plaque), 1981.

Often costing in the thousands of dollars, each sparkling masterpiece takes over ten hours to complete by hand. The process is painstaking and costly. Between seven to thirteen thousand "jewels" are glued on one bag, using the Old World technique that Judith Leiber learned in Budapest. She designed every model and made decisions on every shape and detail. The result was always stunning, recognizable from far away, and does not need additional advertisement or a logo.

Sweet, baby-python evening bag, ornamented by eight onyx-cabochons. Softly pleated skins. Accordion bottom and gussets. Silver filigree frame. Satin interior. Silk-cord tassel strap. (W 7-inch by H 6-inch by D 2-inch). Labeled: Judith Leiber; 1983.

Besides tiny whimsical evening bags, Judith Leiber also developed a trend for capacious carryalls, magnificent day bags in bright designer colors made with luxurious skins, including crocodile, alligator, lizard, karung, whip snake, and ostrich. They are generously accented by colorful, semi-precious gemstones and feature smartly organized interiors—complete with accessory kits and optional shoulder straps. Judith Leiber always sneaks a shoulder strap in every handbag, explaining, *"When a woman has her hands full of packages, she wants to carry her bag on her shoulders. And who has a servant running after them nowadays?"*

Superlative, gathered alligator bag, adorned by an elegant – silver-and-gold – polished frame, with a rose-quartz cabochon. Breathtaking quality! Retractable skin strap; floating hinges marked "Judith Leiber"; lambskin interior. (W 12-inch by H 7-inch by D 4-inch). Labeled: Judith Leiber. 1975.

Opulent, pleated navy alligator pouch, with scalloped frame. The skins are out-of-this-world! Retractable, gold strap; lambskin interior. (W 12-inch by H 8-inch by D 3-inch). Labeled: Judith Leiber; 1982. Shown with a thermoset rose necklace, encrusted with clear rhinestones, by Kenneth J. Lane (K.J.L), ca 1960s.

"In the 1970s and the 1980s, alligator bags were our best sellers. The wives of world leaders, from Nancy Reagan to Raisa Gorbachev, carried alligator bags that I had specially made for them. And when fashionable women around the world saw those bags, they too wanted similar ones. We worked fifteen hours a day, week after week, month after month, turning out intricately made alligator bags. And Fish and Wildlife wanted to put an end to it!" Thus reminisced Judith Leiber in the book *No Mere Bagatelles*, by Jeffrey Sussman. With the help of their attorney, the Leibers were able to withstand the ban on alligator skins and continued manufacturing and selling alligator handbags during difficult times.

Flamboyant, yet sophisticated, her wonderful creations combine the luxury of classic leathers with fantastic craftsmanship and one-of-a-kind details: whimsical accents, gold plating, quilting, gems and jewels, embroidery, braiding, pleating, and trims. The number of styles is mind bending. According to Judith Leiber, she has created more than 5,000 different designs—and most of them became instant collectibles.

Above: Sophisticated, gold ostrich-skin evening purse, with brightly-polished, 24K-plated trim. Complete with original accessories, and price tags from Saks Fifth Avenue (originally $2,180). Faille interior. (W 9-inch by H 6-inch by D 2-inch). Labeled: Judith Leiber. Judith Leiber LLC design, ca 1990s.

Slim, elegant baby-alligator clutch, with a jeweled, multi-stone drop chain, lined in black leather. First class workmanship! (W 9-inch by H 4-inch by D 1-inch). Labeled: Judith Leiber; 1984.

In 1993, the Leibers sold their firm, which since then has changed ownership several times and was finally acquired by the company Schottenstein. Currently operating from New York, they are expanding into the European and Asian markets, and opening a store on Rodeo Drive in Los Angeles. In addition, the company is planning on opening stores in India and Dubai.

Devoted fans of Judith Leiber include celebrities Bette Midler, Mary Tyler Moore, Elizabeth Hurley, Naomi Campbell, and Cindy Crawford, as well as former First Ladies Barbara Bush, Nancy Reagan, and Hillary Rodham Clinton (who often carries her Leiber bags to diplomatic and social events around the world).

Glamorous, python skin clutch treated with unique gold lace finish. Bright, gold-plated trim, removable shoulder strap. Leather interior. (W 9-inch by H 7-inch by D 2-inch). Labeled: Judith Leiber; 1990.

Special Thank You!

Over the years of collecting and researching, I have learned to really appreciate the craftsmanship of exotic skin handbags, especially the ones created by Judith Leiber. Her contribution to the development of her own brand – purely American in style and character – as well as various domestic brands, including Nettie Rosenstein, Koret, Dofan, etc., simply cannot be overestimated.

What intrigues millions of her followers most is not only the brilliance of her designs, but also their innovative construction. Her rare artisan skill to free-hand cut a pattern and create a handbag from start to finish requires an enormous talent – similar to improvisation in jazz!

Her amazing story of the American-dream-come-true and her perseverance in the ever-changing fashion world have secured her a primary position in the history of American handbags. Her brand has become "perhaps the sole survivor of the once teeming and powerful American handbag industry", in her own words. Today, her legacy is being preserved by the Leiber Museum located at 446 Old Stone Highway in East Hampton, New York.

I can't help but share with you that Judith Leiber is also a very kind and warm person who really cares. She kindly agreed to assist me with my project, and checked and corrected the dates of production of her handbags that are featured in this book.

She also mailed to me a signed book of her memoirs, written in collaboration with Jeffrey Sussman, *No Mere Bagatelles*. It is a story of handbag genius Judith Leiber and modernist artist Gerson Leiber—a beautiful story of remarkable survival, perseverance, and eternal love!

KORET
SUCCESS IS IN THE BAG!

When you see the famous Koret Golden Gazelle stamped on the interior of a handbag, you know that you are getting the best quality. Koret, Inc. was founded by Richard Koret in New York City, in 1929. He was a handbag manufacturer, distributor, designer, exporter, and importer. After eight decades of successful and productive business, the firm is still in operation, with Michael Gordon as the current president.

Koret alligator handbag ad, *Harper's Bazaar* 1941.

Luxurious alligator-skin clutch in desirable red, with curvy frame and brass finials. Back handle, softly pleated skins. (W 12 ¼ -inch by H 6 ¼ -inch by D 2 ¾ -inch). Signed: Koret, Irving Detroit. Ca 1940s.

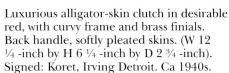

Glossy alligator satchel, with woven-brass handles. Top quality features: self-covered frame; exterior compartments; leather interior; accessories. Mirror pouch is stamped: I. Magnin Inc. & Co. (W 9 ½ -inch by H 7 ½ -inch by D 2-inch). Signed: Koret Made of Genuine Alligator. Ca 1935.

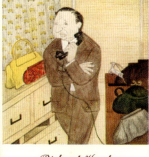

Richard Koret

He is famous for his dramatic, enormous handbags, for using fur, lamés, wonderful leathers with a courageous hand. His bags, his name, and the proud, springing gazelle that is his trademark are known everywhere. But few know that he is small, dark, and shy, and that he refuses to work anywhere but on the twelfth floor.

A commentary to the witty caricature by Aline Fruhauf, published in the October 15, 1940, issue of the *Vogue* magazine, noted that Richard Koret was a short, dark-haired, very shy man famous for his dramatic handbags and impeccable taste. Yet, very few people knew him in person.

Top: Richard Koret ad, *Vogue* October 15, 1940.
Bottom left: Koret handbags ad, *Vogue* 1953.
Bottom right: Koret Rosebud handbag ad, *Vogue* March 1, 1960.

Richard Koret was one of the leaders of the domestic handbag industry and a founder of the National Authority for the Ladies' Handbag Industry (NALHI) that was launched in 1935. A talented trendsetter, he was credited with many innovations in handbag design, such as built-in compartments for combs and glasses. His designs were so highly respected that several of his handbags were used by women's military services during World War II.

Spectacular, woven-straw satchel be-jeweled by substantial, semi-precious cabochons. Very glamorous! Fully leather-lined. (W 11 ¾ -inch by H 8-inch by D 5 ½ -inch). Signed: Koret Made in Italy. Ca 1960s.

A lifelong bachelor, Koret spent his last days in his weekend home in Bedford Hills, New York, where he died in November, 1965, at the age of 63. Although he left no close relatives, his legacy and his passion for the practical beauty of a lady's handbag lives on with his company.

Lovely crocodile-skin satchel, with a unique collapsible frame and double handles. Clean, sleek profile, and beautiful quality! Complete set of accessories. (W 11 ½ -inch by H 6 ¼ -inch by D 3 ½ -inch). Signed: Koret. Ca 1949-1951.

Precious, genuine alligator box-purse, with gold-plated fixtures; lined in black leather. (W 7 ½ -inch by H 6 ½ -inch by D 4-inch). Signed: Koret Genuine Alligator. Ca 1950s.

Classy, full-quill ostrich skin satchel. Curvy lines; beautifully appointed gold-filigree clasp; split, swivel interior coin-purse; leather interior. (W 11-inch by H 8 ½ -inch by D 3 ½ -inch). Signed: Koret Made of Genuine Ostrich.

Over the years, the company has grown and expanded into several production areas. In September 1942, a new branch office was opened in the Merchandise Mart, in Chicago. In August 1948, Mr. Koret formed a new corporation, Tresor, Inc. (33 East Thirty-third Street)—a division of Koret that started the production and distribution of hand-embroidered and beaded evening bags.

Dramatic, ostrich-skin satchel, with a distinct rosebud clasp. High-end details: pleated attachments to the double-handles; roomy, outside compartments; finely tailored, leather interior. Complete with a pair of matching leather gloves. (W 10 ½ -inch by H 14-inch by D 3-inch). Signed: Koret Made of Genuine Ostrich. Provenance: This fabulous set was advertised in *Vogue* March 1,1960 issue (page 111).

Marvelous alligator lunch-box, with a stationary gilt handle, and a key-hole closure. Leather-lined. (W 8 ¾ -inch by H 6-inch w/handle by D 4 ¼ -inch). Signed: Koret Made of genuine alligator. Ca 1954.

Sophisticated, full-quill ostrich pocketbook, lined in scrumptious red leather. Outside compartments. (W 8 ¾ -inch by H 7-inch by D 2-inch). Signed: Koret Made of Genuine Ostrich. Ca 1956.

The successful ownership and long-standing traditions of his company have been maintained through the decades by a dedicated staff, including Mr. Clyde Jennings, formerly a partner and president of Deauville, Inc., who joined Koret, Inc. in an executive capacity in 1951.

The highest standard of quality has always been the trademark of the brand. In the 1930s and the 1940s, Koret offered a wide variety of luxurious styles in crocodile, alligator and ostrich. Cool and whimsical, they had tons of personality. A beautiful alligator purse by Koret was the *It* bag of the 1950s, especially popular with the rich and famous.

The brand's assortment was exceptionally wide: extravagant travel bags and mallettes, sophisticated daytime bags, sensible pocketbooks and clutches, generous totes and stunning evening bags gleaming with gems and gilt. What a kaleidoscope of textures, colors, shapes, sizes, styles, and accents! Each piece was accompanied by the famous Koret signature feature—a tiny coin purse on a delicate gold chain attached to the fitted interior.

Koret alligator handbags ad, *Vogue* April 15, 1938.

Left: Tremendous – highly collectible – alligator travel bag, with a removable document folder marked "Passport Papers", "Tickets", and "Money". Unique features include: a watch (signed Deauville, 7-jewels, Swiss); wide gussets folding inside; incredibly roomy, leather interior. (W 11 ½ -inch by H 11 ½ -inch by D 5 ½ -inch). Signed: Koret Made of Genuine Alligator. Ca 1956.

Right: Spectacular, tall alligator skin frame-bag. Expensive, highly symmetrical belly-cuts on both side, with perfectly matched textures. Distinctive, vertical design. Folding gussets and bottom. Trimmed frame. Ample leather interior, with accessories. (W 11-inch by H 13-inch by D 3-inch). Signed: Koret Made of Genuine Alligator. Provenance: Similar model was advertised by Jay Thorpe (24 West 57) in December 1957.

Later, in the 1950s, their bags crafted of the skins collected from all parts of the globe were sold at Jay Thorpe and Saks Fifth Avenue. Most noted were several models including a Passport-and-Travel satchel with a watch, a compartmentalized interior and hidden pockets; as well as a mini trunk-chest with a gilt-top handle.

Very rare, genuine alligator mallette, with a secret, double-bottom jewelry compartment. Unusual, accordion construction of the bottom. Equestrian style, with multiple belts and buckles. Push-button closure. Immense, leather-lined interior, with a multi-slot folder, marked "Passport", "Tickets", and "Money". Mirror in a sleeve, marked "Saks Fifth Avenue". (W 12 ½ -inch by H 12-inch by D 5 ½ -inch). Signed: Koret Made of Genuine Alligator. Ca 1956.

Their consistently superior quality made it possible for the brand to maintain long-term marketing and licensing arrangements with the world's most renowned French design houses, such as Louis Vuitton, Christian Dior, Pierre Cardin, and Hurbert de Givenchy.

An example of such a successful collaboration was their line of evening handbags from the 1960s made of precious Porosus crocodile adorned by enamel frames, with exquisite, Cartier-style enhancements. Those delicate wonders were made in France per the Givenchy design and distributed in the United States under the Koret name.

Precious, genuine crocodile Porosus cocktail-purse, with an enameled frame, and flower-clasp encrusted with dozens of sparkling marcasites. Leather interior. (W 8-inch by H 6-inch by D 1 ½ -inch). Signed: Koret Made in France. Ca 1960s.

The two featured crocodile evening bags—with the sparkle of white sapphires and rhinestones—were both made in the 1960s. One was created by the American design house of Koret and marked *Koret Made in France*. And, the other—by the French design house of Givenchy, as marked—*Hurbert de Givenchy Made in France*. So very similar, both are breathtaking! You simply cannot take your eyes away from them!

Affluent, baby-crocodile Porosus cocktail-purse, adorned by jeweled, enameled frame. (W 7 ½ -inch by 7 ½ -inch). Singed: Hurbert de Givenchy Made in France. Ca 1960s.

The featured Ghivenchy crocodile evening bag was reportedly acquired from the auction of the personal belongings of legendary Coco Chanel, at the "Auction Extraordinaire Coco Chanel" (Relais Blanc), which took place on October 25, 2002, in Gonesse, France, a small Paris suburb about 14 miles north of the city.

Superlative, crocodile Porosus cocktail-purse, ornamented with a scalloped, bejeweled enameled frame. Textured leather interior. (W 8 ¾ -inch by H 6 ¼ -inch by D 2-inch). Signed: Koret Made in France.

Sassy, genuine python skin and black patent leather satchel. So tiny, yet roomy because of the wide, square gussets. Mirror pouch is stamped: Saks Fifth Avenue. (W 6-inch by H 9-inch x D 4-inch). Signed: Koret Made of Genuine Leather. Ca late 1960s.

As the Koret, Inc. web-site states, over the years, the company manufactured its handbags, luggage and small leather products under several brand names, including Koret USA, Koret Classics and Koret America, following their long-standing tradition of excellence. At one time, it was also known under the variant name of Koret Givenchy, Inc.

Independent from Koret, Inc., a women's clothing company operated in California for several decades, generating tens of millions of dollars worth of business under the name of Koret. After years of confusion, Koret, Inc. finally resolved the conflict of the brand's name ownership by granting the California apparel company permanent permission to use the Koret name for their clothing products, which only increased the exposure of the brand and made its recognition stronger.

L'EDERER DE PARIS

FINEST EUROPEAN HANDCRAFTED L'EATHER GOODS SINCE 1898

Artful vintage skin purses by Lederer de Paris have been coveted by sophisticated shoppers for decades. Meticulously handcrafted from start to finish, they are meant to last. Their construction—a complex engineering marvel—incorporates outstanding techno-designs, finest materials, and superb craftsmanship.

MATCHED ACCESSORIES *of* MATCHLESS BEAUTY •

Lederer DE PARIS

In COLUMBUS
exclusively at
LAZARUS

COBRA at its FINEST—an impressive ensemble for the woman of discriminating taste. Colors: Red, Navy, Grey, Black, Green, Beige, Purple, Tan.
C-521—Stunning quilted bag (11″ x 10″), $39.50*. C-522—Cobra backed snug-gloves, $10.50. C-523—Rakish tam, downy horned pompom, $39.50.
Add 20% Federal Tax.
Please order by number—State second color choice.

GENUINE BENGAL LIZARD — skins of exceptional quality in 8 costume colors: Red, Green, Black, Tan, Navy, Brown, Yellow, Grey.
C-501—Bag of classic smartness (10″ x 9½″), $57.50*. C-502—Fine capeskin gloves, lizard cuffs, $14.75. C-503—Slim umbrella, soft folding cover, $29.50. C-504—Sophisticated lizard hat, $45.50. C-505—Flower, $6.50. C-506—Matching earrings (screw backs), $3.25*.
Add 20% Federal Tax.
Please order by number—State second color choice.

PARTICULARLY FINE LIZARD—In high favor for its smartness, its lasting beauty and long wearing qualities. Colors: Brown, Black.
C-547—Exceptionally spacious bag (13″ x 6″), mock tortoise clasp, $75.50*. C-548—Capeskin gloves with twin lizard buttons, $10.50.
Add 20% Federal Tax.
Please order by number.

Lederer de Paris handbag brochure, ca 1943.

Delightful, structured crocodile Porosus satchel. High-end features: removable watch (marked Made in France); gold-plated trim; popular equestrian style. Tailored, kidskin interior. (W 9-inch by H 11 ½ -inch by D 4 ¼ -inch). Signed: Made in France Especially for Lederer. Ca 1956.

The first Lederer de Paris shop in the United States was opened in New York City, at 711 Fifth Avenue. By the time of its debut in June of 1939, Lederer de Paris, Inc. was operating over twenty boutiques worldwide: in London, Paris, Berlin, Vienna, and Budapest. *"Exclusive imports were planned to be featured in the new store, including original French models in handbags, gloves, umbrellas, luggage, and novelties,"* promised the company's owner, Ludwig Lederer, upon his arrival from France for the shop's opening.

Ultra-rare, priceless baby-crocodile Porosus mallette. Out-of-this-world skins – central belly cuts of unbelievable symmetry, meticulously matched on both sides. Self-covered frame (sliding latches; discreet locking clasp with key); 24K-plated trim. Hard-body construction; tailored gussets. Secret jewelry-box. Superb workmanship! Just takes your breath away when you see it and touch it! (W 13-inch by H 13 ¾ -inch by D 6-inch). Signed: Lederer Made in France 711 Fifth Avenue N.Y. Ca 1964.

An abundance of innovative ideas had always been at the center of the brand's philosophy. In 1944, the company's designers turned tough and long-wearing python and lizard skin into stylish, feminine accessories. They were dyed in unexpected colors: canary yellow, pink, crimson red, purple, and cornflower-blue.

Outrageous, genuine karung clutch of enormous proportions – petal soft and supple – that comes with a matching pair of elbow-length karung-and-suede gloves. Moire-lined. (W 18-inch by H 7-inch by D 4-inch). Signed: Lederer de Paris. Ca 1940s. Shown with a moonstone bracelet by Schiaparelli, ca 1940s. A stunning combination, indeed!

Lederer de Paris was also producing a wide array of spacious day-bags, in alligator, crocodile, and lizard. Refined and exquisite, they were made in France. Today, the awesome vintage bags, especially from the1950s and 1960s, are popular among collectors and can be found in auctions at prestigious auction houses worldwide.

Festive, three-tone, lizard-grain Kelly-style handbag. Gold-plated trim; removable strap; lock and clochette with keys. Lined in beige leather. So trendy! Hard to believe it was made in the 1960s. (W 13-inch by H 9 ¼ -inch by D 4 ½ -inch). Signed: Lederer de Paris Made in Italy. Ca 1960s.

Exquisite, baby-crocodile Porosus frame-bag, with finely crafted details. Outstanding quality! (W 9 ¾ -inch by H 7-inch by D 2 ½ -inch). Signed: Lederer Made in France 711 Fifth Avenue N.Y. Ca 1964.

In 1945, Lederer introduced another innovation: practical, matched accessories in Vinylite, a high-gloss plastic that could be wiped clean with a damp cloth. The gleaming material was worked into umbrellas, hats and handbags (page 123).

Coveted, genuine java-lizard travel bag, with impeccable details. Free-floating hinges. Structured handles. 24K-plated trim. Locking luggage-clasp, with a key. Beautifully appointed, leather interior. (W 12-inch by H 14-inch by D 4 ½ -inch). Signed: Lederer 711 Fifth Avenue Made in France. Ca 1964.

My personal favorites are their superb, architectural pieces from the 1960s, created from Madagascar and Javanese crocodile (currently known as Porosus Crocodile), or Java lizard, in black, brown, navy, gray, or red. They resemble fine cars and boast outstanding details.

Look at this wonder! Its marvelous construction makes one think of a well-tuned racing car. Its frame, plated with 24-karat gold, is carefully polished by hand and assembled with rivets in great precision. The effect looks industrial, modern and trendy. The curved exterior is draped with gorgeous skins. Perfectly symmetrical with tiny, tight scales, it is painstakingly well matched. The gold-plated accents are strategically placed to emphasize its well-balanced proportions and protect it from damage. The gussets are stretched over a robust frame, like an automobile's doors. The bottom is protected from scuffing by hefty bars—its "wheels." The handle is built from several layers of leather shaped into a perfect arch, which makes up its "convertible top". The clasp shuts with a melodic click. Really, it is such a joy to hold this bag, to feel its weight and admire every inch of it—the essence of luxury!

Exceptional, baby-crocodile Porosus top-handled satchel. Outrageously complex construction, with the whole variety of unique details: hard body; trapunto stitching; gilt fixtures; folding gussets; very roomy, finely tailored kidskin interior. Stunning quality! (W 9-inch by H 10-inch by D 4-inch). Signed: Made in France Especially for Lederer. Ca late 1950s-early 1960s.

If you are in the market for a fine, unique vintage handbag with a streak of personality, the Lederer de Paris brand is for you. Full of character, these handbags are as colorful as their founder, Ludwig G. Lederer, a talented person of many passions. *(Continued on page 123)*

Sassy, leather travel-bag, with a removable watch; amazing, gilt accents; and outstanding construction and design. Lined in glove-leather. (W 9-inch by H 6 ½ -inch by D 4 ½ -inch). Singed: Made in France expressly for Lederer. Ca late 1950s-early 1960s.

Handbag and fashion ad, Vogue 1962.
Top: Lucille de Paris clutch. **Bottom:**
Lederer de Paris pocketbook.

Outrageously smart, java-lizard travel satchel, with secret compartments, and accessories. Unique features:
locking front, with the slots for removable holders
(signed in French: Finance, Flamme, Fumee, Fortune).
Silver trim. Leather-lined. (W 9-inch by H 7-inch by D
4-inch). Signed: Made in France expressly for Lederer.
Ca late 1950s-early 1960s.

Ludwig Lederer was born in Budapest, in 1910, and studied at the University of Vienna. Later, he did post-graduate work in navigation and astrophysics at New York University. At the same time, as the owner of Lederer de Paris, Inc., he led a chain of twenty-seven specialty leather shops throughout Europe.

Awesome, baby-crocodile Porosus satchel, styled as a miniature doctor's bag. Unique details: gold-plated trim (ball-pull, studded frame and finials); structured exterior; reinforced handle; tailored, kidskin interior. (W 9-inch by H 11-inch by D 4-inch). Signed: Made in France Especially for Lederer. Ca late 1950s.

During World War II, he was a volunteer and later a civilian instructor of celestial navigation at the U.S. Army base in Greenville, Mississippi. He also served as a lieutenant colonel in the Civil Air Patrol and an executive officer of the greater New York Cadet Training Group. Also, he was quite instrumental in establishing the Civil Air Patrol Cadet Exchange Program.

Right: Duo of flamboyant Kelly-style handbags made of lizard-grained leather. High end features: removable straps; locks and clochette with keys; contrast stitching; leather interior. The blue one is trimmed with chrome (W 11-inch by H 8 ¼ -inch by D 4 ½ -inch), and the red one – gold-plated. (W 12 ½ -inch by H 9 ½ -inch by D 4 ½ -inch). Signed (inside and strap): Lederer de Paris Made in Italy. Ca 1960s.

After the war, in 1947, he sold the leather goods business and moved to Hillsdale, New York, where he operated a commercial dairy farm and raised Holstein cattle. In addition, he was an accomplished scientist who wrote the column, "The World of Science," for various New York, Connecticut and Massachusetts publications in the late 1950s. He was married to Della V. Lederer and died in 1960.

Rare, silk umbrella with faux-crocodile handle, and sleeve, in forest-green. Stamped: Modern MB Umbrella Co. Ca 1940s.

Luxurious, alligator drawstring-bag. Grommets, adjustable drawstring closure; shoulder strap with buckles; unique leather side-and-bottom trim; leather-lined. (W 13-inch by H 10-inch by D 4-inch). Signed: Lederer de Paris Madison Ave at 58 Street Made in France. Ca 1960s.

Since then, the corporation, run by three generations of Ludwig Lederer's followers, has changed ownership several times. Still, it remains in operation worldwide as one of the most distinguished makers of fine leather goods, and it continues to uphold an excellent reputation for quality and exquisite design. *"Always Exquisite, Polished, Streamlined, Refined!"*

L'ESCO

FASHION-TAILORED EXOTIC HANDBAGS

Finely crafted Lesco handbags, marked by a graceful chess horse-head, were swinging from the arms of American women for several decades, starting from the mid-1930s. In 1936, Lesco, Ltd. leased a facility at Rockefeller Center, New York City. A couple of years later, Lesco hired Norman D. Waters Associates to aggressively promote in the media their first line of high-fashion products: attractive leather handbags and small accessories.

Lesco lizard handbags ad, *Vogue* 1949.

Timeless, genuine alligator frame-bag, with tasteful brass trim and top handle. Leather-lined. (W 10 ½ -inch by H 6 ½ -inch by D 3 ¾ -inch). Signed: Lesco. Provenance: Similar style was advertised by B. Altman & Co. in October 1960.

By the mid-1940s, Lesco offered the Bond Street Collection that was composed of an assortment of practical items made in fine English taste. It was on display at Bonwit Teller stores across America. There were smart compacts and matching cigarette cases in intriguing scarlet and navy, made with various reptile skins.

Sweet, alligator-skin purse, trimmed with amber-Lucite. Split gussets. Leather-lined. (W 9 ¼ -inch by H 6 ½ -inch by D 2-inch). Signed: Lesco. Ca 1950.

Lady-like, cobra-skin barrel purse, with wide arm-handle, and solid-brass Retro clasp. Rayon faille interior, a coin purse attached by a cord. (W 8 ¼ -inch by H 6-inch by D 4 ½ -inch). Ca 1953. Provenance: Similar style was advertised by Oppenheim Collins (Brooklyn, New York) in November 1953.

In November of 1946, the fashion presentation "Fashions of the Time" validated the importance of accessories for domestic wear. Among the participating designers was Harry Rosenfeld, as Lesco demonstrated their new collection of over-the-shoulder daytime bags in leathers and skins.

The other innovation introduced by Lesco in 1948 was a dramatic merger of lustrous, colored lizard and snakeskin handbags with matching sling-back shoes, to complement pastel silk and cotton dresses or contrast dark, modest, post-war dresses. Especially glamorous was the line of East Indian Cobra purses in masterfully tanned, fantastic colors: rose quartz, lapis lazuli, topaz, emerald, amethyst, and ruby. Gleaming with color like "Maharajah's treasures," they became an instant hit.

Lesco handbags ads. **Top left:** *Vogue* 1948. **Top right:** *Harper's Bazaar* 1948. **Bottom left:** *Vogue* 1947. **Bottom right:** *Vogue* 1946.

Lesco, Ltd., located at 10 East 34th Street in New York City, was an important player in the alligator handbag market beginning in the late 1940s. Their classic satchels and swinging shoulder bags were sold at stores that included Franklin Simon and Arnold Constable. The brand also produced exclusive assortments for Bonwit Teller, Saks Fifth and B. Altman & Co., in the 1950s.

Classic, beautiful top-handled alligator purse, trimmed with red Lucite bar-frame. Leather-lined. (W 10 ¼ -inch by H 6 ½ -inch by D 3 ½ -inch). Signed: Lesco. American, ca 1957.

Curvy, genuine alligator clutch trimmed with faux-amber. Deep front flap; welted seams; leather interior. (W 10-inch by H 7-inch by D 4-inch). Signed: Lesco. Ca 1963. Provenance: Similar style was advertised in *Sears Catalog* Fall 1963.

A classic vintage Lesco alligator handbag in simple black or brown, properly marked with the brand's logo, is a safe choice today when acquiring vintage to wear. Finely built of quality skins and lined with strong leather, these solid bags will last a long time.

Left: Sleek, high-gloss alligator clutch. Leatherette-lined; welted seams; lever-bar closure. (W 11-inch by H 5-inch by D 2-inch). Signed: Lesco. Shown with a trendy leaf-necklace by Mosell, both ca 1950s.

In 1961, the National Authority for the Ladies' Handbag Industry (NALHI) announced the merger of Lesco, Ltd. with Lona, that was founded two years earlier by the industry veteran Lou Nathan. The new company, Lesco Lona, Inc., moved to 136 Madison Avenue, New York City. Between 1962 and 1968, they produced a large assortment of twin bags, with adjustable shoulder straps and miniature vanities, made with grained alligator, ostrich or lizard. They also made cute turtle skin handbags. Their assortment was sold primarily at the B. Altman & Co., Gimbels, Franklin Simon, Bloomingdale's, and Saks Fifth Avenue stores.

Classic, alligator-skin pocketbook, with folding gussets, leather underlining, and faille interior. Medium glaze. Featured with a silk scarf by Schiaparelli – a great way to remedy the issue of a cracked handle. (W 9 ½ -inch by H 6-inch by D 2-inch). Signed: Lesco. Ca 1965.

Artistic, studded clutch pieced from turtle-skin squares. Zippered top, chain-straps. (W 8 ½ -inch by H 5 ¼ -inch by D 1 ½ -inch). Labeled: Crazygator for Lona Lesco, U.S. Pat. No. R.10739. Ca 1968.

Always check later bags for authenticity, because most of them are reproductions produced from embossed leather or vinyl, not genuine skins, except for genuine turtle mini-bags. By shopping carefully, you will be satisfied with treasures by Lesco.

L'UCIL'L'E DE PARIS

THE EPITOME OF AMERICAN CLASSIC AND PRESTIGE

Highly recognizable among collectors and savvy fashionistas are high-end skin handbags by incomparable Lucille de Paris. For almost three decades, until the late 1960s, they were manufactured in the United States by a New York City company. Lucille Bags, Inc. was located at 30 East 33rd Street.

A fabulous duo of vintage exotics, in stylish black alligator and white ostrich – the ultimate status symbol of the 1960s – made by one of the most prominent makers of that time, Lucille de Paris of New York.

Sleek, sizable crocodile pocketbook in fancy, equestrian style. Clean, elegant lines! Whole, central belly-cut envelopes the front and back. Expandable gussets; leather-lined. (W 10 ¾ -inch by H 11-inch by D 2 ¾ -inch). Signed: Lucille de Paris Made in U.S.A. Ca 1965. Shown with a riding hat by Elsa Schiaparelli (ca 1960s).

Today, Lucille de Paris creations are being regularly offered at reputable auction houses as the best examples of period couture. They always fetch healthy sums—from hundreds to thousands of dollars—especially for rare, custom-made, special-occasion pieces encrusted with jewels and beads. *(See right and following page)*

Breathtaking, mint crocodile Porosus frame-purse, in its original box, with tags and authenticity card. This is the only one – true mint – unused Lucille that I could find for a decade of collecting. Superb! (W 12-inch by H 11 ½ -inch by D 2 ¾ -inch). Signed: Lucille de Paris Made in U.S.A. Labeled: Lucille de Paris style 1664. Price tag: Seideinbach's Alabaster B 1664 $195. Free Sample: "Saphir – The famous universal renovator on the market since 1925. Unique leather cream from France that cleans, polishes and rejuvenates all reptile leathers." Ca 1963-1964.

Elite, custom-made, genuine baby-crocodile Porosus cocktail-purse adorned by an enameled frame, with marcasite in a stunning scroll motif. Silver trim; satin-lined; swivel handle accented by genuine onyx cabochons. (W 8-inch by H 6 ¾ -inch). Signed: Lucille de Paris Made in USA. Ca 1962.

Trio of enchanting, evening chain-purses, from the 1950s, in different skins and colors – with lavish, jeweled frames – lined in satin. Signed: Lucille de Paris Made in U.S.A. **Black:** Baby-crocodile; black-n-gold glass beads. (W 7 ¼ -inch by H 5 ¾ -inch). **Yellow:** Java-lizard; pink-and-green, Aurora Borealis rhinestones; weaved strings of gold-glass beads. (W 8-inch by H 6 ½ -inch by D 2-inch). **White:** Genuine ostrich; pearl-n-gold glass beads, and etched, brass leaf. (W 8-inch by H 6 ¼ -inch).

My love affair with vintage alligator began when I first saw a gorgeous Lucille bag. Since then, dozens and dozens of fabulous handbags have passed my hands. Every time I come across a new Lucille, I become out-of-breath and amazed at how perfect they are.

Voluptuous alligator satchel styled as a capacious doctor's bag. Molded sides, gussets and bottom; distinct, leather-welted seams; gold-plated accents. Lined in tan leather. Amazing craftsmanship! (W 12 ½ -inch by H 8-inch by D 4 ½ -inch). Signed: Lucille de Paris Made in U.S.A. Ca 1949-1953.

Charles Hahn and his wife, Lucille A. Hahn, established the brand in the 1930s, in France, as makers of beaded bags. In the mid-1940s, they moved to New York City, where they founded the company and joined the elite group of prominent domestic makers: Mark Cross, Deitsch Brothers, and Koret. Their mission was to satisfy the growing demand for luxury goods.

Pristine, beaded bridal purse. Etched, gilt-brass frame encrusted with faux pearls. Satin interior, with double-sided mirror, and coin purse. (W 10 ¼ -inch by H 7-inch). Signed: Lucille de Paris Made in France. Ca 1930s.

One of the first advertisements for Lucille de Paris alligator handbags appeared in *The New York Times* in June of 1946. The handbag was marked with a whimsical logo of an alligator with a crown, reading, along with the brand's mark, *Lucille de Paris.* The brand emphasized that their handbags were made with American alligator, exclusively from the United States. Among the early bags sold by Saks Fifth Avenue at Rockefeller Center was a cute, petite shoulder bag in cappuccino alligator, very similar to the one from the featured Lucille de Paris collection, that sold originally for $135.

Lucille de Paris genuine alligator handbags ad, Saks Fifth Avenue, June 1946.

Utilitarian, early genuine alligator shoulder bag, very similar to the one advertised in the Saks Avenue ad in 1946 (above). Shoulder strap; leather interior; brass trim. Lovely and practical! (W 8 ½ -inch by H 10-inch by D 2 ½ -inch). Signed: Lucille de Paris Genuine Alligator Made in U.S.A.

During the 1950s, under the leadership of Charles Hahn, Lucille de Paris successfully produced and distributed exquisite handbags through upscale boutiques across the country. Simple, yet sophisticated lines; highest quality skins; top workmanship; marvelous accents and, above all, a wide array of lush, custom colors were the features highly desired by their customers.

Unique alligator satchel, with wood frame and clasp. Feather-light – no metal parts! Leather interior; expandable gussets. Timeless design! I love to pair it with the Bakelite bracelet, or the delicate necklace from the 1930s, which fits perfectly locked around the handles. (W 9-inch by H 8 ½ -inch by D 3-inch). Signed: Genuine Alligator Made in U.S.A. Ca 1946-1947.

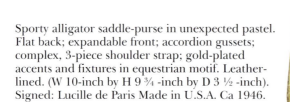

Sporty alligator saddle-purse in unexpected pastel. Flat back; expandable front; accordion gussets; complex, 3-piece shoulder strap; gold-plated accents and fixtures in equestrian motif. Leather-lined. (W 10-inch by H 9 ¾ -inch by D 3 ½ -inch). Signed: Lucille de Paris Made in U.S.A. Ca 1946.

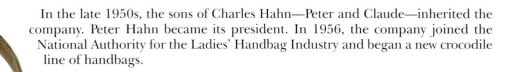

In the late 1950s, the sons of Charles Hahn—Peter and Claude—inherited the company. Peter Hahn became its president. In 1956, the company joined the National Authority for the Ladies' Handbag Industry and began a new crocodile line of handbags.

One of their most successful handbags came from their Fall 1961 collection, presented in the 1961 issue of *Handbags & Accessories* magazine:

Alligator in color makes an exciting array at Lucille Bags, Inc., 30 E. 33rd Street. Prune, bayberry, burgundy, corn-meal, honey and all the newest fall colors are shown. Every shape imaginable: large, small, boxy, pouchy, square, rounded are included in the line. Frames also vary: both covered and not, straight and curved. On the whole, the line is smart, classic and tailored. There is no particular exaggerated trend in shape; good taste in styling is the keynote.

Breathtaking, wide-platform alligator satchel. No metal parts; flap-and-belt closure; intricate, trapunto stitching. Leather-lined, with expandable compartments. (W 9-inch by H 11-inch by D 5-inch). Amazing style! Signed: Lucille de Paris. Ca 1960. Shown with a fantastic, removable fur-clip by Trifari, ca 1950s.

Awesome, alligator briefcase-bag, crafted with pride from a single, whole, impeccably symmetrical, central belly-cut. No metal parts, except for the elegant clasp. Accordion gussets and bottom. Leather-lined interior is separated into three huge compartments, with a zippered envelope in the middle, and a large, framed wallet. Measures enormous W 14-inch by H 15-inch (with handles) by D 3 ½ -inch. Utmost attention to detail! Signed with the dual marks: Lucille de Paris Made in U.S.A.; Mark Cross. Ca 1962. Shown with a lovely hat, by Schiaparelli, adorned by a large, patent bow, and black voile. Provenance: It was advertised in the Harper's Bazaar February 1963 issue.

The demand for beautiful, Lucille de Paris handbags grew steadily. The quintessence of American chic, they became popular all over the world, with celebrities and European royalty.

Connoisseur, genuine alligator satchel, with a front pocket, gold-plated trim, and leather lining. Utmost quality and style! (W 9-inch by H 12-inch by D 3 ½ -inch). Signed: Lucille de Paris Made in U.S.A. Provenance: This very same piece is advertise in the *Vogue* ad, Sept. 1962 (page 139).

Reportedly, a member of the British royal family was seen carrying a brown alligator handbag that looked just like a "Lucille." It appeared that the bag was indeed purchased off the rack at the Saks Fifth Avenue store at Rockefeller Center.

The press at that time commented that Princess Margaret, who came to New York with her husband in November of 1965, visited the Channel Gardens in Rockefeller Center. Upon their arrival, the center's president, Laurence S. Rockefeller—along with Frank E. Conant, president of the Fifth Avenue Association—greeted the royal couple and escorted them across the street to Saks Fifth Avenue. There, the store's president, Mr. Gimbel, and his wife, Sophie (a renowned designer), happily gave them a tour of their store.

Spectacular alligator frame-bag. Shiny, perfectly symmetrical, central belly-cuts. A pull is decorated by a removable rhinestone clip, which I love to add for special occasions. Tan leather interior. (W 13-inch by H 9-inch by D 3 ½ -inch). Signed: Lucille de Paris Genuine Alligator Made in U.S.A. Labeled: Saks Fifth Avenue. Ca 1962. Shown with a pair of classy, vintage, ring-lizard heels by Andrew Geller.

For several decades, the Lucille de Paris brand specialized in the finest alligator, crocodile, lizard, and ostrich handbags produced primarily domestically, or sometimes imported from France. The quality of their craftsmanship was definitely at the level of the most prestigious European houses.

Ultimate, American alligator frame-bag. Elegant style; simple brass clasp; leather-lined. (W 13-inch by H 11 ½ -inch (with handle) by D 3-inch. Signed: Lucille de Paris Made in U.S.A. Ca 1961.

The number of their stock and custom-made models was astounding. It included all imaginable sizes and styles, starting with minuscule evening bags, no wider than eight inches, to enormous travel mallets and briefcases, over 14-inches wide.

Gorgeous pair of special occasion bags, accentuated by black enameled frames, marcasites, and onyx-cabochon. Striking! Etched, silver frames. Impeccable, central belly cuts. Leather interior. Signed: Lucille de Paris Genuine Alligator Made in U.S.A. Shown with a hat-box by Schiaparelli. Small: W 9 ½ -inch by H 7-inch. Large: W 11-inch by H 10-inch by D 2 ½ -inch. Both ca 1956-1957.

Phenomenal, crocodile Porosus frame-bag of enormous size. Huge, central belly-cuts of utmost symmetry are meticulously matched on both sides. Self-covered frame. Leather interior, with multiple compartments, pouches and wallets. (W 14 ½ -inch by H 16 ½ -inch by D 4-inch). Signed: Lucille de Paris Made in U.S.A. Labeled: Bergdorf Goodman. Ca 1959-1960. Shown with Christian Dior glasses, ca 1970s, and a pair of lovely vintage gloves, with faux leopard detail.

Cool, crocodile Porosus satchel, with a front compartment in unexpectedly bright, designer color! (W 12-inch by H 9 ½ -inch by D 3-inch). Signed: Lucille de Paris Made in U.S.A. Labeled: Bergdorf Goodman. Shown with Versace sunglasses. Provenance: Exactly the same model was advertised in the *Vogue* September 1962 issue for $260 (page 139).

Custom-tanned, genuine crocodile satchel, in designer-teal color. Simple, tapered styling. Self-covered frame; elegant, gold-plated clasp. Teal-leather interior. (W 10 ½ -inch by H 10 ½ -inch (with handles) by D 2 ½ -inch). Signed: Lucille de Paris Made in U.S.A. Ca 1967-1968.

There was an endless color palette. Lucille de Paris was one of the first brands to have their bags dyed per order—and they contracted the best tanneries to do the job. Sophisticated evening pastels were particularly popular, but the rarest of all was their specialty: pure white.

The skillful artisans of Lucille Bags, Inc. used ultra-modern equipment to develop several signature features, such as their famous structural handle. Its construction included a flexible metal band to provide support from the inside and maintain the shape for years without breaking.

Extravagant, genuine alligator frame-satchel, in outrageous cobalt blue. Custom-made for an important customer. Stunning all around! Premium, central, belly-cuts of incredible symmetry; solid-brass trim; leather-lined. (W 12-inch by H 8 ¼ -inch without handle by D 2 ½ -inch). Signed: Lucille de Paris Genuine Alligator Made in U.S.A. Ca 1958. Shown with a pair of vintage leather gloves (France, ca 1960s), and a removable, moonstone-n-rhinestone fur clip, ca 1950s.

Other signature features include outside wallet compartments, platform bottoms, smartly organized and accessorized leather interiors, and 24-karat gilt or gem-encrusted clasps on the evening bags.

Precious, genuine ostrich cocktail-purse, with a textured, gilded-frame ornamented with a sparkling rhinestone clasp. Leather-lined. (W 7 ½ -inch by H 6-inch by D 2-inch). Signed: Lucille de Paris Made in U.S.A. Ca 1964.

Pair of superb frame-bags, in brown alligator and taupe crocodile. Impeccable, rosy-tan leather interiors, reinforced handles, and shiny brass trim. Both are signed: Lucille de Paris. Usually, alligator pieces are authenticated as "Genuine Alligator Made in U.S.A.", whereas crocodile pieces are simply marked "Made in U.S.A." Provenance: The taupe alligator style was featured in the Vogue, October 1958 ad (page 51).

The American alligator handbags by Lucille de Paris's—their specialty—almost always bear the authenticity mark, *Genuine Alligator*. Generally, the handbags made with various crocodile skins imported from France—often made per order for important clients—are *not* marked per authenticity. Most bags are also stamped with the country-of-origin mark, *Made in U.S.A.*, in accordance with U.S. export/import regulations.

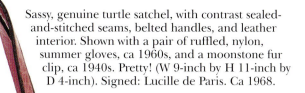

Sassy, genuine turtle satchel, with contrast sealed-and-stitched seams, belted handles, and leather interior. Shown with a pair of ruffled, nylon, summer gloves, ca 1960s, and a moonstone fur clip, ca 1940s. Pretty! (W 9-inch by H 11-inch by D 4-inch). Signed: Lucille de Paris. Ca 1968.

Right: Designer, genuine caiman pocketbook, with bright, gilded accents. Interesting contrast between the delicate, spring color and the rough texture of unglazed skins. Expandable, 3-piece gussets; sealed-n-stitched seams. Ample, leather-lined interior, with multiple pockets. (W 10 ¾ -inch by H 8-inch by D 4-inch). Labeled: Tamed by Lucille de Paris Croco Sauvage & Free. Ca 1949-1950.

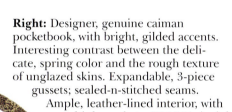

Ring-lizard frame bag lined in passionate red. Dramatic design and style! Platform bottom, tailored body and interior. First-class craftsmanship! (W 10 ¼ -inch by H 15-inch with handle by D 3 ½ -inch). Singed: Lucille de Paris Genuine Lizard Made in U.S.A. Ca 1957.

The handbags made from other exotic skins, such as lizard, turtle or ostrich, are often signed as per their authenticity: *Genuine Lizard; Genuine Turtle,* or *Genuine Ostrich*. Once in a while, a Lucille de Paris handbag is not branded with the company's logo. Those pieces were most likely created per order.

The styles in black were normally lined in black calfskin or kidskin, whereas handbags in costume colors had soft, light-tan linings. In contrast, the pastels were lined in white or matching colors.

Duo of identical, upscale crocodile frame-purses – in black and taupe – created by Lucille de Paris for I. Magnin & Co. Timeless style, and superb quality of skins and workmanship! (W 10-inch by H 9-inch by W 2 ¾ -inch). Signed: Lucille de Paris Made in U.S.A. I. Magnin & Co. Ca 1956.

Their expensive cocktail purses, with beaded clasps, were nicely fitted with exquisite champagne satin. Their lavishly beaded, gilt frames, with delicate snake-chains, were imported from France, a connection with the company's previous beaded-bag business.

Examples of Lucille de Paris production of 1950s-1960s. **Top left and bottom right**: Original, bejeweled cocktail-purses for special occasion. **Bottom left:** Feminine, alligator cocktail-purse, with a replaced beaded handle. (W 8 ¼ -inch by H 11-inch by D 3-inch). **Top right:** Black crocodile daytime handbag, with a removable trembler-clip by Coro (ca 1950s). Provenance: Similar style was advertised in Harper's Bazaar in March 1956.

In 1962, Lucille de Paris produced their in-stock pieces in five prime sizes:

an oversized, 14-inch travel bag sold for $305
a large, daytime 12-inch shopper sold for $260
a medium, 11-inch daytime handbag sold for $185
a demi-sized, 8-inch purse sold for $99.50
a petite, 7-inch evening bag sold for $79.50

In the 1960s, the Lucille de Paris brand gained wide exposure from constant advertising in numerous fashion publications. Their handbags were sold at several upscale department stores, including Saks Fifth Avenue, Crouch & Fitzgerald and Bergdorf Goodman. They could also be ordered by mail or by phone, with convenient delivery.

Right: Impressive, crocodile Porosus satchel, with original, solid-brass handles, and two ample outside compartments. Belt-like closure, with simple, gilt-clasp. Roomy leather interior. (W 11 ½ -inch by H 9 ½ -inch by D 3-inch). Signed: Lucille de Paris Made in U.S.A. Ca 1958.

Left: Lucille de Paris alligator handbag ad, *Vogue* September 1962.

By the mid-1960s, the hype for the crocodile and alligator accessories reached its peak and caused a sharp decrease in the availability of the skins. By 1964, they cost twice as much as in 1961. Finally, in 1969, the ban on alligator and crocodile products had been announced in the U.S.A. Ostrich handbags gained new popularity—for their suppleness and finesse.

Sleek, genuine ostrich equestrian mailbox-purse. Unusual construction of the handles, with the brass bar on the front handle serving as a closure catch. Lined in leather. (W 10-inch by H 9 ½ -inch by D 2-inch). Signed: Lucille de Paris Made in U.S.A. Ca 1962.

As a result of this ban, Lucille Bags, Inc. auctioned their state-of-the-art equipment and shut down their production lines. Sadly, that was the time when most domestic makers of alligator bags had to halt their operation, once and for all. Luckily, some later managed to adapt to new trends and expand in different areas of production, such as Mark Cross. Others, including Lucille Bag, Inc., never resumed operation.

Today, the Lucille de Paris brand is remembered as truly an American brand, one of the biggest names in the international fashion arena that dared to compete with European design houses.

MANON

During the 1950s and the 1960s, a New York company Manon Handbags, Inc. (165 Madison Avenue), a member of the National Authority for the Ladies' Handbag Industry, produced fashionable alligator handbags for sale at upscale Bonwit Teller and Bergdorf Goodman.

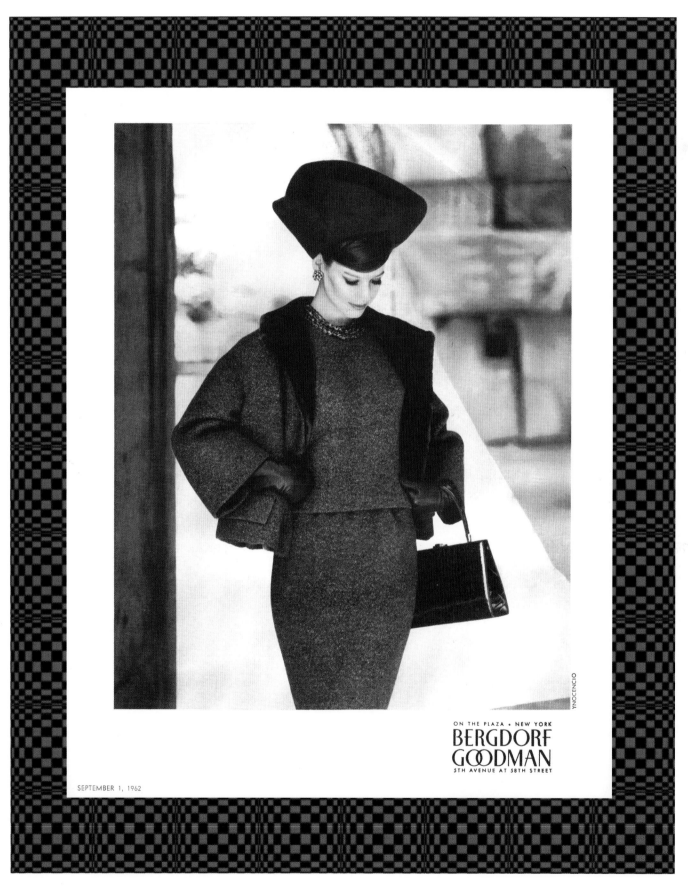

SEPTEMBER 1, 1962

ON THE PLAZA · NEW YORK
BERGDORF
GOODMAN
5TH AVENUE AT 58TH STREET

YNOCENCIO

Handbag fashion ad featuring a crocodile handbag by Manon, sold at Bergdorf Goodman (Vogue, September 1962).

Monumental, genuine alligator daytime bag, with a concealed frame, lever clasp, and strong, top handle. Impeccably-symmetrical, central belly cuts on both sides! Leather-lined, with complete set of accessories. (W 13 ½ -inch by H 15-inch by D 4-inch). Signed: Manon. Ca 1959. Shown with a vintage Bakelite bracelet from the 1940s.

Superb, crocodile Porosus daytime-bag, with a gilded shield-clasp, and leather-lined interior. The example of utmost quality and style! (W 13 ¼ -inch by H 8-inch by D 3-inch). Signed: Manon. Ca 1958. Shown with the bold-n-beautiful, gilt necklace by William de Lillo (ca late 1960s).

Crafted from top-quality skins—quite often in West Germany—their gloriously spacious pieces demonstrated sleek design, outstanding quality and elaborate styling, often accentuated by the elements of equestrian motifs. The brand was one of the few makers to use very expensive, matching central cuts of the underbelly on both sides of the bag. Premium skins and utter attention to detail are the signature features of the brand.

Precious, genuine alligator clutch, crowned by an elaborately-etched gilded frame, with turquoise cabochon. Flat, back-handle. Leather-lined. Original comb. (W 9 ½ -inch by H 6-inch by D 2-inch). Signed: Manon. Ca 1962.

That's how their fantastic Fall 1961 collection was presented in the June 1961 issue of the *Handbags & Accessories* magazine:

"Rich, smooth leathers in the newest colors make a striking bag line at Manon handbags, 165 Madison Ave. Alligators in black and brown are shown in many different shapes. One barrel satchel in brown alligator is particularly nice—the bold-finish clasp is in the form of a buckle... These bags are done in medium sized, tailored lines. Shoes to match will be available... Oxidized frames have become important for fall and Manon puts them to very attractive use... A whole series of (accents) with gold-finish and rhinestone trim makes a lovely cocktail-evening line."

Smart, genuine alligator satchel, in popular equestrian style. Accented by the front-flap and buckles. Leather-lined, complete with accessories. (W 10-inch by H 12-inch with handles by D 4 ½ -inch). Signed: Manon. Ca 1964.

The designs by Manon were quite original and different from other mass-produced bags. Bold yet tasteful, their high fashion details—fully covered frames, brass accents, decorative plaques, belts and buckles, pockets and flaps—enhance their quiet, subdued elegance. Besides glossy alligator and crocodile, the limited editions by Manon were also handcrafted from premium ostrich skin.

Impeccable, genuine ostrich satchel, with outside compartments, and self-covered frame. Fully leather-lined, trimmed with skin. Wide, molded gussets, and bottom. (W 9-inch by H 11-inch by D 4-inch). Signed: Manon. American, ca 1965. Featured with different, removable pieces of jewelry, to create different looks depending on the circumstances: a vintage moonstone-cabochon clip, and a modern Murano-glass necklace. How divine!

Their quality pieces in mint condition are highly prized. Each has an additional skin label, sewn into the top corner seam of the interior—*Genuine Alligator*— indicating its proper authenticity. The featured genuine alligator handbag is one of those statement pieces from the 1960s, which reminds me so much of the trendy bags by Ralph Lauren. So large, yet slim, it can be used as an attaché-case or a fashionably oversized piece for special occasions.

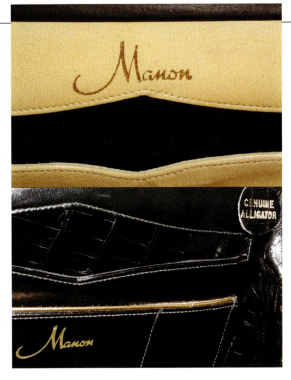

Detail of the Manon's interior.

Chic, genuine alligator daytime purse, with a strong top handle, concealed frame, and a large, bar-clasp in the middle. Leather-lined interior, with a coin purse. Beautiful style and quality! (W 13 ½ -inch by H 12 ½ -inch (with handle) by D 3 ¼ -inch). Signed: Manon. Ca 1959-1961.

If you're looking for a great value, an awesome, versatile piece like this is definitely your best choice. It has it all: the quality, the style, the size, and the character. The luscious and supple skins are amazing, especially considering their monumental size of over 15-inches long and 10-inches high. To build this beauty, two huge central underbelly cuts of over 150 square inches were used. Equal in value to a new handbag worth thousands of dollars, a piece like this could be yours for about $900 retail.

Fancy, genuine anaconda-skin in geranium pink treated with sophisticated, sueded finish. Removable, top handle; gold plated lever-clasp; rayon-faille interior. (W 9 ½ -inch by H 9-inch by D 2 ½ -inch). Signed: Manon. Ca 1964.

Trendy, genuine alligator frame-bag, with unique, secret, squeeze handle-locks. Self-covered frame. Replaced, plastic bamboo handle. Fully leather lined, with skin trim. (W 10 ½ -inch by H 12 ½ -inch (with handle) by D 3-inch). Signed: Manon. Ca 1964. Shown with a plastic, black-rose bead necklace, encrusted with rhinestones, by Kenneth J. Lane (signed K.J.L. for Avon), ca 1960s.

MARK CROSS

THE OUTPOST OF ELEGANCE, THE BAGS OF DISTINCTION

Mark Cross, one of the oldest and most prestigious domestic leather companies, was founded by Henry W. Cross in 1845. As Claire Wilcox mentions in her book, *Century of Bags*, an elegant top-handled purse by Mark Cross was immortalized in American pop culture by appearing in the hand of Grace Kelly's character in the Alfred Hitchcock film, *Rear Window*, when she tucked her slippers and lingerie into it. Although the movie gave the brand a boost, by the time it played in 1954, Mark Cross had been established for almost a century as a fine maker of handbags.

Mark Cross handbags ad, *Town & Country* 1944.

Henry Cross, an Irish saddler, mastered leather workmanship in London before immigrating to the United States in 1845. He started a trunk and harness business in Boston, Massachusetts. His son, Mark, who worked with his father from a young age, later was sent to England to study the craft at a traditional leather-working center.

Upon his return, Mark was joined by Patrick Francis Murphy, who became a major driving force in reshaping the company into a successful retailer of prestigious high-end leather products made in England. When Mark Cross died, Murphy and his son, Gerald, operated the company for many years after it was moved to New York City's Fifth Avenue, near the turn of the 20th century.

For over three decades, this quality purveyor of leather goods concentrated on travel-oriented merchandise. In the 1930s, they shifted their attention to luxurious skin handbags and invested in the development of new technologies, skin treatments, colors, designs, and stylish features.

Glamorous, genuine alligator frame-bag, with a top handle, front pull, and accordion bottom. Lined in luxurious, lipstick-red leather, with multiple compartments, and large coin purse. (W 10 ¼ -inch by H 7 ½ -inch by D 3-inch). Signed: Mark Cross; and a previous owner name. Provenance: Mark Cross Christmas 1956 advertisement, $120.

Their new, highly polished alligator and crocodile models, priced in the 1930s at about $65, boasted unusually pliable skins treated with a novel, high-gloss finish—possible solely due to their new technological process of glazing. They were sold at Saks Fifth Avenue, Lord & Taylor and other upscale stores.

Wartime hardships did not slow down the Mark Cross enterprise. In the fall of 1941, their ads tempted customers to splurge on the luxury of a colored crocodile bag, especially alluring in awesome shades of Pomegranate Red, Malachite Green, Damson Plum, Sable, Horsechestnut, Walnut, and Sunflower Yellow. Mark Cross suggested that a crocodile bag could "do wonders" for your ego, because even when you're not carrying it, you still feel "like an heiress", just knowing that you have it at home.

Mark Cross alligator handbag ad, *Town & Country* 1946.

Luxurious, yellow alligator skin clutch (whole, symmetrical belly-cut), lined in leather, with interior wallet; wood sliding closure. (W 12-inch by H 8 ½ -inch). Dual maker stamps: Selected by Mark Cross Lucille de Paris. Ca 1948.

Right: Magnificent, scarlet alligator satchel of substantial size. Custom-made (owner's name printed on the interior). Spacious, traditional leather interior. (W 13-inch by H 8 ½ -inch (without handles) by D 2 ¾ -inch. Stamped by dual marks: Lucille de Paris and Mark Cross. American, ca 1958.

Spectacular, custom-made crocodile evening-purse. Ornamented by a striking, enameled frame, with a Victorian-style bow, sparkling with marcasites. Swivel handle accented by faceted Aurora Borealis rhinestones. Envelope-style body, with a slim bottom and triangle gussets. Black-satin interior; etched, silver frame. Masterpiece, indeed! (W 8-inch by H 7 ¾ -inch by 1 ¾ -inch). Signed: Mark Cross. France, ca 1955.

The company changed hands several times. In 1960, thirty-two-year-old George Wasserberger and his associates acquired the Mark Cross company for a million dollars from Kleinwort & Son of London. Wasserberger and his brother, Edward, ran the company. The standards of the company and its philosophy remained high.

Paying well-deserved respect to the traditions of the brand, the Wasserburgers were instrumental in developing a new managerial approach. The idea of branching out to unusual accessories proved successful. During a quick tour of the store by a reporter in 1961, he pointed at the pheasant feather ties sold for $25 and proudly remarked that the artist Salvador Dali was among the first to purchase them. The most popular category, however, was still alligator. *"I cannot say alligator is expensive; I can only say the best alligator is expensive,"* George Wasserburger commented once.

Glorious, crocodile Porosus frame-bag in designer green. Highly symmetrical, central belly-cuts are meticulously matched on both sides. Tight scales, and outstanding texture! Silver-tone hardware. Lined in black leather. (W 13 ¾ -inch by H 10-inch by D 3-inch). Dual signatures: Lucille de Paris Made in U.S.A., and Mark Cross. Ca 1959-1960. Shown with a gorgeous, sterling-n-rhinestone châtelaine bracelet by Mazer (signed: Mazer Sterling), ca 1951, which I love to put on for special occasions.

In 1967, the retail store's Fifth Avenue location generated three million dollars in annual sales. In addition, forty other stores across the country were franchised to sell Mark Cross goods. In 1967, the company announced the opening of two additional locations outside of New York City, in San Francisco and Los Angeles.

Top-of-the-line, genuine crocodile Porosus shopper. Compact, yet capacious! Marvelous skin; tailored gussets; roomy, outside compartments; huge, leather interior, with a framed wallet. Grommeted handle mounts; rolled arm-handles. Famed French craftsmanship, indeed! (W 9-inch by H 7 ¼ -inch by D 3 ½ -inch (opens to whopping 12-inch wide!). Signed: Mark Cross Made in France. Ca 1965-1966.

Striking, spacious satchel made of baby-crocodile Porosus skins – a single, whole, belly-cut of astounding symmetry. Immense style! Custom-made for an important customer and stamped by the owner's name. Classy navy-blue. 18K, rose-gold plated hardware. Deep, outside compartments; secure, push-button clasp; kidskin interior, in fashionable tan, trimmed with navy skin. (W 11 ¾ -inch by H 9 ¼ -inch by D 5 ½ -inch). Stamped: Mark Cross Made in Italy. Ca 1962.

Classic, genuine crocodile frame-bag – a twin to the identical piece in black, with red lining (page 145). Simple and beautiful! (W 10 ¼ -inch by H 7 ¼ -inch by D 2 ¾ -inch). Signed: Mark Cross. Provenance: Mark Cross Christmas 1956 advertisement, $120.

In 1968, the brand enjoyed truly phenomenal success. In August, they announced a huge sale in *The New York Times*, in order to move quickly their remaining alligator inventory, in response to the ban. As per the emotional testimony of a couple of participants, the "mob scene" at the store *"seemed second only to the storming of the Bastille."* The sale, advertised as *"the 120-minute handbag snatch,"* in reality lasted only twelve minutes. The sophisticated Fifth Avenue emporium—known for their quality leathers for over 100 years—at the time of the sale looked like a one-dollar store, where about 250 women and a couple of devoted husbands battled for 120 handbags. Among them were six alligator bags marked down to $35 from the original price of $460.

In the process, the salesgirls got trapped behind the counter by the charging crowd and then were replaced by men. Within a matter of minutes, most of the inventory was gone. A customer's own purse with wallet and money was stolen and another customer's arm was bitten by *"an irate customer attempting to corner the market with six bags in tow."* The police were called and 40 additional handbags were thrown in to calm down the crowd. By the time police arrived, the eye of the storm had passed. One of the husbands who arrived to buy "under orders," emerged three hours later with an alligator handbag: *"My wife told me to buy anything as long as it's alligator. She told me to push like everybody else."*

Truly, the sale was a "howling" success, as the press reported. To the question whether he was going to have another one soon, George Wasserberger replied: *"Well, yes, but not tomorrow."*

In April of 1970, the Mark Cross company announced a clearance of crocodile handbags in confirmation of their effort to support conservation measures to preserve endangered species. *"Crocodiles are in trouble, and we're going to stop selling the products in all seven of our stores,"* announced the company's president. The sale in the summer of 1970 marked the end of the era of crocodile handbags at Mark Cross.

About forty years later, the Mark Cross brand is still strong and vibrant, as a part of the Sarah Lee conglomerate. Vintage pieces by Mark Cross—handbags, purses, wallets, travel bags, luggage and suitcases—are extremely desirable and collectible today. Especially valuable are alligator, crocodile and ostrich handbags and luggage, quite difficult to find in mint condition. If you stumble across a vintage Mark Cross exotic skin handbag, be prepared to pay a handsome price for a piece of American fashion legacy.

Sweet, genuine alligator satchel, with a flip-clasp. Prominent positioning of the umbilical scar under the clasp. Trapunto stitching; brass trim; leather-lined; with accessories; swivel, structured handle. (W 11 ¼ -inch by H 6 ½ -inch by D 3-inch). Dual signature: Lucille de Paris and Selected by Mark Cross; also Made in USA. Ca 1949.

MARTIN VAN SCHAAK

NEW YORK'S MOST EXCLUSIVE PURVEYOR OF FINE HANDBAGS

"Too rarefied to operate from anything as public as a showroom, he preferred to call on his society clientèle in their own homes. Any bag that bears his name is a fortuitous find."—Tracy Tolkien, fashion collector, consultant, and author

Martin Van Schaak crocodile handbag ad, *Harper's Bazaar* 1956.

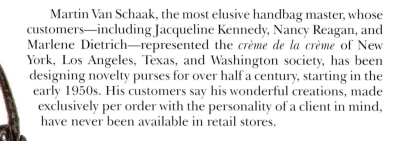
Martin Van Schaak, the most elusive handbag master, whose customers—including Jacqueline Kennedy, Nancy Reagan, and Marlene Dietrich—represented the *crème de la crème* of New York, Los Angeles, Texas, and Washington society, has been designing novelty purses for over half a century, starting in the early 1950s. His customers say his wonderful creations, made exclusively per order with the personality of a client in mind, have never been available in retail stores.

Very rare – absolutely remarkable – baby-crocodile Porosus satchel, elegantly appointed by a gilded coral-branch, sparkling with rhinestones. Custom-made, museum-quality piece – no doubt about that! Trapunto-detail on the front; swivel handle; kidskin interior. (W 9 ½ -inch by H 8 ½ -inch). Signed: Martin Van Schaak New York. Ca 1956.

Prestigious, genuine java-lizard satchel, from the estate of an heir of the Reynolds aluminum fortune. Impeccable style! Gilded accents. Roomy outside compartments; spacious interior, with multiple compartments. (W 10 ¼ -inch wide by 14-inch high (with handles) by 4-inch deep). Signed: Martin Van Schaak. Ca 1966.

I acquired a taste for the exquisite novelties of the maestro when I had a rare chance to purchase a Martin Van Schaak bag. It was a sublime, ca. 1966, navy java-lizard satchel, lined with emerald-green leather, which I bought from the estate of an heir of the Reynolds aluminum fortune. That bag was so different from anything I had seen before, a true masterpiece of sophistication and beauty!

Stunning, java-lizard satchel, with a lovely,
carved Bakelite-rose, with a gilded leaf.
Easy-to-reach, outside compartments.
Leather-lined. (W 9-inch by H 11-inch).
Signed: Martin Van Schaak. Ca 1964.

Since then, I have bought every intact vintage piece by the
incomparable Martin Van Schaak, if I could afford it. In 2001,
his new custom-made creations cost between $1,200 and $2,000.
His vintage pieces from the 1950s and 1960s could be found for
several hundred dollars, when in good to excellent condition.
His extremely rare, unique alligator pieces in mint condition
could go as high as several thousand dollars apiece.

Elite, rare, crocodile Porosus satchel, ornamented
by a fabulous, gilded shell-clasp. Dual handles,
exterior compartments lined in moire; leather-
lined interior. (W 10-inch by 13-inch high (with
handles) by 3-inch). Signed: Martin Van Schaak
New York. Ca 1965.

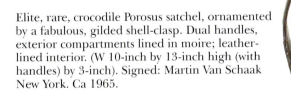

Special, genuine cobra skin evening-clutch in rare yellow.
Pleated, buttery-soft skins; welted seams; removable strap,
with toggle-holders; leather-and-moire lined. Fabulous
frame with a precious-wood inlay, in gorgeous mosaic
motif. (W 9 ¼ -inch by 6 ¾ -inch). Signed: Martin Van
Schaak New York. Ca 1960s.

Trendy, java-lizard cocktail purse, with a wonderful, metal handle made of textured, gilded and silver beads. Outside compartments, leather interior. (W 8 ¼ -inch by H 9 ½ -inch by D 3 ½ -inch). Signed: Martin Van Schaak New York. Ca 1960s.

Classic and traditional, they are not without occasional little "fantasies," as Van Schaak used to say himself. Crafted by skilled European artisans working on Long Island, New York, each is a one-of-a-kind design. Besides custom designs, you could also choose from his stock items, which were sold by appointment only.

His vintage styles usually come in several basic designs, crafted of luxurious materials, with glistening jewelry enhancers. Among them are a double-handled Pullman, a top-handled satchel, a classic clutch, a messenger shoulder bag, a bracelet bag, and a petite evening bag. Crisp lines and sleek profiles define the quintessence of the brand's image.

Collection of daytime handbags, from the 1950s-1960s. All signed: Martin Van Schaak New York. Top left: Elegant, genuine karung bracelet-purse. Bold, gilded, filigree Peacock ornament (2-inch in diameter). Framed; outside compartments; leatherette interior. (W 8 ¾ -inch by H 9 ½ -inch (with handles). Top right: (a) Striped silk-velvet clutch, with two rhinestone-studded buckles. Outside compartments; satin-lined. (W 8-inch by H 6 ½ -inch). (b) White, java-lizard arm-purse, accented by a whimsical ornament: a smiling, 3-inch dolphin (blue-n-green cloisonné, gilded brass, ruby cabochon eye). Adjustable, swivel strap; framed; leather-lined, coin-purse. (W 8-inch by H 6 ½ -inch). Bottom left: (a) Ample, white leather tote, with black patent handles, gilded accents, and two outside compartment. Leather-lined. (W 9 ½ -inch by H 12 ½ -inch (with handles). (b) Burgundy leather tote, accented by a large, gilded jewelry detail. Leather-lined. (W 9 ½ -inch by 13-inch by 4-inch wide.

MARTIN VAN SCHAAK NEW YORK

Superlative exotic skins, book-binding leather, cut velvet, brocade, satin, and beaded silk were the main materials used by Van Schaak in the 1950s to 1960s. Lizard skin was his daytime favorite. The frames for his handbags were crafted per-order in Paris. The roomy interiors of a smart layout were lined with practical calfskin or satin, in jewel tones, and signed in gold *Martin Van Schaak New York*.

Cheerful, genuine java-lizard arm-purse, in sunny yellow. Fancy front detail; adjustable, swivel strap; leather lined, with original mirror. (W 9 ¾ -inch by H 7 ¼ -inch). Signed: Martin Van Schaak New York. Ca 1960s.

Precious, genuine java-lizard frame bag, ornamented by a whimsical, jeweled accent: a parrot (encrusted with multiple colored rhinestones). Split handle; jade-cabochon finials; enameled frame; gilded trim; Kelly-green leather interior. (W 9 ½ -inch by H 7 ½ -inch by D 3 ½ -inch). Signed: Martin Van Schaak New York. Ca 1956.

The cornerstone of his fabulous vintage designs is a sizable, 24K gold-plated ornament encrusted with sparkling crystal rhinestones, glass gems or colorful enamel. Whimsical and artful, they usually depict various animals—such as tigers or elephants—as well as birds, fish and dolphins. Their uniqueness lies in their oversized proportions and highly artistic designs. They are never static, but rather fluid and expressive, conveying motion in progress.

Absolutely fabulous, genuine java-lizard cocktail-purse, accented by an amazing jeweled detail: a flaunting peacock (gilded green-and-blue cloisonné, pave rhinestones). Two large outside compartments; gilt snake-chain; leather-lined. Signed: Martin Van Schaak New York. Ca 1960s.

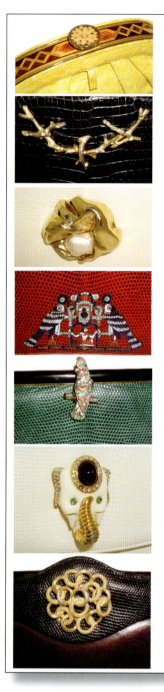

Collage of remarkable handbag-jewelry by Martin Van Schaak, made in France, ca 1950s-1960s.

Divine, genuine python chain-clutch. Flap closure is ornamented by a marvelous jewel: a ram-head (gilded black enamel, emerald-cabochon eyes, dozens of clear pave-rhinestones, large ruby cabochon on the forehead). Welted seams; accordion gussets, bottom; pleated front; leather-lined, mirror. (W 10-inch by H 7-inch by D 4-inch). Signed: Martin Van Schaak New York. Ca 1950s.

Bold and modern in spirit, his handbag jewelry doesn't just blend or complement, but stands out and works in contrast with the traditionally quiet styling of his handbags. Used purely as decoration on some of the pieces, the jeweled ornaments play a functional role, especially while being incorporated into a handle's design. Each ornament is attached to the body of the bag by means of special "holders" before sewing its sides together.

So distinct and glamorous, the Van Schaak handbags are always practical and spacious. Daytime satchels and totes come in a roomy 11-inch size, sometimes with adjustable shoulder straps. Evening models are conveniently small, less than 9-inches wide.

Artistic, one-of-a-kind genuine java-lizard satchel, created in a doctor's bag style. Tons of character! Rolled handle is held by special, jeweled holders: elephants (W 1 ¾ -inch by H 1 ¼ -inch), articulated with meticulous attention to detail. Impressive combination of brushed-metal textures, in gold and silver. Self-covered frame; wide, molded gussets; five gold-plated protective feet on the bottom; push-button clasp; exceptionally roomy leather interior, with mirror. (W 11-inch by H 13 ½ -inch (with handle) by D 4 ½ -inch). Signed: Martin Van Schaak New York. Ca 1950s.

Luxurious, genuine java-lizard clutch, with a fan-clasp, and removable shoulder strap. It was inspired by the famed Art Deco style, and boasts clean geometrical lines and features (zig-zag flap, gilded trim, and compact size). Expandable, dual-gussets. Leather lined, with two large compartments. (W 9 ½ -inch by H 6 ¾ -inch by D 2 ½ -inch). Signed: Martin Van Schaak New York. Ca 1950s.

Refined, ring-lizard satchel of a sleek design, with high-fashion accents. Outstanding quality and style! My favorite combination of silver and gold accents – in the form of stylized bows – on the belted handles. Fully leather-lined, with original accessories. (W 11-inch by H 10-inch by D 4-inch). Signed: Martin Van Schaak New York, ca 1966.

During my research, I could not help but notice how scarce information about Martin Van Schaak is. You can imagine my excitement when I discovered a couple of newspaper articles from the 1960s where he was mentioned as "the best-kept secret." A slender, brown-haired man, Martin Van Schaak—who described himself as "half-French, half-Dutch"—arrived in America from France in the mid-1940s. In 2001, he celebrated his eightieth birthday. He reminisced that in 1943 he sold his first purse to the wife of the Dutch ambassador, and, from then on, he has been designing for the most fashionable women of America.

He hardly ever advertised, and did not sell his designs in stores. His important customers—ladies of means and fame—usually discovered him by seeing his fabulous creations carried by others. Happy to get his name and telephone number, they would make an appointment to visit him at his Upper East Side apartment in New York—an elegant enclave tastefully decorated with picturesque oriental rugs, French furniture, and original oils on the walls painted in raspberry-red. After discussing a client's preferences, Mr. Van Schaak would set up a date to visit her at home. He used to show up with four commodious suitcases stuffed with 120 sample bags: *That's because, when most ladies say they want a black bag, they end up buying a red or a green one.* In the 1960s, his made-per-order handbags cost upward of $125. You could also buy his stock handbags that were produced in limited editions. A man of sophisticated taste, he believed that black, beige, navy and brown—especially the chocolate brown, with no red hues—were best for daytime wear. For cocktails, ruby-red and emerald-green were his preference, to be matched with a black dress, *"...much younger than black from head to toe. And you can match your jewelry – rubies or emeralds – to your bag."*

Fun, lizard-print leather chain-bag, accented by an amazing, jeweled clasp: a 2-inch elephant head (white enamel; large, gilded ruby-glass cabochon; emerald-glass eyes; and pave-rhinestones). Leather-lined, two interchangeable straps (leather and gilded-link strap). (W 9 ½ -inch by H 6-inch). Signed: Martin Van Schaak New York. Ca late 1960s.

He usually called on his California and Illinois customers in summer and fall, and his Texas clientèle—in winter and early spring. *"During those months, there isn't a soul in New York who can afford my pocketbooks,"* noted Van Schaak. *"Besides, America has a lot of chic women outside of New York, and they deserve to have beautiful things."* Among his most prominent clients of the 1960s were actresses Dina Merrill and Marie Oberon, as well as Mrs. John F. Kennedy. To his delight, shortly before her trip to India in the 1960s, Jacqueline Kennedy invited Mr. Van Schaak to visit her at the White House, and purchased eight handbags from him.

Practical, java-lizard shoulder bag, with adjustable, buckled strap. Impressive clasp: a fox (molded and embossed brass). Accordion gussets; welted seams; large, back pocket; leather interior, with two compartments separated with a zippered envelope. (W 9 ¾ -inch by H 8 ¼ -inch). Signed: Martin Van Schaak New York. Ca late 1960s.

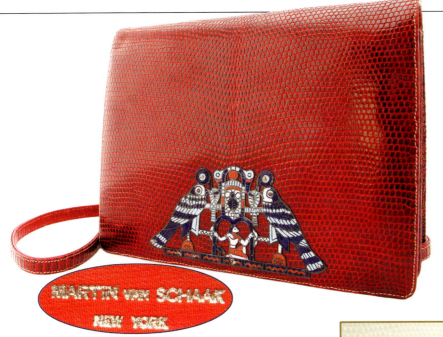

Early in his career, he had shops at various addresses on Madison Avenue in New York City, but eventually gave them up because of the *"lack of the temperament to be a shopkeeper,"* as he admitted himself. He was also offered an opportunity to sell at Neiman Marcus and considered it briefly, but then told Stanley Marcus that he would rather know the women he created for personally.

Sleek, genuine java-lizard clutch, in trendy Art Deco style. Beautiful, symmetrical belly-cuts! Lovely, cloisonné detail in Egyptian motif (4 ½-inch wide by 2 ¼-inch high). Removable strap; silver-tone hardware. Leather lining. (W 8-inch by H 6-inch). Signed: Martin Van Schaak New York. Ca 1950s.

Despite his busy schedule, which included numerous sales trips across the country to visit with his clientèle, Van Schaak was actively involved in charitable activities conducted by prominent members of New York society.

Exquisite, special occasion pieces by Martin Van Schaak, ca mid-1950s. **Left:** Lizard-printed leather clutch, with a removable shoulder strap. Outstanding, jeweled accent: a Buddha head (W 2-inch by H 3 ½-inch). Carved-jade face (a rhinestone in the forehead), with an intricate, gilded filigree head-piece. (W 9 ¼-inch by H 7-inch by D 2 ½-inch). Leatherette-lined. **Right:** My favorite, emerald satin cocktail-purse crowned with a clear Lucite lift-frame, studded with sparkling rhinestones. Satin-lined; trapunto stitching. (W 8 ½-inch by H 8-inch).

Timeless, genuine java-lizard pocketbook, ornamented with brightly polished, gilded hardware and glossy Lucite. Accordion gussets and bottom; leather-welted seams; front-flap closure; leather-lined, with multiple compartments backed with satin; original oval mirror in a satin sleeve. (W 11-inch by H 6 ½-inch (without handle). Ca late 1960s.

In the early 1960s, among collections of other contributors— important designers from New York, Florida, Chicago, and California—he provided his precious handbags for the Christmas shopping center, "Les Boutiques de Noel." It was arranged at the New York townhouse of the Baron and Baroness Philippe de Rothschild. Proceeds from the sale were donated to the Cancer Care of the National Cancer Foundation.

Today, Martin Van Schaak's vintage handbags are the most exclusive collectibles and rarely available in the secondary market. Each represents a keen understanding of the materials and the virtuoso use of various textures and colors—to communicate the utmost harmony.

Every Van Schaak handbag is a smart investment worth from hundreds to thousands of dollars when in pristine condition. They are an important slice of international fashion to add to an expert collection with pride!

NETTIE ROSENSTEIN

HEIRLOOM QUALITY OF STRONG, IMAGINATIVE DESIGNS

"Nettie Rosenstein is a past master in the art of elimination of superfluous details. She makes every fold and every seam contribute to the architecture of her design."—Virginia Pope, fashion editor, *The New York Times*, 1940

A Nettie Rosenstein Bag

Nettie Rosenstein alligator handbag ad, *Harper's Bazaar* 1946.

Rare, genuine crocodile Porosus handbag in a highly unique style, with a large front medal detail and pull closure. Semi-hard construction; oval, platform bottom; complex, tailored gussets. The back and the front-flap are cut from the whole central belly-cut that boasts beautiful symmetry. Roomy interior is lined in British-tan leather, with multiple, tailored compartments, and original mirror backed with leather. The handbag is missing the handle. (W 9 ½ -inch by H 9 ½ -inch by D 4 ½ -inch). Signed: Nettie Rosenstein. Ca 1946.

A purist and a perfectionist, fashion designer Nettie Rosenstein was known for the subtlety and finesse of her garments. Not only her distinguished, ready-to-wear clothes and the highly imaginative jewelry made history in American fashion. This multi-talented designer also made her mark as a creator of the most innovative and luxurious handbags. The understated grace and superior quality of her skin, leather, velvet, and beaded handbags, designed from the 1940s to the 1960s, created an unprecedented demand among collectors. On a good auction day, her rare and very scarce alligator handbags, in mint condition, could fetch thousands of dollars.

The Nettie Rosenstein handbags were available at Saks Fifth Avenue at Rockefeller Center. Her lines were simple. Her mediums were satiny calf, luxurious suede, and the supplest alligator. Her finely tailored, curved underarm styles and flat parcels were most meticulous and outstanding. Her distinguished alligator chest-boxes did wonders for fashion.

Legendary Nettie Rosenstein, whose successful career lasted for six decades, from 1916 to 1975, was born Nettie Rosencrans in Vienna, Austria. Her family moved to New York City in the 1890s, where they settled in Harlem and ran a dry-goods store. Like her three siblings, she graduated from a public high school. Without ever taking sewing or drawing classes, at the age of eleven, she began designing clothes for others—at first for her dolls, then for friends, family and, ultimately, for the public.

Top: Nettie Rosenstein ad, *Vogue* October 15, 1940. **Bottom left:** Nettie Rosenstein dress ad, *Vogue* October 15, 1941. **Bottom right:** Nettie Rosenstein fashion ad, *Harper's Bazaar* 1944.

As Nettie Rosenstein admitted, her most effective instructor was the trial-and-error-method, because she made no sketches and worked with materials by draping them on the model. Since the beginning of her career, her high-end fashion reflected the essence of her personality—simplicity and understated chic, rather than theatrical drama.

In 1916, she married Saul Rosenstein and opened a business under the Rosenstein's name in a leased apartment on 117th Street, near Lenox Avenue, in New York City. Within three years, the enterprise expanded to fill the entire four-apartment building and employed a staff of fifty. Soon, I. Magnin approached her with the irresistible offer to sell her fashion in their stores under the *I. Magnin* label.

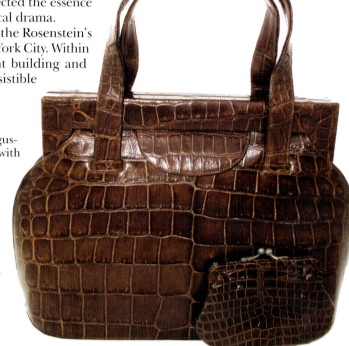

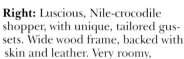

Right: Luscious, Nile-crocodile shopper, with unique, tailored gussets. Wide wood frame, backed with skin and leather. Very roomy, leather-lined interior. (W 12 ½ -inch by H 13-inch high with handles). Signed: Nettie Rosenstein. Amazing, virtually unused condition! Provenance: Similar style was advertised by Saks Fifth Avenue in September 1950.

Above: Adorable, leather pocketbook with a trendy bamboo handle; black leather interior, and original accessories. (W 8 ¼ -inch by H 9 ½ -inch by D 3 ¾ -inch). Signed: Nettie Rosenstein. Italy, ca 1968.

By 1927, Mrs. Rosenstein had developed a reputation for great designs and good business sense. However, after running her firm for almost ten years, she retired to raise her son and daughter. Three years later, in the midst of the Depression, she returned. At first, she designed for another company, and later, in 1939, she decided to re-launch her enterprise under her own name. Her new line of women's apparel thrived.

In the 1940s, when the trend was to maintain high profits at the expense of quality by minimizing the investment in workmanship, the fashions by Nettie Rosenstein, Inc. catered to the taste of the well-to-do minority. For her devoted clientèle, she created elegant and expensive garments with feminine, softly tailored lines—the trademark of her brand. Her simplicity of design did not come cheap. In 1942, Bonwit Teller featured her new creation—a divine little black dress. *"It's what you leave off a dress that makes it smart,"* Nettie mentioned, defining her vision.

Nettie's handbag operation was productive during the 1950s and the 1960s. The refined lines of her exquisite garments were successfully transferred into the widest array of new handbag styles. Among her favorites were larger, curved satchels; precious, miniature treasure chests; and enchanting boxes—slanted or curved—decorated with wonderful heraldic emblems. They were produced in limited editions—a new collection for every season—and sold for high prices. In the 1950s and 1960s, her popular leather bags sold for $50–$250, ostrich bags for $150–$250, and superb alligator handbags for $300–$550.

Curvaceous, genuine alligator top-handled satchel. No metal parts! Strong, self-covered frame, with a wood clasp wrapped in skin. Rounded, molded gussets. Very roomy, leather-lined interior, with multiple, neatly stitched compartments. Wonderful quality throughout! (W 13-inch (widest parts) x H 8 ½ -inch by D 4 ½ -inch). Signed: Nettie Rosenstein. Ca 1947.

Nettie's favorite materials for daytime handbags were exotic skins of alligator, crocodile and ostrich, as well as polished calf and patent leather, or suede. Evening models of silk, satin, gold brocade, English mohair, cashmere, or French velvet were lavishly hand-beaded or masterfully hand-embroidered. Similar to the Rosenfeld and Koret brands, her expertly designed evening purses were adorned by exquisite gilt jewelry accents.

Razzle-dazzle, gem-studded and hand-beaded evening purse. Silk-lined. Features gold-glass beads; faux turquoise beads; Aurora Borealis rhinestones; small pronged rhinestones; and faux pearls. Stunning! (W 11 ½ -inch by H 4 ½ -inch by D 3-inch). Signed: Nettie Rosenstein. Ca 1951-1952.

Fantastic, genuine java-lizard satchel, with an impossibly beautiful, ornamented brass-frame (hand-engraved and embossed). Truly a piece of art! Tailored, wide, one-piece bottom and gussets. Faille interior, with open pouches and a zippered compartment. (W 11 ½ -inch by H 7 ½ -inch by D 5 ½ -inch). Signed: Nettie Rosenstein. Labeled: Neiman Marcus. Ca 1961.

Nettie's sublime sense of style was also reflected by her choice of the material for the interiors. Her neutral spring purses, on occasion, could be lined with silk faille in unexpected shades of mustard, peach, or violet.

Spectacular, baby-crocodile Porosus briefcase-bag. Amazing quality and size! Fabulous texture and symmetry! Tailored, 3-piece, accordion gussets. Three-compartment interior is lined with kidskin, with wallet compartments. Custom-made for an important customer and stamped with her name. (W 13 ½ -inch by H 10-inch by H 5 ½ -inch (opens to whopping 10-inch). Signed: Nettie Rosenstein Made in Italy. Ca 1963-1964, Italy.

From 1950 to 1975, artful accessories by Nettie Rosenstein were sold in various stores, including Bonwit Teller and Saks Fifth Avenue. However, her most impressive collections were created exclusively for Bergdorf Goodman. In 1958, she included the "Pleasure Giving" pouch in alligator or ostrich, in the choice of sizes, 13-inch by 10-inch, or 10 ½-inch by 8-inch. In 1959, the $300 Diplomatic Pouch in alligator was *far too distinctive to travel incognito.* In 1960, a new version of a box-bag led a collection of so-called "Consequential Curves."

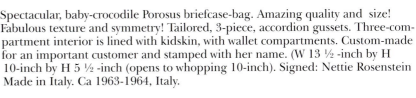

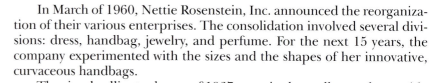

In March of 1960, Nettie Rosenstein, Inc. announced the reorganization of their various enterprises. The consolidation involved several divisions: dress, handbag, jewelry, and perfume. For the next 15 years, the company experimented with the sizes and the shapes of her innovative, curvaceous handbags.

The simple alligator boxes of 1967, seemingly smaller on the outside (as per the late 1960s fashion), but roomy on the inside and outfitted with a mirror and a coin purse, were representative of the brand's philosophy *"how to have fashion and function all wrapped up in one handbag."*

Luxurious, glossy baby-crocodile Porosus satchel, with curvy, compact body, and wide, tailored gussets. Architectural, metal handle wrapped with skin. A very roomy, leather-lined in interior, of complex design, with multiple compartments and neat decorative stitching. Outstanding quality and style! (W 9-inch by H 8 ¼ -inch by D 3-inch). Signed: Nettie Rosenstein. Ca 1967.

Museum quality, baby-crocodile Porosus satchel, with a curved Bakelite handle. Top-notch quality and style! Severely tailored design. Molded, boat-like bottom and gussets; wealth of welted seams; self-covered frame; discreet, push-button closure. Jewelry-quality, highly-polished, gilded handle mounts. Amazingly detailed leather interior, trimmed with matching skin: pleated pouch, multi-layered compartments, accessories. (W 10 ½ -inch by H 10 ½ -inch by D 4-inch). Signed: Nettie Rosenstein. Provenance: In 1967-1968, similar styles were offered by Bergdorf Goodman for over $600!

Executed with the unmistakable Nettie's cachet, its elegant exterior in splendid Porosus Crocodile, tanned a neutral beige, accentuates the gleaming mock-tortoise handle. The 4-inch gussets provide additional room to its chic shape. Sold for $545 in the late 1960s, the current value of this masterpiece (in unused, mint condition) has been appraised at several thousand dollars.

Refined and good to the very last line, every alligator or crocodile bag by Nettie Rosenstein is a rare find worth keeping, even if not in perfect condition. Minor flaws, such as insignificant wear or scuffing, do not affect the value considerably and can be easily remedied. Mint examples of rare design are considered to be exceptionally valuable, museum quality collectibles.

PAL'IZZIO
VERY NEW YORK!

Palizzio, Inc., which became a quintessential New York brand, was formed in the early 1940s. In 1943, they leased a facility at 19 Waverly Place, New York, to launch a production of trendy handbags and shoes. The line was widely promoted by *Vogue* and *Harper's Bazaar* magazines, and quickly found its market among a younger, fashionable crowd looking for style and quality at a reasonable price.

Palizzio handbags and shoes ad, *Harper's Bazaar* March 1961.

Special, hard-to-find, 3-piece set consisting of two handbags and a pair of matching heels – in an original storage box. Made of quality tegu-lizard. Beautiful, pliable, glossy skins! Small pocketbook, with a brass lever-clasp, is lined in faille (W 8 ½ -inch by H 6 ½ -inch by D 3 ½ -inch). Huge frame-bag is lined in beige leather, and trimmed with golden cord; complete with a set of original accessories (a coin purse and mirror). Heart-shaped gussets and bottom. (W 14-inch by H 11-inch by D 4-inch). Signed: Palizzio. Ca 1960.

Classic, genuine alligator pocketbook. Simple and sleek! Gold-plated hardware; lined in rust leather, with gold-cord trim. (W 12-inch by H 8-inch by D 3 ½ -inch). Signed: Palizzio. American, ca 1963.

Pair of exotic-skin handbags from the 1950s. **Left:** Soft pouch in python. Leather gussets; zippered top; optional leather strap; faille interior. (W 10 ½ -inch by H 6 ½ -inch by D 2 ½ -inch). Labeled: Palizzio Accessories. **Right:** Slim, java-lizard frame-bag, lined in leatherette. (W 7 ¾ -inch by H H 9 ½ -inch).

Palizzio, Inc. included the Palizzio Shoe Factory and the Capri Handbag Factory of New York, as well as the Matrix Shoe Factory of Rochester, New York. The smart business arrangement made it possible for the brand to establish production of fashionably unique, matching ensembles.

Roomy, two-tone, leather satchel printed with lizard pattern. Pretty design, and a very generous size. Lined with faille. (W 10 ¼ -inch by H 11-inch by D 4-inch). Signed: Palizzio. Ca 1960s.

Sassy, genuine cobra-skin shoulder bag. Front, flap closure; faille-lined. Original tag. (W 9 ¾ -inch by H 6-inch by D 3-inch). Labeled: Palizzio Accessories. Ca 1960s.

Until 1957, the company was headed by Leo Gordon. In the 1960s, Ralph M. Abrams served as president of Palizzio Shoes, Inc. Later, in the 1970s and 1980s, Leon Rubin headed Palizzio, Inc.

Pair of trendy cobra clutches. Blue: leather gussets, rayon interior (W 9 ¾ -inch by H 6-inch). Green: leather gussets, bottom and retractable shoulder strap; rayon interior (W 12-inch by H 8-inch). Labeled: Palizzio Accessories; ca 1960s.

This vanguard brand collaborated with a number of talented New York designers, including Anne Klein, who—in April of 1965—showed her swank collection of leather and suede garments and accessories. Famous for snappy-yet-elegant clothes for the young, with a hint of Western influence, she promoted the complete look, including the bags and shoes made for her by Palizzio. The collection was a roaring success!

Fashionable, raw silk pocketbook, accented by gilded details, with accordion gussets, lined with moire. (W 8 ¾ -inch by H 6-inch by D 2 ½ -inch). Signed: Palizzio. Ca 1969. Shown with a glistening rhinestone-flower bracelet, by Kenneth J. Lane (signed K.J.L, ca 1960s-1970s).

Colorful, perma-suede satchel in fresh, spring colors, lined in faille. (W 10 ½ -inch by 7 ¾ -inch by D 3-inch). Signed: Palizzio. Ca 1967.

Sleek, genuine karung clutch. Retractable top handle, lined in champaign satin. (W 12 ½ -inch by H 6-inch by D 3-inch). Signed: Palizzio Very New York. Ca 1956-1957.

The Palizzio company specialized in sophisticated, easy-on-the-eyes, matching handbag and shoe ensembles made of high quality alligator, lizard and snake skins, commonly in subtle, understated colors; and also fun, younger looking pieces, in vibrant colors, made of raw silk and faux suede and skins. Their pretty designs were available in the best department stores and luxury boutiques, including Saks Fifth Avenue.

RENDL' ORIGINAL'
HIGH-END, CASUAL EXOTIC SKIN BAGS

Very fine and stylish handbags of reptile and ostrich skin—the ones on the list of desirable collectibles—were produced by Theodore Rendl Co., in New York, starting in the 1940s. In March of 1940, the company leased space at 7 West 30th Street for handbag manufacturing. By 1945, the business had grown considerably and moved to 165 Madison Avenue. In the 1950s, Rendl became a member of the National Authority for the Ladies' Handbag Industry.

Museum-quality, baby-alligator cocktail-purse, adorned by a striking frame treated with marvelous, reverse-etching, and accented by a tall, Bakelite clasp. So delicate! Fully lined in two-tone leather. (W 8-inch by H 10 ½ -inch (without handle) by D 2 ¾ -inch). Signed: Rendl Original. Ca 1955-1956.

Fashionable, baby-crocodile Porosus cocktail purse. Superior, central belly-cuts of utmost symmetry, on both sides. Tightly-scaled pattern! Unusual, bridge-handle, with a sweet, bow-detail. Leather-lined, with multiple compartments trimmed with skin and gold-cord. (W 8 ½ -inch by H 15-inch (with handle) by D 2 ¾ -inch). Signed: Rendl Original. Provenance: Similar piece was advertised in the *Harper's Bazaar* March 1956 issue.

Pair of oversize alligator frame-bags – a perfect option for everyday use. The choicest, symmetrical, belly-cuts are used to create these beauties. Both are leather-lined, with original accessories. Black: W 13-inch by H 11-inch (18-inch with handle) by D 4-inch. Brown: W 13 ¾ -inch by H 12-inch (with handle) by D 2 ¾ -inch. Both are signed: Rendl Original. Ca late 1957-1958.

This wonderful brand specialized in luxurious handbags at the upper end of the quality spectrum and commanded top prices, which their dedicated customers were eager to pay without hesitation. They were sold in the best department stores nationwide, such as Saks Fifth Avenue and B. Altman & Co.

Curvy, genuine alligator pocketbook. Elegant style and features. Very pretty! Conveniently wide arm-strap. Two-part, leather interior, complete with accessories (coin-purse, comb and mirror). (W 10-inch by H 6 ½ -inch by D 3 ½ -inch). Ca 1960s.

Exceptional, custom crocodile wristlet, adorned by a curved Celanese plastic frame. Softly pleated skins; loop-closure; faille-lined, with set of accessories. Special style, amazing quality! (W 6 ¾ -inch by H 8 ½ -inch (without handle) by D 5-inch). Signed: Rendl Original. Ca 1947.

Fairly spacious, Rendl purses always look feminine, refined and sophisticated. Carefully thought through, their designs are usually geared toward comfort, yet often they incorporate "unnecessarily" luxurious details—expensive in execution—to add flavor to their casual appearance.

Attractive, supple crocodile arm-purse, with a top handle and roomy, leather-lined interior, trimmed with skin. Leather gussets; gold-plated trim. (W 8-inch by H 7 ½ -inch by D 4 ¾ -inch). Signed: Rendl Original. Ca 1946.

Luxurious, matte crocodile Porosus, top-handled satchel. Unique details: curved, self-covered frame, with two-tone clasp; expandable front-pocket, with a flap, and snap closure; deep, open-pouch on the back; two-tone, leather-lining trimmed with skin. Complete set of accessories. (W 10-inch by H 9 ½ -inch by D 3 ½ -inch). Signed: Rendl Original. Provenance: Similar piece was advertised by Saks-34th in 1949-1951.

The core of Rendl design is a clean, geometric shape—rectangular or square—with well-defined horizontal or vertical lines that accentuate bold, architectural structure or intentionally curved edges to soften it. Handles were crafted with the idea of extending or balancing the construction. Exteriors were cut from whole skins, with no seams or undesirable patching.

Slim, genuine alligator purse accented by an unusual, enameled frame in amber-brown, with square flat handles. Exquisite style! Folding gussets; fully leather-lined; solid-brass trim. (W 11-inch by H 13-inch by D 2-inch). Signed: Rendl Original. West Germany, ca 1956.

Boxy, genuine crocodile arm-bag, with very wide body and spacious, leather-lined interior. Interesting, folding top-closure, with a gold, twist-clasp. Complete with accessories. Glowing – supple and cushioned – skins! (W 7 ¼ -inch by H 6-inch by D 4 ¼ -inch). Singed: Rendl Original. Ca 1946-1947.

The Rendl brand is distinctive by its creative use of skin patterns. Only the hides of impeccable symmetry—proportioned to the size of the bag—were handpicked for each item. Each was centered to enhance their impeccable design. There is no attempt to save on quality here!

Superb, genuine alligator frame-bag, with a wide, swivel handle. Leather-lined; complete with the set of original accessories, and a pair of gloves, trimmed with matching skin. Finely tailored, soft gussets and accordion bottom. Remarkable quality! Exceptionally supple skins! (W 8 ¾ -inch by H 13-inch by D 3-inch). Signed: Rendl Original. Labeled: Crouch & Fitzgerald New York. Ca 1948.

In ostrich bags, a clever application of cuts with mixed textures—full quill and smooth—often creates a strong visual effect. No two bags by Rendl Original are alike. A curved, rocking bottom was an innovation of the brand and the company's signature feature.

Luxurious, ostrich top-handled handbag. Marvelous, full-quill skins. Rocking bottom; swivel handle; self-covered frame, with a trendy, large gilt lever-clasp. Ample leather interior, trimmed with skin. (W 12-inch by H 8-inch by D 3-inch). Signed: I. Magnin & Co. Rendl Original. Ca 1957.

Special, genuine alligator lunch-box, with swivel-handles; wide-split interior – in green leather – and central, zippered envelope. Hard-sided construction. (W 9-inch by H 6-inch by D 3-inch). Signed: Rendl Original. Ca 1950.

The traditional layout of their finely fitted leather interior is complex and incorporates plenty of multi-level pouches piped in gold cord. The contrasting trim prevents soiling. A large coin purse on a brass chain and well-adjusted gilt fixtures complete the picture-perfect alligator handbags by Rendl.

Spacious, black crocodile Porosus satchel in a style of a popular doctor's bag. Wide, tailored gussets; leather-lined interior; trapunto details; pendant-pull. Well-built, structured top handle. (W 9 ¼ -inch by H 5 ½ -inch by D 4 ¼ -inch). Beautiful workmanship! Signed: Rendl Original. Ca 1949.

Exotic, lizard frame-bag, with gilt trim. Interesting texture and markings! Light-beige leather interior, trimmed with skin and gold cord, complete with accessories, including a lovely shell comb, encrusted with rhinestone and faux pearls (signed 'Handmade in France'). Lovely! (W 9-inch by H 13 ½ -inch (with handle) by D 3-inch). Signed: Rendl Original. Ca 1954.

Fairly scarce, decadent Rendl exotics in mint condition are a delightful addition to any comprehensive collection. They would set you back over $900 for a rare piece of unusual design, such as the handbags featured here.

HARRY ROSENFEL'D
SENSIBLE GLAMOR OF STYLISH DECORATIONS

Harry Rosenfeld handbags are some of my personal favorites. I developed a crush on this brand years ago when I acquired a stunning, jeweled Rosenfeld piece in black Porosus Crocodile, from the estate of an avid traveler and collector of antique and vintage fashion.

Rosenfeld handbags are truly magnificent. Each is a one-of-a-kind treasure, unsurpassed in quality, style and craftsmanship. When a vintage Rosenfeld bag is swinging from your arm, you feel fabulous. Try it and you will know what I mean.

Sublime, genuine alligator evening purse by Harry Rosenfeld, crowned by an enameled frame jeweled with quartz rhinestones. Ca 1956.

Harry Rosenfeld was involved in the handbag industry of New York City since 1916. He was a founder and first president of the handbag company bearing his name, Harry Rosenfeld Handbags, Inc. Starting from 1935, the company was located in New York City at 135 Madison Avenue. It also was a member of the National Authority for the Ladies' Handbag Industry (NALHI).

Harry Rosenfeld's impact on handbag design was profound, and resulted in his numerous signature styles. He is credited with the development of elaborate treatments of leather and fabrics, along with the use of unique embellishments for purses. His last personal contribution to the handbag fashion world was a practical, 1941 silhouette: *"We have evolved this type of defense bag, larger than a canteen, with plenty of pockets, realizing that style must now be practical."*

Harry Rosenfeld died from a heart ailment at his home on Park Avenue in July of 1942; he was only 42 years old. Since then, Harry Rosenfeld Handbags, Inc. had been headed by its second president, Milton S. Graber.

Above: Timeless, genuine alligator skin satchel, with a front swagger-pocket, structured handle, and two-tone leather interior. Beautifully appointed, brown enameled frame – a uniquely Rosenfeld's feature. (W 10-inch by H 8 ½ -inch by D 4-inch). Signed: Rosenfeld Genuine Alligator. West Germany, ca 1958.

Group of collectible handbags by innovative Rosenfeld, from various decades. **Top left:** "The Chain Bag" – smart, genuine suede duplet. Larger framed pouch (with a skinny, long, doubled strap) is W 7-inch by H 6 ½ -inch by D 1 ¾ -inch. The smaller one is attached by chains. (W 7 ¾ -inch by H 5 ½ -inch by D 1-inch). Signed: Rosenfeld (larger one). Provenance: The same style was advertised by B. Altman & Co. in September 1950. **Top right:** Special, leather shoulder bag of highly unusual design. It features a leather shell, with a bold, multi-dimensional Lion-Sun motif, embossed on a gilded plate. Inside, there's a leather coin purse that can be pulled out. Satin-lined and signed: Copyright 1973 Harry Rosenfeld Inc. Long, decorative strap. (W 6 ½ -inch by H 7-inch by D 3 ¼ -inch). **Center:** Amusing, leather shoulder bag decorated with a multi-dimensional, fox-pendant. Incredible craftsmanship! Gilt hardware. Two smaller fox-finials serve as strap attachments. Faille interior. (W 10 ¾ -inch by H 9-inch by D 3-inch). Signed: Copyright 1972 Harry Rosenfeld. **Bottom left:** Darling, genuine leather coin-purse, with a cage-hinge closure, adorned by butterscotch Bakelite. (W 3 ½ -inch by H 3 ¾ -inch by D 2-inch). Signed: Made in Italy for Rosenfeld. Ca 1960s. **Bottom right:** Cute, java-lizard purse, with a faceted onyx tassel-clasp. Satin-lined. (W 8-inch by H 6 ½ -inch by D 2-inch). Signed: Rosenfeld. Labeled: Made in U.S.A. Ca 1950s.

Phenomenal, ultra-rare piece made of expensive American alligator. Unique, multi-dimensional construction. Round body; football-like bottom, with plenty of welted seams. Generously pleated, central belly-cut on the front, with the umbilical scar displayed on the bottom. Self-covered, square frame. Amazing, gilded-brass disks are holding a very wide, cuff-like handle. Black leather interior with red trim; original comb. (W 9-inch by H 12-inch by D 5-inch). Signed: Rosenfeld Original. Provenance: This very same style was advertised by B. Altman & Co. in November 1946.

The emphasis of Rosenfeld's lines was the originality. In order to develop their luxurious styles, the company contracted skilled artisans from Europe: France, Belgium, Germany, and Italy. Talented designers created a variety of limited editions offered at Saks Fifth Avenue, B. Altman & Co., Lord & Taylor, Bonwit Teller, and other prestigious boutiques. They were sold side-by-side with handbags by Lucille de Paris, Koret, Coblentz, and Rendl. Made to impress and last for generations, they commanded top prices and attracted smart buyers willing to invest in their uniqueness and quality.

B. Altman & Co. advertisement of the Rosenfeld's new collection of fine alligator handbags: "Masterpieces in the aristocrat of leathers, done by Rosenfeld. Each one is a long-term investment in fashion, quality and durability". November 1947.

Decadent, ample, genuine crocodile pouch of unique design. One-of-a-kind, arch-handle is made of brass, of two parts: one is wrapped with the skins, and the other is accented by two halves of Bakelite, riveted together. Huge, supple, central belly-cuts are arranged horizontally – unusual! Leather-lined interior, with original coin purse. (W 9-inch by H 18-inch (with the handle) by D 3-inch). Signed: Rosenfeld. Ca 1953.

In 1947, the Rosenfeld company was asked to take part in the Bloomingdale's "Woman of Fashion, 1947" collection, which was presented later by the store to the Metropolitan Museum of Art on its 75th Anniversary. The collection included a complete wardrobe, typical of the best examples of 1947 fashions, by twenty-four leading American designers. Among them were Harry Rosenfeld, Richard Koret, and Nettie Rosenstein. Now a part of the permanent collection of the Costume Institute of the Metropolitan Museum of Art, the exhibit became a great inspiration for designers, artists and students of art.

Divine, museum-quality genuine crocodile handbag. Artistic, multi-dimensional fish-details (gilded metal cast). Very special, unique styling! Flat back, with pleated, molded-and-tailored front, and flap-closure (snap underneath). Crescent-like bottom; brown leather interior. (W 8 ¾ -inch by H 13-inch (with the fish) by D 3 ½ -inch). The handle is 6-inch drop. Labeled: Rosenfeld Original. Provenance: This very same handbag is featured in the *Vogue* ad 1946 (right).

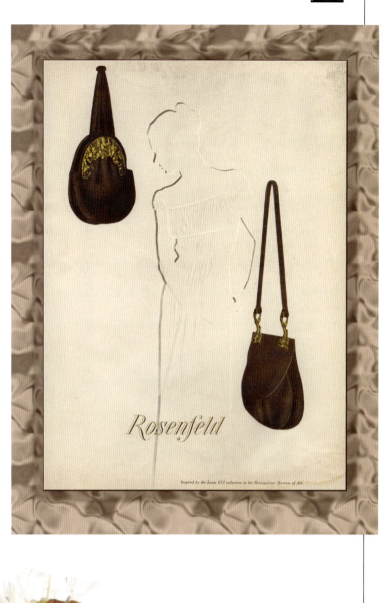

Rosenfeld

Special, football-shaped genuine alligator arm-purse, accented by a sizable, solid, faceted, clear-Prystal clasp that reflects light like real crystal. So unusual! Gold-plated frame; leather interior; very special construction of the body, with multiple welted seams. (W 10-inch by H 9-inch by D 6-inch). Labeled: Rosenfeld Original. American, ca 1944-1945.

The signature style of a Rosenfeld bag lies in its distinctive character, elaborate design and unique decorative features. Milton Graber frequently attended Paris trade shops to find high-fashion ornaments. In 1948, a peculiar situation arose when he visited France to purchase French Colonial citations, which could be used as handbag decorations—as he was told. He purchased the whole lot and his designers later created a collection of handbags to feature those citations. They retailed for about $60 apiece, a huge amount of money in the 1940s. Graber's creative initiative was eventually reported to the American government as a violation of the provision of the International Convention for the Protection of Industrial Property. A representative of the French government notified local stores that the distribution of the Rosenfeld bags with the French medals was in violation of the law—and they should be withdrawn from sale. The company communicated their disagreement to Congressman Sol Bloom. We don't know exactly how the story ended, but, since then, Rosenfeld handbags enjoyed an enormous commercial success and their sales rose substantially throughout the country.

Above: Pair of ultra-rare, identical shoulder bags in red crocodile and black leather, lavishly ornamented by an amazing brass detail: an Imperial Eagle. Mind-bending workmanship of embossing and etching! Shapely bodies, with rounded, 1-piece gussets, and a curvy, platform bottom. No clasp under the front flap – it stays closed under its own weight. Leather lined. (W 9 ½ -inch (widest parts) by H 9 ½ -inch by D 3 ½ -inch). Signed: Rosenfeld. Ca 1946.

To create their fascinating styles, the firm invested a lot of time and money in research of the period fashion. They collected their own handbags from previous years by offering a participation in their "recycling" program. In 1953, they announced that they would send new fall samples to customers who would supply them with their old pieces made between 1935 and 1945—to be able to trace the evolution of their designs. In response, their customers submitted thirty-five older bags, which the company accepted and replaced with new ones. One resourceful lady brought in a fifteen-year-old purse that she had purchased a week before from a thrift shop—to replace it with a new, expensive alligator bag.

Spectacular, genuine alligator arm-purse with a massive, enameled frame and lipstick-red leather interior. Tailored design, with welting and trapunto. Curved, platform bottom. (W 10-inch by H 8-inch by D 4-inch). Signed: Rosenfeld Genuine Alligator. West Germany, ca 1958.

Rosenfeld was in the vanguard of setting trends in handbag decorations. Significant events of the 1950s found their reflection in the constant change of their fashionable motifs and themes.

This particular piece – so impressive and sublime – was created for Tiffany & Co., and was sold in their store in New York in 1943. Included is a card in a Tiffany envelope that reads: "Your Rosenfeld handbag is fashioned from the finest Mexican skins, Baran Alligator, acclaimed the aristocrat of all leathers, polished to pliant perfection, a cherished possession to treasure." Superb, high-fashion style! Valuable features: pliable, premium skins; generous pleating; tailored construction of the exterior and interior (moire, with tan leather). The jewel-crown of the piece is its clasp – a uniquely shaped Bakelite ornament, trimmed with hammered brass. (W 16 ½ -inch by H 8-inch by D 4-inch). Singed: Rosenfeld.

In 1953, following up on their phenomenal success, the company opened a new subsidiary, Rosenfeld Imports, Inc. In order to accommodate their imports, specialized departments were installed in many stores across the country. As a result, their sales immediately increased, about four times.

Sassy, genuine crocodile pocketbook, in neutral navy-blue, with sexy-red leather interior. Interesting positioning of the central belly-cut – it runs horizontally, not vertically. Distinctive scale-texture! Unique design: boat-like shape; bold, gilded bracket-closure; massive handle-mounts. Welted seams. (W 12-inch by H 11-inch (with handle) by D 2 ¾ -inch). Signed: Rosenfeld. Ca 1956.

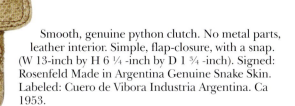

Smooth, genuine python clutch. No metal parts, leather interior. Simple, flap-closure, with a snap. (W 13-inch by H 6 ¼ -inch by D 1 ¾ -inch). Signed: Rosenfeld Made in Argentina Genuine Snake Skin. Labeled: Cuero de Vibora Industria Argentina. Ca 1953.

Built with utmost attention to detail, highly collectible Rosenfeld exotics often sport elaborate, 24K gold-plated hardware and accents; lacquered enameled frames; gorgeous rhinestone or jewel-encrusted clasps; Lucite or Bakelite accents; fancy fittings; piped seams; trimmed edges; accessories; and unbreakable, rolled handles with metal rod inserts.

Close-up of the opulent ornamentation by Rosenfeld. The enameled frame is intricately engraved and etched, and prong-set with unusually large, quartz rhinestones. What fire! Pleated, supple skins; satin-lined. Superb craftsmanship! (W 9 ½ -inch by H 8-inch by D 2 ½ -inch. Signed: Rosenfeld Genuine Alligator. France, or West Germany, ca 1956.

Pair of glorious alligator frame-bags, with identical, enameled frames: black on black, and white on yellow. Leather interior; gilt-brass trim; protective feet on the bottom; reinforced, semi-structural handles. (W 11-inch by H 10-inch by D 3-inch). Signed: Rosenfeld Genuine Alligator. Ca 1954-1956.

Pair of giant, identical hobo-bags, with bracelet handles. Stunning presence! Black Nile crocodile (left), and velvet-and-leather (right). Unique detail: enormous, round bodies; folding half-gussets; neat, trapunto stitching; belt-closure with a snap; brass bracelet-handles draped with skin; humongous, leather-lined interiors. Huge, central belly-cuts of superior symmetry painstakingly matched on both sides: W 16-inch by H 15-inch by D 2 ½ -inch! Considering its sheer size, the value of this breathtaking piece can be estimated in many, many thousands. Black-and-red leather interior, with large, framed wallet; huge zippered compartments. Signed: Rosenfeld. Labeled: Joseph shoes. Ca 1958.

Superb, symmetrical skins—brightly polished, and treated with a bombe finish—are the cornerstones of the Rosenfeld's style. Carefully matched belly-cuts of premium hides—Mexican alligator, Porosus crocodile, Tortuga turtle, Java lizard, and African ostrich—were sourced from all over the world. No wonder each Rosenfeld handbag looks like a million bucks and costs a small fortune!

Above: Divine, genuine alligator pocketbook, with classic features and detail. Tightly-grained, whole, central belly-cut is used on the front and back. Superb symmetry! Strong, brushed-and-polished brass flip-clasp. A smart top-handle is attached to a metal-bar riveted to the top – it will last forever, without any damage. Two-tone (brown and tan) leather interior, with multiple compartments. (W 11 ½ -inch by H 13-inch w/ handle by D 3-inch). Signed: Rosenfeld Genuine Alligator. Ca 1965-1967.

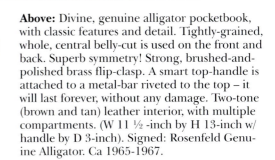

Ultimate, genuine American alligator briefcase, lined in red leather. Top-quality, huge and flawless central belly-cuts of impeccable symmetry. Outrageously expensive and valuable! Front swagger pocket. Self-covered frame. Platform bottom. Luggage-type, rolled handle. Gold-plated hardware. Original accessories. (W 15 ½ -inch by H 13-inch (with handle) by D 3 ½ -inch). Signed: Rosenfeld Genuine Alligator. Ca 1958-1959.

When shopping for a divine Rosenfeld, always look for their famous fan logo, with the word *Rosenfeld*, as well as their reliable authenticity marks—*Genuine alligator*, *Genuine ostrich*, *Genuine turtle*, or *Genuine lizard*—stamped in gold on the interior.

Chic, genuine alligator pocketbook with no metal parts whatsoever! Whole, central belly-cut of utmost symmetry is used to create the body of the piece. Exceptionally expensive feature! Belted front closure. Folding gussets and bottom. Black leather interior trimmed with contrast red-leather. (W 10-inch by H 7-inch by D 3-inch). Signed: Rosenfeld Genuine Alligator. Ca early 1963-1964.

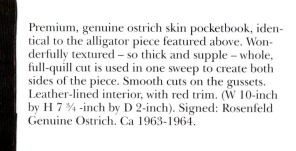

Premium, genuine ostrich skin pocketbook, identical to the alligator piece featured above. Wonderfully textured – so thick and supple – whole, full-quill cut is used in one sweep to create both sides of the piece. Smooth cuts on the gussets. Leather-lined interior, with red trim. (W 10-inch by H 7 ¾ -inch by D 2-inch). Signed: Rosenfeld Genuine Ostrich. Ca 1963-1964.

Beware of pieces altered by means of added embellishments or replaced handles not original to the handbag. Such a bag would be less valuable than a similar one in original, unmodified condition. To distinguish the difference, inspect how the "jewel" is attached. If it is glued directly to the skin, it is not original. Please note that Rosenfeld did not produce large alligator day-bags with chain straps. If you see such a bag, with an added jewel or a replaced handle, don't pay a full asking price. Ask for a bargain.

Trio of genuine turtle handbags, from 1968. **Top left:** Black piece in equestrian style, with plenty of decorative details. Expandable front pouch that can be unbelted. Wide, doctor's bag style gussets. Protected bottom. Push-button clasp. The plastic handle is a well-matched replacement. (W 9-inch by H 7-inch by D 4 ½ -inch). Singed: Rosenfeld Genuine Turtle. **Center:** Structured taupe bag, identical to the black one, but with the original top-handle. High-gloss finish. (W 9-inch by H 6 ½ -inch by 4 ½ -inch). Signed: Rosenfeld Genuine Turtle. Labeled: The Elaine Shop at the Diplomat the Bal Harbour Shops Hollywood Beach Hotel. **Bottom left:** Sexy-red cocktail purse, with expandable front pocket, flap-closure; self-covered, padded frame; gilded trim. Lined in black leather. Beautiful, pliable skins, with distinct markings. (W 8 ¼ -inch by H 7-inch by D 3-inch). Signed: Rosenfeld Genuine Turtle, I. Magnin & Co.

Fantastic, genuine alligator frame-bag, with massive, brightly-polished brass frame. Stunning, premium skins, with expensive bombe finish. Two-tone, leather interior. Impressive quality and attention to detail! (W 11 ¾ -inch by H 11-inch (without the handle) by D 2 ½ -inch). Signed: Rosenfeld. Ca 1958.

In the early 1970s, the Rosenfeld company ceased production of alligator handbags, but continued to manufacture various leather goods for at least two more decades. The company's undeniable success of that period is attributed to its collaboration with one of the most glamorous New York costume jewelry designers, Kenneth J. Lane, who created a fantastic line of bejeweled evening purses for Rosenfeld. The collaboration with another costume jeweler, Marcel Boucher, created examples that incorporated high quality jewelry accents, such as the featured black leather piece with an engraved silver plate. Absolutely fabulous!

A pair of masterpieces by incomparable Rosenfeld created in collaboration with famed jewelers, Marcel Boucher and Kenneth J. Lane, in the 1950s-1960s. **Top:** Petite, sharkskin-grained leather pocketbook, accented by a stunning, jeweled Lion's head bracelet-handle. It is composed of a flexible, beaded arch, connected by a pair of finely crafted lion heads, gleaming with polished gilt, and a handful of pave-rhinestones and emerald-cabochon eyes. Satin-lined. (W 7 ¾ -inch by H 7-inch (with the handles) by D 3 ½ -inch). Provenance: I was very lucky to find an original Bonwit Teller's ad, from September 3, 1969, where they advertised the very same cocktail purse – a great provenance of this unique collectible. **Bottom:** Opulent, genuine leather handbag, with a structured body, and a finely-polished nickel hardware. It is accentuated by the outstanding jeweler's detail: an intricately etched silver plate depicting a pastoral scene. Superb quality! The plate is signed in three places: Boucher (top), Pastorale (bottom), and B. Wicker Gr. (bottom right corner). Faille-lined. (W 14-inch by H 6-inch without handle by D 4-inch). Signed: Rosenfeld. Ca 1950-1955.

Don't confuse a vintage garment label of Henry Rosenfeld or cheap bags made in China by MaryAnn Rosenfeld for the high-end brand of Harry Rosenfeld. Neither of them has any connection to the renowned Harry Rosenfeld Handbags, Inc.

Equestrian, genuine alligator framed satchel. Gorgeous, shimmering skins! Bright, gilded hardware. Strong, self-covered frame and wide gussets. Leather-lined, with an original coin purse. (W 8 ½ -inch by H 6 ½ -inch by D 4 ½ -inch). Signed: Rosenfeld Genuine Alligator. Ca 1964.

Today, if you are ready to invest in the best vintage, a superlative Rosenfeld is definitely for you—the true status symbol among discriminating collectors! They exude panache and scream old money. Every piece in pristine condition is a collector's dream—and a smart investment opportunity!

Impeccable, genuine alligator satchel, lined in beige leather, with original accessories. Attractive, equestrian motif typical for this brand: front belt-details; fancy, gold-plated trim; structured, riveted top handle. (W 9-inch by H 10-inch by D 4 ½ -inch). Signed: Rosenfeld Genuine Alligator. Ca 1964.

SOUTH AMERICAN IMPORTS
LUXURY HANDBAGS AT MODEST PRICES

The 1940s brought war to the doorsteps of most European countries and cut back European exports of luxury goods. In the meantime, the demand for luxury was on the rise in the United States. In 1940, when it was impossible to import crocodile handbags from France, the U. S. Department of Commerce explored new opportunities in Central and South America—especially Brazil, Argentina, Uruguay, and Mexico. There they found ideal perspective markets for the development of manufacturing high-end goods to replace European imports.

Impressive, genuine alligator vanity-duplet, in delicious crimson-red – a real piece of art! Glossy, bright skins. Finely polished gilded trim. Heavenly-soft, suede interior. The vanity compartment is conveniently located under the flap, and closes with a snap – for easy reach. Complete with the set of original accessories, and moire (coin purse, comb, etc.). Generously sized, 11 ½ -inch by 8 ½ -inch by 3-inch. Labeled: Marroquineria Fina La Creacione Made in Uruguay. Ca 1950s, Uruguay.

Voluptuous, genuine alligator wrist-bag, in collectible forest-green. Pleated sides; gilded trim; wide top wristlet-loop; push-button clasp; leather interior with original coin purse; round bottom. (W 8-inch by H 8 ¾ -inch by D 4-inch; L 7-inch wristlet). Signed: Mago, Real Alligator, Industria Argentina Made in Argentina. Ca 1949. Original price tag for $64.45.

Shirred-and-draped, genuine alligator vanity wristlet – true blast from the past! Unusual construction and details. Wide arm-handle is attached to the vanity-lid, with the mirror underside. Wide platform-bottom. Sliding pin-closure, with a chain-pull. Brass trim. Suede interior and gussets. Boxy and robust! (W 8-inch by H 8 ¼ -inch by H 5-inch; L 5-inch wristlet). Argentina. Provenance: Similar piece was advertised by Gimbels in their November 29, 1947 sale, for $45.

Special, red alligator dressmaker-bag, with curvaceous, rounded body; massive dome-frame; unusually structured clasp; softly pleated skins, and two wide arm-handles. Suede-lined, multiple skin-trimmed compartments. (W 9-inch by 14-inch with handles by 4 ¾ -inch deep). Labeled: Cuero Caiman Industria Argentina. Argentina. Provenance: Similar style was advertised by Saks-34th in February 1949 ("Valentine Sale").

As reported in the *New York Times,* a new corporation was founded—the Block International Corporation—to create merchandise in Latin American countries for mass distribution in the U.S. It was set up under the auspices of a program of the Inter-American Development Commission. The company sent agents to facilities in Brazil and Argentina to select samples of snakeskin and alligator products. The first shipment of the selected merchandise was sold with great success. After that, retailers were encouraged to buy from various Latin manufacturers. The first South American handbags were introduced to the North American market in 1941 by Lord & Taylor stores at modest prices and in rich colors.

In early 1940s, American women worked hard on factory assembly lines wearing masculine work clothes. After a hard-days work, they wanted to feel feminine and pretty. A sharp increase in spending money on glamor was noted. Reportedly, the sale of luxury goods more than doubled by 1943. Furs were flying off the racks. Diamonds were selling like rhinestones. The stores could not keep alligator handbags that cost up to $150 apiece.

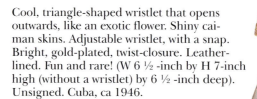

Cool, triangle-shaped wristlet that opens outwards, like an exotic flower. Shiny caiman skins. Adjustable wristlet, with a snap. Bright, gold-plated, twist-closure. Leather-lined. Fun and rare! (W 6 ½ -inch by H 7-inch high (without a wristlet) by 6 ½ -inch deep). Unsigned. Cuba, ca 1946.

Interesting, genuine alligator-n-leather arm-purse, with unique hardware. Bold, brightly-polished buckle, with a chained, bullet-pin closure. Removable handle – trimmed with gilded hardware – is attached to the handbag by chained toggles. It can be removed through the grommets on the top of the bag, to convert the purse into a clutch. Smart! (W 9 ½ -inch by H 7 ½ -inch). Unsigned. Ca late 1949. Based on the quality of the skins, general design and especially the style of the hardware, it was most likely crafted in Mexico, inspired by famed French workmanship.

The spenders represented women of all walks of life: newly wealthy war workers, middle-class women whose earnings increased drastically, women who became executives when men went to fight in the war, and women whose husbands' businesses were booming.

Left: Distinct, genuine full-quill ostrich bracelet purse, with a molded, natural-bamboo wristlet. Pretty! Fully lined in gray leather. (W 10-inch by H 15-inch). Labeled: Made by Prado Bags Marca Reg. 11635 Hecho en Mexico. Ca 1950.

Above: Sleek, brass-trimmed, genuine alligator clutch, lined in leather. Interior compartment is trimmed with gold-n-red cord – a unique feature typical of Cuban-made alligator products. Welted seams. Great design and proportions. First-class quality! (W 12-inch by H 4 ½ -inch). Signed: Genuine Alligator Made in Cuba. Ca 1950s.

Macy's advertisement of the fabulous collection of South American alligators, February 1944.

High-volume South American handbag imports helped to satisfy the new spending habits. In the late 1940s, Prado Bags from Mexico, Industria Argentina from Argentina, and Madeleine Pegs from Mexico were the major Central and South American exporters to the United States. Their products came in enormous quantities and retailed in department stores such as Lord & Taylor, Macy's, B. Altman & Co. and Oppenheim Collins, and were sold by mail-order.

Except for valuable Mexican crocodile, South American skin bags were primarily made with affordable but brittle caiman skin. Substantially inferior in quality to true crocodile, they compensated by a blinding sheen of their finish, cheerful colors and a wide assortment of styles, including shoulder bags, box-bags, envelopes, clutches, satchels, and frame-bags.

Above: Lady-like, soft and shiny red crocodile arm-purse. No metal parts! Wide, heart-shaped, double gussets. Welted seams. Rolled arm-strap attached by skin loops. Skin-loop closure, with a long, wood button. Incredibly spacious, leather interior. (W 9 ½ -inch by H 6-inch by D 5 ½ -inch). Signed: Abtik, Mexico. Ca 1944.

Pliable, genuine alligator duplet-clutch, with a wristlet-handle. Pleated skins. Duplet frame reveals two separate, suede-lined compartments; two lift-clasps, decorated with carved Bakelite button-accents. (W 13 ½ -inch by H 8-inch). Signed: Real Alligator Industria Argentina Made in Argentina. Ca 1948.

Unique, genuine alligator satchel, with an unusual sliding closure. Art Deco-styled brass frame features a sliding pull that opens or closes the frame. Leather handles. Leather-lined; trimmed with matching skin. (W 9 1/2-inch by 8-inch (without handles)). Signed: Industria Argentina. Ca 1953.

Lord & Taylor and Macy's ran regular promotions of South American imports, selling huge amounts of inventory every month. In October of 1947, the imports sold rapidly at a high rate of 1,500 bags in four days, priced a mere $39.50 apiece. For Christmas, Macy's brought 1,000 more bags for only $19.98 apiece, and these flew off the racks within days!

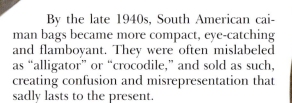

By the late 1940s, South American caiman bags became more compact, eye-catching and flamboyant. They were often mislabeled as "alligator" or "crocodile," and sold as such, creating confusion and misrepresentation that sadly lasts to the present.

Gleaming, convertible, genuine alligator clutch. Sleek design, great quality! Swivel, gilded handle can be positioned upwards, or downwards – to be used as a clutch or an arm-purse. Clever! Leather-lined. (W 11-inch by H 7-inch). Labeled: VACA Industria Argentina E 5490. Argentina, ca 1950s.

Therefore, when buying an Argentine handbag today, remember that even if it is marked *Alligator* or *Crocodile*, it may be made with inferior, less expensive caiman. Generally, caiman bags from Argentina or other South American countries are not as valuable as European or American alligator or crocodile counterparts.

Delightful, genuine alligator cocktail-purse, with an unusual cube-and-pin closure, and a relief detail on the front. The wire handle is a well-matched replacement. Lovely, top-quality skins! (W 8-inch by H 10 ½ -inch). Signed: Madeleine Pags Genuine alligator Hecho en Mexico. Ca 1950s.

Glossy, genuine alligator frame bag – beautifully styled and crafted with a keen attention to detail. Blue-gray leather interior; polished, gilded trim. (W 9 ¾ -inch by H 6 ¾ -inch). Dual labels: El Trebol Buenos Aires (skin label seen in the picture) and Yacare Overo Industria Argentina 1307. Brazil, ca 1960.

When shopping for a quality handbag, it is safer to select the tightly grained, top-quality Mexican crocodile, such as that made by Prado Bags. Erroneously marked as *Mexican Alligator* or *Baby Alligator*, those marvelous pieces usually come in black or brown, accented by tasteful, finely crafted solid brass details and are lined in colored leather. Largest handbags of this type in mint condition could retail for upwards of $800 apiece.

Above: Luscious, top-quality, genuine crocodile clutch in desirable red, lined in quality leather, with an original leather coin-purse. Very soft and pliable. Welted seams, simple brass-plate closure. Roomy interior with a zippered compartment. (W 12-inch by H 7-inch). Signed: Creaciones Del Prado Hecho en Mexico. Ca 1952. Amazing craftsmanship influenced by French artisans!

Above: Luxurious, genuine alligator duplet in collectible emerald-green. Belted, adjustable shoulder strap; tall, two-piece, wood frame; tailored, leather interior; solid brass hardware. Fabulous, petal-soft skins! (W 9-inch by 8-inch by 3-inch). Signed: Genuine Alligator Hecho en Mexico. Ca 1949.

Right: Generous, navy-blue genuine crocodile duplet, trimmed in brass and lined in leather. Expensive, central belly-cuts on both side. Beautiful relief-stitching. Soft and cushioned – quality piece! Duplet frame provides individual access to both parts of the interior. (W 12 ½ -inch by H 7 ½ -inch). Signed: La Popular Hecho en Mexico. Ca 1950.

Right: Superb, rich-looking, genuine crocodile skin satchel. Premium-quality craftsmanship, so similar to French! Beautiful symmetry of the belly skins. Bold, brass clasp. Self-covered frame; welted seams. Generous, leather interior. (W 13-inch by H 9-inch by D 2-inch). Labeled: Gambin Hecho en Mexico. Ca 1959.

Above: Sweet, tapered genuine crocodile frame-bag, with stylish bar-clasp and unique relief-stitching. Buttery-soft, top-quality skins! Leather-lined. (W 10-inch by H 8-inch). Labeled: Marion's. Mexico. Provenance: Similar piece was advertised by Bloomingdale's in November 19, 1944, for $39.00.

The South American exotic skin handbags were successfully imported to the United States until the early 1970s, when the ban on alligator and crocodile species affected the trade in general. It forced retail stores to stop trading in skin products from South America.

VARIOUS BRANDS

Most customers who look for a strong, vintage handbag for every day use favor the fine, affordable alligator or crocodile pieces by various New York makers from the 1950s and the 1960s. They include Bellestone, Manon, Prestige, Finesse, Revitz, Sterling U.S.A., Escort, and Vassar.

As a booming business in the late 1950s, alligator handbags were regarded as a sound investment. They represented the highest status symbol—a must have for the daytime attire—and were marketed as an important gift-giving opportunity, ranking as high as minks, diamonds, cars, and chateaus.

An astounding variety of satchels, boxes, pouches, and totes—in all imaginable styles, shapes, and sizes—was sold ranging from $15 to $375, depending on their quality and workmanship. Inferior caiman bags imported from South America by Macy's were sold for a mere $15–$40 apiece.

The demand for quality handbags reached its peak in 1957, when a new wave of domestic manufacturers entered the market to capitalize on the trend for luxury goods made of exotic skins. Among them were Bellestone, Manon, Prestige, Finesse, Revitz, and others established between 1957 and 1959.

Several existing brands, such as Sterling U.S.A., Escort and Vassar, had increased their capacity to strengthen their position in the mid-priced market. Each brand had its own market niche, and targeted a specific sector of buyers.

Bellestone, Manon, Sterling U.S.A. and Escort used domestic or Peruvian alligator skins, tanned domestically. Their handbags would

then be made per order in the U.S. or overseas—for example, in Belgium for Bellestone. Those beautifully detailed handbags were sold at B. Altman & Co., Gimbel's, Macy's, Orbach's, Oppenheim Collins, Franklin Simon, and Saks-34, in the range of $55 to $150, depending on the brand and model.

The Prestige brand—located in New York City at 38 West 32nd Street—brought back the fine French imports, along with Finesse and Revitz. Styled out of top-quality Javanese and Madagascar crocodile skins—so soft and plump, with tight markings—their top-quality purses of streamlined silhouette were particularly fashionable and expensive, and ran upwards of $175. In the late 1950s, they were sold at Saks Fifth Avenue, Bergdorf Goodman, Lord & Taylor, and Tailored Woman.

For comparison, in 1958, a mid-sized American Alligator pochettes by Lucille de Paris, or the same size French-made crocodile satchels by Coblentz, Prestige, or Finesse—all cost the same average amount of about $165 apiece.

Lucille de Paris alligator handbag ad, Bergdorf Goodman, *Vogue* August 15, 1960.

BEL'L'ESTONE

      Bellestone Bags, Inc., a member of the National Authority for the Ladies' Handbag Industry (NALHI), was located at 38 West 32nd Street, New York City, in the 1950s and 1960s. Their lines of beautiful, lady-like, exotic skin handbags were often manufactured in Belgium. Unfortunately, information about the owners of the brand was not forthcoming. Because Deitsch Brothers Co. also had close business ties with Belgium, it may be that Bellestone Bags, Inc. was their other production line.

Collection of glossy, lady-like alligator handbags by Bellestone, from the 1950s-1960s.

Oversized, genuine alligator shopper, with a deep swagger pocket, double handles, and a strong, brass frame. Roomy, leather-lined interior, with original accessories. Very capacious! (W 14 ¼ -inch by H 10 ½ -inch by D 4-inch). Signed: Bellestone. Ca 1959.

Fantastic, shiny alligator saddle-bag, accented by unusual for this brand equestrian-motif hardware. Curved bottom, front flap, and a unique shoulder strap that fastens through the bracket on the right gusset. Bright, gilded trim. Typical for this brand light-colored interior. (W 10-inch by H 9-inch by D 3 ¼ -inch). Signed: Bellestone. Ca 1967.

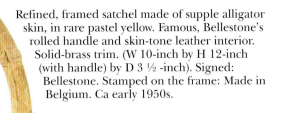

Refined, framed satchel made of supple alligator skin, in rare pastel yellow. Famous, Bellestone's rolled handle and skin-tone leather interior. Solid-brass trim. (W 10-inch by H 12-inch (with handle) by D 3 ½ -inch). Signed: Bellestone. Stamped on the frame: Made in Belgium. Ca early 1950s.

Bellestone's rounded handbags were offered in a great array of styles and sizes by Bonwit Teller and other upscale boutiques. Made of beautifully tanned alligator, crocodile, turtle, lizard or snake skins, they gleamed in rich shades of classic brown or fashionable black. Substantial in size and depth, with expensive frames opening wide to disclose a handsome lining, a Bellestone purse was a great complement to every costume—the exclamation point to any outfit!

Their spectacular pieces with unique, rolled handles crafted around a rubber core—exceptionally strong, flexible and durable—were produced in Belgium. So glossy and roomy, highly practical and robust, they represent one of the best vintage choices for everyday use. If you find one of those delightful pieces, check its frame to confirm its authenticity. Close to the hinge, there should be a *Made in Belgium* triangular mark.

Glossy, genuine alligator skin satchel, in desirable olive. Rolled handle; wide, doctor's bag-style body; typical Bellestone leather interior, with a coin purse. Solid brass hardware. (W 10 ½ -inch by H 12-inch by D 4-inch). Signed: Saks Fifth Avenue. Stamped on the frame: Made in Belgium. Ca early 1950s.

The quality of the glazing is definitely their best signature feature. Their alligator skins are usually treated with a highly reflective, intense glaze. Their pliable crocodile handbags boast a mellow, well-fixed, gleaming finish. And, their lizard skins are always nicely polished.

Glamorous (quite rare for this brand), genuine alligator cocktail-purse, adorned by a sparkling, rhinestone clasp. Enameled frame; polished silver trim; swivel handle; satin interior, with accessories. (W 7 ½ -inch by H 7 ½ -inch by D 2 ½ -inch). Signed: Bellestone. Ca mid-late 1950s.

Curvy barrel-bags – genuine alligator (left) and tegu-lizard (right) – both with wide, molded gussets; rolled handles; solid-brass fixtures; and shiny finish. Fully lined in Bellestone leather, with original accessories. (W 12-inch by H 11-inch by D 4 ½ -inch). Signed: Bellestone. Ca early 1950s.

Dramatic, genuine crocodile cocktail-purse, adorned by a fabulous, three-dimensional, gilded rose-clasp. Masterful, jewelry-quality workmanship. Gorgeous, healthy skins. Leather interior. (W 8 ½ -inch by H 8 ¼ -inch by D 2 ¾ -inch). Signed: Bellestone. Ca 1964.

Special, genuine tegu-lizard purse in metallic lavender. Lady-like styling, and unusual color. Glove-leather interior. (W 8 ½ -inch by H 6-inch by D 3 ¼ -inch). Signed: Bellestone. Ca mid-1950s.

The other distinctive feature that helps identify unsigned pieces by Bellestone is their leather interior, complete with a set of accessories: a leather coin purse, a faux tortoise comb, and a mirror encased in matching plastic. The styles in shades of brown are normally lined in rosy beige, while the black ones—in black or red. Rare pieces in designer colors, such as yellow, navy or olive, usually come with a neutral beige interior.

Pair of impeccable alligator handbags, complete with original accessory-kits. Left: Substantial, shiny piece of simple, timeless design. Flat handle; brass trim, protected bottom. (W 13-inch by H 8 ½ -inch by D 3 ½ -inch). Right: Compact barrel-bag, with a decorative, two-tone metal frame. Famous Bellestone rolled handle. (W 9 ½ -inch by H 11 ½ -inch by D 4-inch). Signed: Bellestone. Ca mid-late 1950s.

The traditional Bellestone interior layout includes three pockets on one side: a shallow pocket for a comb (marked by the brand's bell logo), a deeper pocket for a mirror, and a larger compartment with a plastic zipper. On the other side, there is a large pocket for a coin purse. All pockets are corded to prevent scuffing. Very strong and practical, the Bellestone interior usually shows less wear than any other brand, even after years of use.

Duo of solid, identical, genuine alligator frame-bags, in classic black and brown. (W 10-inch by H 13-inch by D 3 ¾ -inch). Signed: Bellestone. Stamped (on the frame): Made in Belgium. Ca early 1950s.

Cute, genuine karung pocketbook in unexpected turquoise, with a swivel top handle, lovely clover wire-clasp, and leather interior (W 8 ½ -inch by H 6-inch by D 3-inch; 5-inch drop handle). Marked: Bellestone, and J. Miller (store label). American, ca 1968.

Classic, genuine tegu-lizard frame bag in collectible color, with brass hardware and leather interior. (W 9 ¼ -inch by H 7 ¼ -inch by D 3-inch). Signed: Bellestone. Labeled: Saks Fifth Avenue. Ca 1956.

Every Bellestone handbag in mint, unmodified condition—complete with a set of original accessories—is a desirable addition to your collection or wardrobe. Look for unique pieces in designer colors, with unusual clasps or frame decorations. The more intricate the ornaments are, the more valuable the bag is. Beware of later alterations—chain straps or glued-on brooches or clips. They decrease the value of a collectible. Check the handle and gussets for damage. Rare pieces in mint condition can bring upwards of $950 retail.

STERLING USA

"A triumph of meticulous, long wearing, American craftsmanship!"

Sterling Handbag Co. was incorporated by H. A. Richard, in September 1932. Initially, they were located in New York at 70 Pine Street. The company specialized in various leather goods, particularly in alligator handbags.

Sterling handbag and Palizzio shoes ad, Vogue, August 15, 1960.

In the late 1940s, their reptile line was represented by Frank-Samberg Co. In 1951, they moved to a new facility at 347 Fifth Avenue, where they manufactured luxury products until 1955, in association with Gamma Leather Goods, Co. In 1956, they joined the National Authority for the Ladies' Handbag Industry (NALHI); and, in 1961, they moved to 25 West 31 Street in New York.

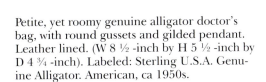

Shiny, genuine alligator pocketbook, with a lovely, arching Bakelite top handle. Deep front flap; delicate, squeeze clasp; tailored, 3-piece gussets; leather-lined. (W 9 ¼ -inch by H 9 ¼ -inch by D 4-inch). Signed: Leather Lined Himelhock's Detroit. Ca 1968.

Petite, yet roomy genuine alligator doctor's bag, with round gussets and gilded pendant. Leather lined. (W 8 ½ -inch by H 5 ½ -inch by D 4 ¾ -inch). Labeled: Sterling U.S.A. Genuine Alligator. American, ca 1950s.

Strong and capacious, deluxe Sterling bags are very similar to the Vassar brand in their appearance, style and quality. Stylishly fashioned and carefully crafted from quality skins, classic Sterling bags are easy to identify by the brand's glued-on fabric label "Genuine Alligator by Sterling U.S.A." The largest pieces of unusual design, in mint condition, could bring upwards of $700 retail.

Glossy, genuine alligator pocketbook, with a rolled, structured handle, and a tiny, gilded lever-clasp. The back and front are tailored from the whole belly-skin. Scalloped flap is reinforced by an underlying brass rod covered with matching skin. Unique, high-quality feature! Leather-lined interior. (W 10-inch by H 6 ¾ -inch by D 3 ¼ -inch). Labeled: Sterling U.S.A. Genuine Alligator. Ca 1964.

Stylish, genuine alligator pocketbook, with a
scalloped flap, double-pockets on the front, and
squeeze clasps. Large outside compartment; very
roomy, leather-lined interior; and a top handle.
(W 9 ½ -inch by H 7-inch by D 4 ½ -inch). Signed:
Sterling USA Genuine Alligator. Ca 1965.

Different, genuine alligator frame-bag composed of
riveted, skin-squares. Leather bottom and gussets. (W 9
¼ -inch by H 7-inch). Labeled: Sterling USA Genuine
Alligator Leather Lined. Ca 1960s.

In addition, consider examples of the beautiful and
usable vintage pieces by other makers, such as Escort
Bag and Finesse. (*Continued on following two pages*)

Immense, genuine alligator top-handles
satchel of enormous size! Lady-like styling; wide, rounded gussets, self-covered
frame. The spacious interior is fully
lined in tan and brown leather. (W 15
¼ -inch by H 8-inch by D 4 ½ -inch).
Signed: Escort Bag. Ca 1958-1959.

Elegant, genuine alligator frame-bag, with interesting, gold-plated trim. Tons of style! Leather lined. Beautiful quality! (W 12-inch by H 9 ½ -inch by D 3-inch). Signed: Escort Genuine Leather Lined. American, ca 1960-1962. Shown with a pair of white kidskin gloves, accented by faux pearls, ca 1960s.

Attractive, genuine tegu-lizard frame purse, with wide leather gussets. Complete with original accessories, including a plastic comb and round mirror signed: Escort Mam'selle. Petal-soft, belly-cuts of symmetrical pattern; stylish trapunto stitching. (W 10-inch by H 8-inch by D 3 ¼ -inch). Signed: Escort Bag. Ca 1956.

ESCORT
BAG

Superb, crocodile Porosus doctor's bag, trimmed with gilded brass. Curvy lines throughout! Beautifully constructed, molded gussets; self-covered frame; structured top handle. Kidskin-lined. Comes with an original storage box. (W 9 ½ -inch by H 7-inch by D 4 ¾ -inch). Signed: Finesse. Ca 1950s.

Shapely, genuine python hobo, with glamorous, silver and gold-plated shoulder straps. Leather and leatherette lined; self-covered frame on snaps. (W 12-inch by H 8 ½ -inch by D 3-inch). Labeled: Finesse LaModel New York. Ca 1970s.

Duo of exotic chain-bags – with jeweled frame – by Finesse la Model, ca 1970s-1980s. **Left:** Black karung. Gold-plated trim; black-and-clear rhinestones, onyx cabochon. Leatherette-lined. (W 8 ¼ -inch by H 6 ¼ -inch by D 2 ¾ -inch). Signed: Finesse La Model (gilt plaque). **Right:** Golden-metallic python. Gold-plated frame in Egyptian motif. Pleated skins. Champaign satin interior. (W 9-inch by H 6 ¾ -inch by D 3 ½ -inch). Signed: Finesse La Model (gilt plaque).

Sleek, pastel genuine python clutch, with a retractable shoulder strap. Collapsible frame, leather-lined interior. The seams are welted with purple leather. (W 12 ¼ -inch by H 7-inch by D 3 ½ -inch). Signed: Finesse La Model New York (gilt plaque). Ca 1970s.

VASSAR

AWESOME CARRYALLS—ULTIMATE PROFESSIONAL L'OOK

Vassar is a popular vintage brand, which for the last few years has become quite desirable among women who buy vintage for a practical reason: to wear it. Known for their durability and streamlined appeal, Vassar satchels, shoppers and swaggers are truly the ultimate for daytime wear. Exceptionally solid and roomy, they were made to last.

The Handbag . . Reflecting timeless, tasteful styling and achieving a magnificence that endures. Its appointments: a golden-toned frame, a handsome clasp, two inside pockets, and a mirror. Lined with smooth leather. About 11x6x2 inches.
N 88 G 246E—Sport rust
N 88 G 247E—Black
N 88 G 248E—Red
Shipping weight 2 lbs. 8 oz. $44.90

The Pump . . pure classic lines created with a touch of timeless fashion genius. Highlights: its nipped toe, squared throatline. Soft glowing, exquisitely matched Alligator skins shape upper. Featherlite® combination last, cushioned forepart. Supple leather lining. Flexible leather sole.
Sizes AAA (very narrow) in 7 to 9.
     AA (narrow) width 6 to 9.
     B (medium) 5 to 9 and 10.
Half sizes, except 9½. State size, then width.
2¼-INCH SLENDER HEEL
N 54 G 44060F—Sport rust
N 54 G 43050F—Black
N 54 G 45100F—Red
Shipping weight 1 lb. 4 oz. $34.97
2¾-INCH SLENDER HEEL
N 54 G 44049F—Sport rust
Shipping weight 1 lb. 4 oz. $34.97

The Glove, a smart, slender tailored beauty of imported capeskin. Full piqué seams; Bolton thumb. About 13 in. long. Hand wash.
Sizes 6½, 7, 7½, 8. State size.
88 G 5720F—Dark brown   88 G 5719F—Black
Shipping weight 3 oz. $7.90

The Necklace . . 12K Gold Filled. Surface excitement in the look of matte against glisten of smooth beads. 15¾-inches long.
4 G 5831E—Shipping weight 13 oz. $15.00

Matching Earrings . . polished, ¾ inch diameter beads. Screw-back.
4 G 5832E—Shipping weight 4 oz. $4.00

Catalog numbers with "E" on these two pages have 10% Fed. Exc. Tax included in price of item.

ALLIGATOR

PCORM
AEDSL6 SEARS 27

Vassar alligator handbags ad, Sears, Roebuck & Co. Catalog, Fall/Winter 1963.

The brand was manufactured by Vassar Bag Co. of New York. Early records date to 1932, when Vassar Bag Co., which produced leather goods and ladies' handbags, was incorporated by Exco Lawyers Albany Service, 116 Nassau Street, with the initial capital of $25,000.

A year later, in February 1933, they rented a manufacturing facility at 44 West 28th Street in New York City. In October of 1933, Vassar advertised their line "import reproductions" in the Business and Trade section of *The New York Times*. A large and successful American maker of reptile handbags, Deitsch Brothers, advertised their imported handbags in the same issue, side by side with Vassar. Later, the Vassar Bag Co. joined the National Authority for the Ladies' Handbag Industry (NALHI).

Trio of very collectible Vassar alligator shoppers, in different styles and colors.

Vassar products were often distributed by Sears Roebuck and Company, and by Montgomery Ward catalogs. In the 1950s and 1960s, they were also sold by B. Altman & Co., Lord & Taylor and Bergdorf Goodman. Today, they are popular with customers who acquire vintage collectibles not only for display, but also for use. What can be more rewarding for a vintage brand from the 1930s than to see its resurrection and growing respect from a new generation of women who appreciate quality, uniqueness and beauty?

Made with alligator or lizard skin, the luxurious Vassar creations incorporate the best qualities to survive heavy use and time. By far the strongest among other vintage brands, they are elegant and sophisticated, substantial and attractive, boasting fashionable styling and quality details. Quite often, you can find them in the oversized version of 14-inches by 10-inches, designed as sturdy swaggers with commodious, slightly tapered, deep bodies and strong handles to fit over the shoulder. Their lines are sleek, and their profiles are well defined. On rare occasions, they feature tortoise-shell plastic that was molded into frames during wartime, due to restrictions of the use of metals.

Impressive, genuine alligator satchel with gorgeous, arched Bakelite handles. Spacious! Fully leather-lined, with a front snap-closure. (W 11-inch by H 13-inch by D 2 ¾ -inch). Signed: Genuine Alligator by Vassar. Ca 1940s.

Usually thick and tough, yet flexible and cushioned, Vassar hides were treated with high-gloss sheen, typical for this brand. It usually maintains its look with no signs of dullness or dryness for many years.

The overall construction of the featured beauty is brilliant, designed to maximize its capacity and strength. Its wide, robust body is built on a brass frame expanded by floating hinges to allow the gussets to open to a whopping 8-inch width. A secure clasp in an attractive Art Deco motif is solid brass, with a large exterior pocket on the front, and a footed bottom.

Enormous, genuine alligator shopper, with a tapered body, shiny brass trim and strong double-handles. Famous floating hinges! Leather interior, with multiple, fancy compartments and pockets, including a deep wallet compartment, with a snap closure. (D 14-inch by 10 ¼ -inch by D 4 ¼ -inch). Signed: Genuine Alligator by Vassar. Provenance: Similar piece was advertised by Franklin Simon in November 25, 1956.

Vassar is one of the few vintage brands that had bags properly marked per the material. If the handbag was made with alligator skins, it is usually embossed on the inside with the *Genuine Alligator by Vassar* mark. If it was made with lizard skin, it is usually marked *Genuine Lizard by Vassar*. This is why Vassar handbags are the safest choice for beginning collectors.

Their coloration is always modest and subtle. Alligator in basic black is primarily lined with strong, glossy black or rust-colored leather. Once in a while you can find a rare example lined with contrasting red leather. Brown shades of the skins are diverse and include luscious chestnut, mahogany, redwood, burgundy and their multiple variations, fully lined in cheerful saddle leather with a glossy finish and gold piping. Rare pieces in red alligator could be lined in red or black leather. Taupe or brown lizard bags come with brown or saddle leather lining. Their finely polished hardware—including unique floating hinges and exquisite finials—is usually made of solid brass.

Magnificent, genuine alligator skin shopper, with self-covered frame. Beautiful, solid-brass clasp, strong double-handle, leather interior. (D 12-inch by H 10 ¼ -inch by D 4-inch). Signed: Genuine Alligator by Vassar. Ca 1956.

Sleek, genuine baby tegu-lizard. Classic frame-bag style, with top handle and self-covered frame. Lined in two-tone leather and leather-ette. (W 11 ¼ -inch by H 7-inch by D 3-inch). Unsigned Vassar. Ca 1964.

For the last couple of years, classic shoppers by Vassar from the 1950s have come back into vogue with New Yorkers. You can sometimes find them at auctions for about $850–$1,000 for the largest, spectacular models in mint condition.

CHAPTER FOUR
EXOTIC SKINS

"All that Glitters is not Gold"

ALLIGATOR CROCODILE TURTLE OSTRICH LIZARD SNAKE

For many centuries, various leathers have been at man's disposal primarily for utilitarian purposes. Exotic skins, on the other hand, have been solely about aesthetics and social status. Their appeal is in their rarity and uniqueness. What an abundance of eye-catching patterns and textures! Only Mother Nature could create such serene beauty.

The leather of certain reptiles, such as alligator and crocodile, have been particularly desirable since they were first introduced in the late 19th century as the most valuable classic leather for making accessories. The process of harvesting wild skins was very involved and dangerous—thus extremely expensive—causing a limited supply and sharply growing demand.

As a result, the uncontrollable appetite for the natural beauty of exotic skins brought some fauna species to virtual extinction. From thousands of recognized reptile species—including turtles, lizards, snakes, and crocodiles—several hundreds are listed as threatened in the *2008 IUCN Red Book of Threatened Animals*. Consequently, the urgency of the problem has prompted the implementation of high-scope environmental programs, conducted worldwide, in order to recuperate the endangered species and to develop a ranching industry.

Yet, the very sensitive issue of harvesting wild skins for illegal trade remains. That is why "recycling" of vintage exotic-skin handbags could be regarded as a contribution to the preservation of endangered species.

The variety of exotic skins used for decades is astounding. There are literally dozens of wild reptile, fish, bird, and animal skins of all imaginable types and sizes that artisans of the past were able to utilize in their search for perfection—an artful exotic-skin handbag!

Here, however, we do not promote any articles made of skins from endangered species prohibited from trade under the Endangered Species Act—such as turtle, leopard, zebra, elephant, etc. We concentrate on alligator and crocodile, as well as reptiles often confused with alligator and crocodile. We also examine their qualities and features, to help readers learn to identify them properly and verify their value and price.

Exotic skin handbags ads. **Top left**: Lesco lizard handbags, *Vogue* March 15, 1946. **Top right:** Pichel ostrich handbags, *Harper's Bazaar* 1944. **Bottom left:** Chandler's Rajah lizard handbag, *Harper's Bazaar* October 1944. **Bottom right:** Chandler's cobra handbags, *Vogue* 1946.

Handsome group of exotic-skin handbags from the 1960s, all with arched, stationary handles. **Left:** Genuine python satchel, with a removable shoulder strap. (W 12 ½ -inch by H 13 ½ -inch by D 4-inch). Unsigned; Egypt. **Center:** Genuine ostrich-skin double-handled satchel. (W 12-inch by H 12-inch by D 4-inch). Unsigned; England. **Right:** Genuine baby-caiman, tailored shopper. (W 12-inch by H 11 1/2-inch by D 2 ½ -inch). Unsigned; Hong Kong (England).

Terminology

Prior to analyzing the qualities and attributes of different skins used for making handbags, it is necessary to take a close look at the industry terminology, which is, unfortunately, quite confusing. Partially because of the language barriers inherent to the export-import operations; but particularly because of the difficulty in coordinating numerous industries involved in the extensive production process, which starts in the wild or on a farm where skins are harvested, and ends in the distribution chain where consumers can buy a finished product.

Different species of reptiles come from various parts of the world where people speak different languages. To identify them, specialists use both Latin and English terminology, as well as their native languages. In addition, tanning and fashion industries apply their own terms to market their product. And, finally, advertisers add confusion by using catchy marketing sound bites to create consumer interest and promote sales.

At each step of this complex process, various terms and names are used to identify the same product, often causing misrepresentation among manufacturers and consumers. That is why it is important to know basic terminology when entering a market of vintage exotics, in order to navigate with confidence and avoid costly mistakes caused by misrepresentation.

American Crocodile

It is particularly important to remember that some species are still considered endangered and prohibited from trade. One of them is a crocodile species, the American Crocodile (*Crocodylus acutus*). Due to its mixed freshwater and coastal habitat in the Southern United States, as well as in Central and South America, it is known under several common names, such as American crocodile or American Saltwater Crocodile, South American Alligator or Central American Alligator, as well as Cocodrilo americano, Crocodile d'Amérique, Cocodrilo de Rio, Crocodile à museau pointu, Lagarto Amarillo, or Lagarto Real. A product bearing one of these names is eligible for confiscation by the U.S. Customs officials.

The following table outlines several common reptile skins presently allowed for trade. Also included are their different names—common and Latin—and a brief description of their features and qualities.

Common Name	Species/Latin	Origin	Features
ALLIGATOR			
American Alligator Mississippi Alligator	*Alligator mississippiensis*	Southeastern U.S.A. freshwater	Classic leather Quality belly skins
CROCODILE			
Crocodile Porosus Saltwater Crocodile, Australian Saltwater Crocodile, Javanese Crocodile	*Crocodylus porosus*	Australia, Indonesia, Papua New Guinea	Top classic leather Largest species No ventral osteoderms Oval flank scales, tile-like rectangular, small and even belly scales
Nile Crocodile Madagascar Crocodile	*Crocodylus niloticus*	Central and South Africa, freshwater	Classic leather No osteoderms*
Morelet's Crocodile Mexican Crocodile, Baran, Cocodrilo de Morelet, Soft Belly Central American Crocodile	*Crocodylus moreletii*	Belize, Guatemala, Mexico, freshwater	High quality No ventral osteoderms
Large Scale Crocodile New Guinea Crocodile	*Crocodylus novaeguineae*	Indonesia, New Guinea, freshwater	Valuable, but not as much as Porosus
Johnston's Crocodile Australian Freshwater Crocodile	*Crocodylus johnstoni*	Northern and Western Australia, freshwater	Ventral osteoderms in belly scales in adults
CAIMAN			
Yacare Caiman Caimán del Paraguay, Jacaré, Lagarto	*Caiman crocodilus yacare*	Argentina, Brazil Paraguay	Osteoderms Flanks used
Common Caiman Caiman Blanco, Caiman de Brasil, Lagarto Blanco	*Caiman crocodilus crocodilus*	South America, freshwater	Osteoderms Lateral flanks used
Brown Caiman American Caiman, Lagarto Negro	*Caiman crocodilus fuscus*	South America, freshwater	Osteoderms Flanks used
LIZARD			
Ring lizard Juvenile Water Monitor	*Varanus salvator*	Asia	Bright yellow "flower" markings
Java Asian Water Monitor	*Varanus salvator*	Asia	High-quality fashion skin
Common Teju/Tegu Colombian Tegu	*Tupinambis teguixin*	South America	Quality leather
Argentine Red Tegu	*Tupinambis rufescens*	Argentina	Quality leather
Iguana Green or Common Iguana	*Iguana iguana*	Central, South America	
SNAKE			
Karung	*Acrochordus javanicus*		Smooth leather
Python Indian, Royal, Reticulated	*Python molurus, regius Python reticulates*		
King Cobra	*Ophiophagus hannah*		

***Osteoderms**: Small armor bones that develop in ventral scales in the skin along the back of some crocodiles and all caimans, usually absent on smaller alligators; large alligators typically have some osteoderms in the throat area. Not desirable for handbag making as they affect flexibility and reduce value.*

American Alligator
A True American Classic

If you are looking for a beautiful, environmentally conscious and durable classic leather to last a lifetime, try the American Alligator (*Alligator mississippiensis*). Indigenous to the South-eastern part of the United States, where it inhabits freshwater swamps and marshes, rivers and lakes, the American alligator has always been an important part of culture in the South.

Alligator skin—*"a uniquely American product"*—is one of the most valuable classic leathers, second only to the scarce Crocodile Porosus (*Crocodylus porosus*). Priced around $6 a foot in the 1960s, American Alligator's price per foot rose to over $40 in the late 1980s, in accordance to research conducted by the Louisiana Fur and Alligator Advisory Council (FAAC). Today, trendy purses by renowned European fashion houses, priced from $2,000 to over $60,000 apiece (e.g. Hermes creations), have established it as the top luxury product. The *"mink of the exotic leathers,"* the American Alligator is truly an American classic, and the efforts toward its preservation became a success story of modern wildlife management.

Shenanigan's alligator and lizard handbags ad, *Town & Country* 1949.

Swatches of genuine alligator skin (various cuts and colors).

Group of glossy, genuine alligator handbags, from the 1950s-1960s. **Top left:** Kelly-style purse, with gold-plated trim, lock and clochette with keys; leather-lined. Italy. **Center:** Timeless frame-bag by Lucille de Paris. Leather-lined. Bottom left: Classic black frame-bag by Deitsch, with top handle and leather interior. **Bottom right:** Large, curvy frame-bag by Deitsch, with folding handle and trapunto stitching.

The Endangered Species Act

Data recently compiled by the FAAC confirms that American Alligator has been hunted in the wild since the 19th century. During the first quarter of the 19th century, they were hunted by the thousands. The earliest record of alligator products, such as shoes, boots and saddles, dates back to the 1800s. During the American Civil War, alligator leather was used to make boots for soldiers. In the late 1860s, alligator products began to rise in importance for fashion accessories. In 1893, Hugh M. Smith, M.D., of the Fisheries Commission of South Atlantic States, expressed concern regarding a decline in the alligator business in Florida due to unprecedented demand for the skins: "…*Since 1880 not less than 2,500,000 alligators have been killed in the state, and it is not surprising that the supply has been greatly reduced.*"

FAAC further reports that through the 1930s, millions of mature alligators were hunted for their skin. Later, through the early 1960s, hunters took from the wild even smaller alligators. As a result of a lack of regulations, the population of the Louisiana alligator had dwindled to a mere 100,000 animals. Consequently, in 1962, the State of Louisiana banned the hunting of alligators. In 1967, the alligator was put on the federal Endangered Species Act list. The necessary legistative initiatives were introduced in 1970 to support the development of commercial harvesting. From 1962 to 1972, extensive research was conducted of the population of the American Alligator and its reproduction to protect the species as a sustainable resource.

The appropriate corrective legislation, as well as support of the industry, created the proper environment for the promotion of conservation measures, which resulted in the successful rescuing of the American Alligator from extinction.

A vivid example of such support was expressed by one of the largest and the oldest retailers of alligator products, Mark Cross, Ltd., in a letter published in *The New York Times* on September 8, 1970, "*An open letter from Mark Cross to the conservation-minded public.*" George Wasserberger, the company's president, confirmed their decision to discontinue selling alligator products, in accordance with the Mason Law that declared illegal the trade in crocodile, alligator and other endangered species.

In 1987, Louisiana successfully pioneered the farming programs. After twenty years of hard work in preservation, the U.S. Fish and Wildlife Service finally pronounced the American Alligator was fully recovered and consequently removed it from the list of endangered species. Since then, alligators have been successfully farmed in Florida, Georgia, Louisiana, and other states under established conservation programs. Today, the current alligator population in Louisiana alone is between one and two million.

On the other hand, the American crocodile from Florida is still listed as endangered and prohibited from trade. Therefore it is important to differentiate between the two species, and not confuse the endangered American Crocodile with the American Alligator, which is no longer endangered and thriving in the swamps of Florida and Louisiana.

Recent market research has revealed that the public is largely unaware of these changes. To eliminate confusion, the FAAC has created the Retail Education Program. Its specialists conducted an in-store training program of sales managers, marketing VP's and buyers, both in Canada and the United States.

Presently, both the alligator and the crocodile skin trade are carefully regulated by the Convention for International Trade in Endangered Species (CITES). Legal crocodile skins come from many countries, including Australia and South Africa. Tanzania exports only wild crocodile, and Madagascar deals in both wild and ranched crocodile.

CROCODILE

Alligators and crocodiles are the crocodilian species that share similarities, yet are somewhat different in appearance. Alligators live in fresh water in a subtropical climate, and they have rounded snouts. Crocodiles, on the other hand, live in salt water in a tropical climate, and have pointed snouts. Alligator skin has no hair follicles (ISO), whereas crocodile skin has ISOs on each scale.

Distinguishing Alligator, Crocodile and Caiman

An ISO is an integumentary sense organ, a small sensory pore (hair follicle) located close to the edge of the scale that assists crocodiles in detecting change in water pressure. It helps them to locate and capture their prey. A major difference between the two is that crocodiles have ISOs on every scale of their body—one to four on the lower part of the ventral scales—whereas alligators do not have ISOs. Therefore, it is not difficult to distinguish the two. If the scales of the skin have tiny follicles close to the edge, you know the skin comes from a crocodile, not an alligator.

Swatches of genuine crocodile skin (various cuts and colors).

Most "alligator-crocodile" confusion is purely cultural in nature. Europeans call all crocodilians "crocodiles," while Americans refer to them as "alligators." Ironically, the situation contributes to frequent mislabeling of final products. For example, in Italy, if you purchased an alligator handbag labeled "crocodile," it can be confiscated by U.S. Customs officials because of the ban on the trade of some types of crocodile, such as American Crocodile (*Crocodylus acutus*). Therefore, it is important to educate yourself on this point before traveling to Europe, so you can stay away from potential problems.

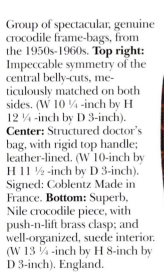

Group of spectacular, genuine crocodile frame-bags, from the 1950s-1960s. **Top right:** Impeccable symmetry of the central belly-cuts, meticulously matched on both sides. (W 10 ¼ -inch by H 12 ¼ -inch by D 3-inch). **Center:** Structured doctor's bag, with rigid top handle; leather-lined. (W 10-inch by H 11 ½ -inch by D 3-inch). Signed: Coblentz Made in France. **Bottom:** Superb, Nile crocodile piece, with push-n-lift brass clasp; and well-organized, suede interior. (W 13 ¼ -inch by H 8-inch by D 3-inch). England.

In the 1960s, Peter Hahn, president of Lucille Bags, Inc., believed that some shops called their bags crocodile "for snob appeal"—just because the handbags were imported from Europe, where people primarily used the word "crocodile." In his opinion, the terminology was not as important as the origin of the skins: alligators from Florida yielded first class skins, while scorned caiman from Argentina was brittle and hard. The best were the flank skins from Brazil, while short-in-supply Mexican crocodile was especially desirable for its fine texture and suppleness. As Hahn noted, crocodile skin could be of high or low quality, depending on its origin (Asia, Africa, or Northern Australia).

How Skin Becomes Leather

Exotic leather is a material created by nature and preserved by tanners. Its natural qualities make it superior to man-made synthetics. Extraordinarily strong, flexible and durable, if cared for properly, leather ages gracefully and lasts for many years. Every skin has its own specific markings, with some areas being thinner, grainier, or softer. These inherent inconsistencies add to the unique appeal of its natural beauty.

The conversion of a skin to finished leather is achieved through tanning, which is a chemical process for curing skins to prevent deterioration and enhance its strength while enabling it to withstand natural elements. The specific type of tanning and finish determines the quality of the leather, in terms of texture and surface perfection. Finish is the result of a variety of treatments, such as glazing or polishing to improve and enhance the skin's appearance, applied after the initial dying and tanning.

On its long journey from marsh to market, this leather goes through more than twenty different hands. That is why it is so valuable and expensive. Trappers and farmers collect and grow the skins to insure premium quality. It takes courage and skill to trap and handle a fierce animal that could injure or even kill a trapper.

Tanners process the measured and graded skins by soaking, dyeing, oiling, and glazing them. Each craftsman takes great care and pride in his work. The process requires several months and involves many steps, such as preservation, pre-tanning, wet-finishing, and dry-finishing.

In all, tanning skins takes an army of specialists and professionals: hunters, farmers, graders, legislators, designers, manufacturers, exporters, importers, marketers, and retailers. The costly and time-consuming stages of the tanning process explain the high prices of alligator products.

Quality control is a priority at every step. Manufacturers select the right sizes and types of leather suitable for production. Artisans cut it to yield the greatest symmetry (an art by itself) and create the articles that become prized possessions and pass from one generation to the next.

CAIMAN

Adding to the confusion is the fact that American Caiman (*Caiman crocodylus fuscus*) can be also mislabeled as "crocodile." The difference between the two is obvious. The crocodile skin is highly pliable, smooth and soft. On the other hand, the caiman skin is brittle and predisposed to cracking because of its bony plates (ossifications). As a low-grade material, caiman is less expensive.

In the 1930s and 1940s, caiman was often used in Florida for making large, stiff-looking handbags and briefcases. From the late 1940s through the late 1960s, inexpensive caiman bags from South American countries were sold as "alligator" or "crocodile." Currently, you can see it in a lot of handbags imported from Asia, Germany and Italy. If caiman bags are labeled as crocodile and priced accordingly high, it is a consumer who incurs losses. That is why, prior to paying for crocodile or alligator accessories, be sure to double-check the skin for authenticity and remember that the price should be set based on the skin type, origin, grade, overall quality, and condition.

 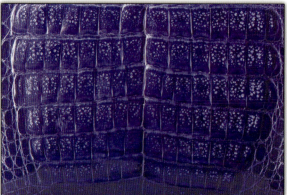

Swatches of genuine caiman skin (various cuts and colors).

Group of practical, caiman-skin handbags. **Top left:** Coral shoulder bag, with outside back-pocket, long strap, leather interior. Folding, accordion gussets. (W 9 ½ -inch by H 11-inch by D 4 ½ -inch). Clasp stamped: Paloma Picasso. Interior marked: Genuine crocodile Made in Italy; ca 1980s. **Top right:** Cute, turquoise camera-bag. Two-tone leather interior. (W 6-inch by H 5 ½ -inch by D 3 1.2 -inch). Italy, ca 1980s. **Bottom right:** Sleek, structured pocketbook, made of full-size baby-caiman cuts. Two-tone, contrast finish (gloss and matte). Two large outside compartments. Hong Kong, ca 1960s.

TURTLE

Vintage as Recycling—a Sensitive Incentive

Unfortunately, there is a long-standing misconception regarding sea turtle skin, which was banned from trade in the early 1970s by an international agreement through CITES (Convention on International Trade in Endangered Species of Fauna and Flora). Glossy and pretty, turtle skin is often mistaken for alligator or crocodile, and sold as such. The difference between the two is obvious: turtle has distinct, angular scales randomly arranged in swirl patterns, whereas alligator has oval or rectangular-tiled scales neatly arranged in a symmetrical, vertical design.

Soft and leathery turtle skin comes from leatherback sea turtles over six feet long, that inhabit the Atlantic, Indian, and Pacific Oceans. Once in abundance, leatherback turtles now are endangered. The United States and 115 other countries have banned the import and export of the sea turtles through CITES, in order to encourage the development of breeding programs and educate the public about their impact.

Nevertheless, enforcement of the trade restrictions is not an easy task. Every year, contraband reptile products, worth millions of dollars, are smuggled across international borders. Sea turtle leather accessories are among the items most commonly seized by U.S. Customs and Fish and Wildlife Service (FWS) officers. The World Wildlife Fund urges the public to become educated before traveling abroad and to be aware of the laws that govern the trade. *"When in doubt, don't buy,"* the FWS counsels American travelers.

Today, the production of accessories from turtle skin is not permitted in the United States. But in the 1960s, several leading handbag brands, including Rosenfeld, Saks Fifth Avenue and Lucille de Paris, specialized in the manufacturing of cute, colorful purses made with turtle leather. They were usually made in France. To assure authenticity, they were labeled *Genuine turtle.*

 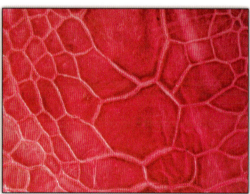

Swatches of genuine turtle skin (various cuts and colors).

Adorable, faux-turtle vinyl satchel. Molded plastic frame and handle, lined in navy faille. (W 7 ¼ -inch by H 7 ¼ -inch by D 3-inch). Unsigned; ca 1968.

The year 1967 was noted in fashion history as the year of the turtle, when a rash of advertisements proclaimed turtle leather as the new "status symbol" in accessories. To the untrained eye, turtle skin remotely resembled alligator, and its price was considerably lower. The quality of turtle products ranged from hopelessly dreadful to relatively fine.

The fashion industry itself was quite indifferent toward the new skin. Jacomo and Gucci companies did not believe in it. *"We don't consider that they are in our class,"* a spokesman for Gucci announced. George Wasserberger, president of Mark Cross, stated his position slightly differently. *"I don't think the poor turtle makes a very handsome handbag. The crocodile has a more symmetrical, even graining."*

Turtle skin made its debut in the American market when French tanners came up with the idea of using the skin of turtles that were hunted in Caribbean waters for their meat. The idea was prompted by necessity, to find a new reptile as a substitute for scarce and expensive alligator. At that time, the best baby alligator handbag could cost about $1,400.

The best sea turtle hides came from Mexico and Honduras. They were sold in pairs, because only the soft and pliable skins from turtle legs could be used for making handbags. Turtle skins did not really compete with the best alligator and crocodile skins from Louisiana, Madagascar, Singapore and Java; rather, it competed with low-grade, South American caiman skins.

The first collection of French-made, pastel-colored turtle handbags was introduced by Saks Fifth Avenue in March of 1966, at a price from $50 to $180. Frank McIntosh, Henry Bendel's accessories merchandise manager, quite liked them: *"Turtle is the current bally-hoo topic. It looks marvelous; it's on the scene in color. But you don't relate turtle to alligator. Alligator is in a class by itself. It's the Rolls Royce. Turtle is the Skylark or Riviera Buick."* The industry observers maintained that the only reason for the turtle's success was its price, which was about a third of that for alligator. Both collections sold fast, but prompted protests from conservationists.

As a sensitive alternative to genuine turtle, embossed cow hide and vinyl imprinted with the turtle pattern was introduced a year later. Handbags made with leather printed with the turtle design were then sold by Saks Fifth Avenue and Neiman Marcus. The adorable chartreuse evening bag featured on page 216 is printed vinyl. Currently, any articles made with real turtle skins, new or vintage, are prohibited from trade in the United States.

Duo of pretty genuine turtle handbags, from the 1960s. **Left**: Charming, purple clutch in Art Deco style, lined in black leather. (W 8-inch by H 5-inch by D 1 ½ -inch). Italy. **Right**: Smart duplet, with two separate flaps, closures, and interiors. gold-plated trim; leather-lined; accordion gussets and bottom. (W 7 ¼ -inch by H 6 ¼ -inch by D 3 ½ -inch). Signed: Rosenfeld Genuine Turtle. Ca 1968.

OSTRICH

Ostrich *(Struthio camelus)* is the world's largest flightless bird, indigenous to the Savannah areas of Africa. It is not an endangered species. An ostrich can live to be 70 years old, weighs up to 350 pounds, and yields about 12 to15 square feet of leather.

Ostrich farming was established in South Africa in the mid-1800s. By the turn of the 20th century, ostrich farming became one of the largest businesses on the African continent. A smaller, easily handled bird, the South African black ostrich was cross-bred and brought to the United States in 1882.

Soon thereafter, ranching ostrich was developed in Arizona and Florida, and later extended to Texas, Nevada, and Utah. Presently, about 60,000 birds are harvested annually worldwide, including South Africa, Zimbabwe, Namibia, Tanzania, Kenya, and Israel, for leather and meat. The industry has been tightly regulated by numerous world and national associations, to avoid overproduction. Japan and various European countries are the major importers of ostrich handbags and boots, which are sold for $1,000 to $8,000 apiece .

Only second to classic alligator and crocodile in value, ostrich is regarded as one of the most durable leathers because of its unique fiber pattern. In most leathers, the fibers lay parallel to each other. In ostrich, fibers have a crisscross pattern that makes the leather stronger and more flexible. Plump and thick, ostrich leather is full of natural oil that resists drying or cracking. Its longwearing properties, attractive quill pattern, and especially its suppleness make ostrich ideal for manufacturing garments, footwear, handbags, luggage, and furniture.

In handbag making, ostrich leather comes in three general cuts: a full quill cut (crown or diamond area of the hide), a smooth cut, and a leg cut. Today, ostrich can be tanned in a wide selection of colors and finishes.

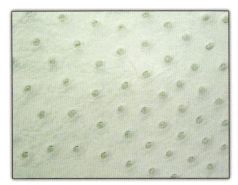  

Swatches of genuine ostrich skin (full-quill, leg-, and smooth cuts).

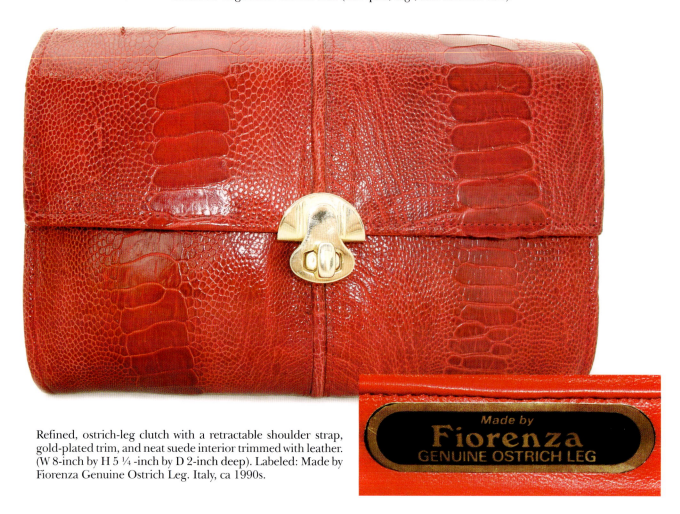

Refined, ostrich-leg clutch with a retractable shoulder strap, gold-plated trim, and neat suede interior trimmed with leather. (W 8-inch by H 5 ¼ -inch by D 2-inch deep). Labeled: Made by Fiorenza Genuine Ostrich Leg. Italy, ca 1990s.

Made by
Fiorenza
GENUINE OSTRICH LEG

Full-quill cuts have a distinct "bubbly" appearance, with quill marks arranged in neat patterns. In vintage handbags, the prime skins were mostly used as front and back panels. Supple, smooth cuts were used for bottoms, handles and gussets. Thus, on a genuine ostrich skin bag, a combination of different cuts and patterns can be seen. They indicate that the material is genuine, not embossed leather or vinyl. Like fingerprints, genuine skins display unique markings, never uniform and never repetitive.

It is important to always confirm the authenticity of an ostrich bag, because it could be a fake. In the 1950s and 1960s, several vintage handbag makers and brands, including Koret, Rendl and Saks Fifth Avenue, produced a great number of affordable, embossed imitations.

While examining a handbag made with embossed leather (cowhide, pigskin, or lambskin), you can see the same repetitive "quill" pattern throughout its different parts, including the bottom and the handle. On a genuine skin bag, however, its different parts are made from different patterns: quill and smooth. In addition to a careful check for the pattern similarity and repetition, one can feel the skin with your fingers and weigh it in your hand. By touch, genuine skins are soft and silky, and exceptionally light in weight. Embossed pigskins and cowhides are rough in texture and quite heavy in weight.

Look inside the interior of the handbag. Expensive genuine ostrich purses are usually finely fitted with high-quality suede or genuine leather. Older pieces from the 1920s can be lined in fine silk moiré. Embossed leather handbags are often lined in rough, glazed leather or leatherette, or rayon faille.

The authenticity issue is especially important if you are buying a vintage ostrich handbag online or from an unconfirmed source. Failure to recognize the fake could cost you dearly. Note that most vintage makers did not sign their genuine or embossed products. Only a couple of them, such as Rosenfeld and Corbeau, consistently labeled their bags *Genuine Ostrich*. It is unsafe to buy a vintage ostrich purse from an unreliable source, unless the bag is made by a recognizable top brand, such as Hermes, Judith Leiber, or Lucille de Paris.

Group of trendy, full-quill ostrich handbags, from the 1960s. **Top center:** Structured, bracelet satchel, with leather gussets; suede-lined. (W 12-inch by H 12-inch by D 4-inch). England. **Bottom left:** Rich, frame-bag fully lined in scrumptious suede. (W 11-inch by H 7-inch by D 3 ½ -inch). Stamped on the frame: England. Signed: Genuine Ostrich Leather. **Bottom right:** Soft, cuff-wristlet, with softly-pleated skins; black leather interior. (W 11-inch by H 8 ½ -inch, 6-inch high cuff). Signed: Genuine Ostrich Made in Italy. Ca 1969.

L'IZARD

For millions of years, some of the oldest inhabitants of this planet are lizards. They have occupied almost all continents, except Antarctica and some Arctic regions of North America and Asia. More than 95 percent of living reptiles are descendants of early lizards, with several thousand lizard species in existence today. They range from tiny, three-inch lizards to huge, almost ten-foot-long Komodo dragons of South East Asia.

Lizard skin has been used for the longest time to make boots and shoes, handbags and luggage, garments and vanity items. Nearly indestructible, lizard skins are praised for their beautiful textures, variety of tightly grained patterns, and, above all, their strength and durability.

The most commonly used lizard skins—java, ring, tegu, and iguana—come from the largest lizards of Asia and South America. Different in appearance and quality, they have a similar, smooth, "beaded" texture formed by tiny, round scales. The best skins have been supplied from India since the 1920s, tanned in various shades, for ladies' and children's shoes and purses.

Swatches of genuine lizard skins (**top:** ring, java, iguana; **bottom:** tegu, java).

Below: Pair of colorful, genuine java-lizard satchels, from the 1960s, by incomparable Martin Van Schaak.

Java lizard (*Varanus salvator*) is a fashion term for lizard leather harvested from the largest lizards in the world—huge, over six-feet-long, Water Monitors that inhabit the Asian subcontinent. Water Monitors are not endangered and commonly are hunted for skin and meat. Annually, over a million skins are legally exported, mainly from Indonesia, by the fashion industry of Europe, Japan, and the United States. Mostly, medium-sized skins are harvested for their pliability.

The delicate, caviar-like scales are arranged in perfectly uniform patterns. Smooth, soft and supple, this high-fashion leather is often dyed in pastel colors and treated with a high-sheen finish. It is also remarkably tough and longwearing, as evident by antique 19th-century java-lizard purses and wallets, fitted with sterling fasteners. More often than not, they hardly show any wear or age. Exquisite java pieces by renowned Hermes, Gucci, Lucille de Paris, Lederer, Rosenfeld, Judith Leiber, and especially by Martin Van Schaak are highly collectible and routinely fetch healthy sums at auctions.

The **Ring lizard,** or Rajah lizard as it was known in the 1940s, is one of the most attractive and expensive lizard leathers. It comes from juvenile Asian Water Monitors that have light-colored, ring-like markings on a darker background. These distinct markings disappear when the lizard reaches adolescence. Dyed in various shades and colors, it boasts a beautiful, two-toned pattern composed of tiny, bead-like scales arranged in circles—like a handful of beautiful flowers scattered over an ocean of beads. Martin Van Schaak, Hermes and especially Judith Leiber have used ring lizard leather quite extensively in their fabulous creations. Flamboyant and cool, the designers' ring-lizard handbags, circa 1940s to 1960s, are always in demand with collectors.

Tegu-lizard (*Tupinambis teguixin*), meaning "giant lizard" in the Amazonian dialect, a large, over five-feet-long lizard second only to the Water Monitor, comes from South America. Leather from the Tegu-lizard is often called "teju." In Argentina and Paraguay, the tegu-skin trade has become a multi-million dollar industry. The largest importers of this skin are the United States, Hong Kong, Mexico, and Canada.

Supple and smooth in texture, this elegant leather is primarily supplied in central underbelly cuts, composed of neat and tidy ridges of slim, vertical scales at the center surrounded on both sides by smaller, rounded scales. In the 1940s to 1960s, there were several domestic brands that specialized in making tegu-lizard bags: Lucille de Paris, Saks Fifth Avenue, Vassar, Escort, and especially Palizzio. Their excellent, bold pieces in solid colors are still beautiful and useful today.

This lizard leather is often misrepresented as "baby alligator" in online auctions. In the 1940s, it was occasionally referred to as "alligator lizard" or "lizagator"— merely to emphasize its sheer size. It has nothing to do with alligators. Watch for such misrepresentation when shopping for expensive, real baby alligator bags, as they could be made from cheaper tegu-lizard.

A 1949 *Vogue* magazine advertisement (see page 124) shows beautiful handbags made with tegu-lizard in exotic colors of Ming green, Manchu red and Tang Brown. Its outdated marketing terminology reads: *"In gentle accord with a season of unfettered fashion – the quiet richness of alligator-lizard perfectly executed by Lesco."*

Above:
Elite, genuine ring-lizard frame bag, with platform leather gussets. Top-notch quality! Suede-lined; welted seams; riveted top handle; etched, gilt trim. (W 11 ½ -inch by H 6-inch by D 3 ¼ -inch). England, ca 1960s.

Pair of tailored, genuine tegu-lizard arm bags. **Left:** Three-tone purse, with a structured top handle. Gilt trim, suede-lined. (W 10-inch by H 7-inch). Labeled: Made in England Genuine Lizard. Ca 1960s. **Right:** Structured wristlet, with central, belly-cuts of symmetrical pattern. Signed: Styled by California Alligator Co. American, ca late 1930s.

Below: Shapely, genuine iguana-lizard wristlet, with a massive black Bakelite frame. Faille-lined. (W 8 ½ -inch by H 7 ½ -inch by D 4 ½ -inch; 7-inch wristlet). American, ca 1940s.

Iguana lizard (*Iguana Iguana*) skin is often mistaken for tegu. Somewhat alike in appearance, with round scales arranged in neat rows, it is quite different in quality, due to some roughness of the scale pattern that is less refined and less symmetrical. This leather comes from a four-feet-long common iguana indigenous to the rainforests of Central and South America. Hunted for meat and skin, it is used for making belts, boots and handbags and comes in basic, dark colors. Once in a while, you can find an older collectible piece with natural markings and coloring, such as the featured wrist purse on a black plastic frame, circa 1940s.

Vintage, brand-name, lizard handbags in excellent condition are strong and can be recommended for everyday use. Before purchasing one, carefully examine the handle. Most damage, such as cracking and breaks, happens here and reduces its value. Be aware of altered bags decorated with glued-on adornments or chain-straps that have less value.

SNAKE

Man has always been fascinated with this regal reptile, not only by the air of mysticism surrounding it, but also by its mesmerizing beauty. Snake skin has been used as currency and for adornment since early ages. It is impossible to describe the great variety of snake-skin patterns, textures and colors. Here we concentrate only on the most commonly used and widely recognized patterns of karung, python, and cobra. These leathers are imported from South East Asia, Indonesia, India, Pakistan, and Africa.

Swatches of genuine snake skins (top: natural python, cobra, dyed python; bottom: karung).

Karung (*Acrochordus javanicus*) is a popular snake skin, distinct by its tiny, smooth, dot-like scales similar to a lizard's. Tidy and pretty, perfectly uniform with a delicate, silk-like texture, karung has been consistently used by prominent couture houses. Judith Leiber loves it in outrageous colors for her luxurious evening bags lavishly ornamented by semi-precious gems. Her artistic pieces in karung are highly collectible.

Darling, genuine karung clutch, with a butterscotch plastic frame. Softly pleated skins; satin-lined. (W 12 ½ -inch by H 7 ½ -inch by D 3 ½ -inch). Signed: Ruth Saltz. Ca 1960s.

Python skin boasts the most impressive and bold markings. Elaborate geometric patterns are fantastic, with designs in contrasting colors. When used for garments, the luscious, wide skins are often treated with a water-resistant finish. Popular species include Python Indian (*Python molurus*), Python Royal (*Python regius*), and Python Reticulated (*Python reticulates*). In the 1940s, Argentine python was used for shoes.

Left: Group of sassy, genuine python clutches. **Top:** Pleated envelope, with snap-frame. Skin shoulder strap; leatherette-lined. (W 12 ½ -inch by H 7 ½ -inch by D 2 ½ -inch). Signed: Bags by Supreme. Ca 1960s. **Center left:** Tailored envelope trimmed with plastic. Suede-and-leather lined; metal strap. (W 11 ¾ -inch by H 7-inch by D 1-inch). Signed: Bags by Varon. Ca 1960s. **Center right:** Structured clutch, with a lovely buckle closure. Welted seams; leatherette-lined; link-chain strap. (W 14-inch by H 7-inch by 1 ½ -inch). Signed: Bags by Varon. Ca late 1950s. **Bottom left:** Large pleated pouch, with a removable skin strap; gold-plated trim; leather-lined. (W 10 ½ -inch by H 8-inch by D 4-inch). Signed: Colombetti Milano Made in Italy (plaque). Ca 1980s. **Bottom right:** Small soft pouch, with shoulder strap; leather-lined. (W 8-inch by H 6 ½ -inch by D 3-inch). Labeled: Parri's Florence. Italy, ca 1970s-1980s.

King Cobra (*Ophiophagus hannah*) comes from Indonesia in back-cuts or front-cuts of smooth texture. Since the turn of the 20th century, cobra skin has been widely used for handbags, shoes, belts or garments, often dyed in radiant colors for spring and summer fashions, *"to capture the carefree mood of carnival and dramatize your newest sprig costumes."* Cobra was simply referred to as "snakeskin" in 1949 *Vogue* magazine advertisements for gorgeous Deitsch handbags.

Flamboyant and intriguing, mint vintage snakeskin bags are fun additions to your collection, if they are made by popular brands and demonstrate unique designs, colors or details.

Below: Smart, genuine python convertible clutch. Folding, gold-plated bracket-handle; suede-lined. Made of two, whole cuts. (W 11 ½ -inch by H 7-inch by D 2-inch). Labeled: Genuine Snake. England, ca 1960s.

Set of rich cobra-skin handbags, from the 1950s. **Top:** Sumptuous, brown chain-bag, with softly pleated skins, plastic frame, and chain-strap. Faille interior. (W 13-inch by H 10-inch by D 3-inch). Stamped (frame): Made in France. **Bottom:** Three-tone, convertible clutch, with two optional handles. Suede-lined. (W 10-inch by H 6 ¾ -inch by D 2-inch). Labeled: Made in England Genuine Snake.

Snakeskin handbags generally cost about a forth of the price of a good quality alligator handbag. Gorgeous, suede-lined python clutches made in England in the 1960s are remarkably modern and beautifully styled. They are a welcome addition to a modern wardrobe for relatively little money, about two hundred dollars.

Imitations
Embossed Leather and Vinyl

Embossing is a process of printing exotic skin patterns on various materials, such as pigskin, cowhide, lambskin, or vinyl. Such embossed materials are called faux.

Since the early 1900s, the industry had the capability of producing faux materials to imitate the look of precious alligator skins. With a sharp increase in travel among women before World War I, the demand for a durable, yet affordable and attractive travel bag was on the rise. As a result, various manufacturers started producing stylish embossed accessories. The new imitation material was called 'alligator grain' or 'alligator finish'.

At the turn of the 20th century, in mail order catalogs, such as the Sears, Roebuck Catalog 1902, alligator grain bags were advertised right next to genuine. Faux travel bags were sold for only 34 cents for a 14-inch model, and club bags in selected 'alligator grain' goatskin - for only $1.50. In comparison, genuine alligator club bags cost almost four times as much, $5.20 for a 16-inch model. Remember that the first substitute for leather, Keratol, was introduced as early as the beginning of the 20th century, in the early 1900s. That prototype of vinyl was primarily used to make suitcases. It was advertised as "a new fiber that looked like leather and was equal to it for wear."

Reptile handbags ad, *Sears, Roebuck Merchandise Catalog*, Fall/Winter 1963.

In the 1920s, a wide array of materials was manufactured to imitate genuine skins and leathers, to satisfy the growing demand for affordable accessories. Animal grain prints were often embossed on Fabrikoid (imitation leather), cowhide, goatskin, or leatherette (old vinyl). The common grain patterns included alligator, ostrich, walrus, Galuchat, or shark, as advertised in the Montgomery Ward Fall–Winter, 1928–1929 catalog.

Since then, virtually every maker offered practical and soil-proof embossed leather handbags. Koret and Dofan sometimes marked them *Genuine Leather*, as opposed to *Genuine Alligator*, or *Genuine Ostrich*. Other brands, including Saks Fifth Avenue, unfortunately did not mark their embossed products produced in the 1930s-1960s. Fine and elegant, they were made to look like the "real thing".

Early, alligator-grain clutch made of a single leather-cut imprinted with alligator pattern. Laced seams, suede interior, lever-clasp. Please note the reverse, repetitive pattern of the "scales", especially vivid on the bottom part. (W 12 ¾ -inch by H 7 ½ -inch). American, ca early 1930s.

Especially common were embossed leather handbags by Bienen-Davis, Koret, Dofan, and Finesse. They were mostly produced in the late 1960s, after the ban on genuine alligator skins. Koret's embossings were often signed *Genuine Leather*, while Bienen-Davis, Dofan, and Finesse's faux pieces were usually unsigned.

One of the indicators of a cheap imitation made of faux material is its fabric lining. Normally, expensive leather lining was reserved for genuine skins. Once in a while, you can find an embossed leather bag lined in low-grade leather. There is another universal feature characteristic of faux bags—an abundance of decorative stitching and patching. Generally, expensive skins were used as whole cuts, with a minimum of undesirable patching.

In the 1940s, faux products were primarily advertised as reptile-grained vinyl, baby-gator print vinyl, lizard print, or cobra-print vinyl.

The quality of vintage embossing varies greatly, depending on the manufacturer. Usually it is not difficult to distinguish what is fake and what is real, even if it is not signed. However, sometimes the fakes look so real that they can fool even an expert. While considering to buy a vintage exotic skin handbag, check its authenticity. Faux pieces are cheap and not desirable. To determine whether your bag is genuine, use the simple authenticity tests provided on the following page.

Above: Cute, tiny, vinyl box-purse printed with alligator pattern. Accented with pave-rhinestones. Satin-lined. (W 5-inch by H 5-inch without handle, 8-inch with handle by D 3 ¾ -inch). Signed: MM (Morris Moskowitz). Ca late 1960s.

Sizable, vinyl satchel printed with ring-lizard pattern, lined in moire. Coin purse, and comb. (W 13-inch by H 9-inch by D 3 ½ -inch). Tag: Calcutta Lizadex Made in England. Ca 1950s.

AUTHENTICITY TEST

Gloss: Embossed leather and especially vinyl are often treated with extremely high gloss.

Smell: Use your nose. Embossed leather smells "sour." Vinyl, as a manmade material made of oil, has a strong "chemical" smell.

Pattern Quality: Embossing (printing) has dull, shallow definition of the edges between the scales, whereas the grooves between the scales of genuine skin are deeper and better defined, with crisp edges.

Pattern Repetition: Carefully examine various parts of the bag for pattern repetition. Like fingerprints, every genuine skin has a unique scale-pattern. Thus, you will never see the same pattern on different parts of the genuine bag. On the embossed bag, the same pattern can be seen on its different parts, over and over again.

Pattern Symmetry and Cuts: Genuine skins come in symmetrical central cuts (expensive) or outside-the-pattern cuts (less expensive). Central cuts are usually positioned right in the middle of the bag creating a meticulously symmetrical design, with larger scales in the center graduating into smaller scales on the sides. If you see a reverse pattern, with smaller scales in the center and larger on the sides, the material is definitely embossed, not genuine.

Lining: Genuine skins are often lined in top-quality suede, or leather. Small evening bags can be lined with fine silk, satin, or moiré. Embossed handbags are mostly lined in leatherette (vinyl made to look like leather), or fabric (faille), and very rarely in low-grade leather.

Craftsmanship: Genuine skin handbags are generally much finer in quality because of the handmade workmanship and attention to detail.

Nail Test: Feel the surface with a fingernail to check if it can snag the edge of a scale. Test the bottom or the gussets where larger tile-scales can usually be found. Even the smoothest skins have sharper scale-edges that can be very slightly "lifted." Embossing is always evenly smooth on all parts of the bag.

Weight: Weigh the bag in your hand. Genuine skins are lighter than dense embossed pigskin, cowhide, or vinyl. They are also thinner and more delicate than early embossed materials.

Always take time to examine the vintage bag before paying for it. As the old saying goes, *"Better safe, than sorry."*

Super rare, museum-quality, genuine alligator arm-purse, adorned by a distinct, molded Bakelite frame, with a front adornment. Unique, split arm-handle; bold, intriguing design. Loud, Schiaparelli-fuchsia leather interior! Gold-trimmed interior, complete with accessories. (W 11-inch by H 8 ¼ -inch without handle by D 3-inch). One-of-a-kind, indeed! Ca 1946-1948.

CHAPTER FIVE

FOUR CS TO REMEMBER
CIRCA, CONDITION, CRAFTSMANSHIP, COLOR

"You Get What You Pay For"

Do you know why some alligator handbags are more expensive than others? It is because of their circa (age), condition, craftsmanship, and color. Remember these four *C*s and you will never fail to get the best value.

The first *C* to consider is the age of the item, or the circa, which plays an especially important role for serious collectors. For example, older pieces from a desirable era, such as 19th-century luggage or ornate Art Deco envelopes from the 1920s, are very valuable as collectibles. If you're looking for a strong, casual vintage alligator bag, get a trendy purse from the 1950s or 1960s—they are ultimate for everyday use. Funky, colorful skins from the 1940s are the best conversation pieces, while dramatic novelties from the 1950s are simply the best for special occasions. Confirmed circa, as well as its documented provenance, adds greatly to the appeal of a collectible.

Imagine you have come across a good-looking vintage alligator bag. How do you know that it is truly a great find? First, confirm its authenticity using our simple test (opposing page), to be absolutely sure that it is genuine, not fake. Then, inspect its condition by following the steps outlined below.

In vintage handbags, quality is all about 'condition, condition and condition.' If the handbag is in a miserable state and literally falling apart, you definitely do not want it. The second *C*—condition—is the most important factor influencing the price. Pristine pieces in immaculate, un-restored, original condition are always more expensive—several times more, to be exact. Damage, flaws, repairs, alteration, and additions decrease the value dramatically.

How well the bag is made—its craftsmanship—is the third *C* to always keep in mind. Workmanship is very important. Craftsmen, like artists, take incredible pride in their craft, which takes a lifetime to master. The level of craftsmanship, as well as the quality of its design, can be established by inspecting specific features, as outlined below. The quality of skins also matters. They come in various grades rated based on their flexibility and elasticity, symmetry and pattern. Some species are much more valuable than others. You wouldn't pay as much for a rhinestone bracelet as you would for a genuine diamond bracelet, correct? Then why pay more for an inexpensive Argentinean caiman bag if you can get a precious Crocodile Porosus or American Alligator one for the same price?

The fourth *C* to remember is the color. For instance, designer colors are always in high demand, hence more expensive. In casual handbags, classic black is more desirable than brown. The size of the bag made of whole skins is also important in setting the price. To put it short, remember the four *C*s and you will know exactly what you are buying. Let's take a more in-depth look at the four *C*s. This will assist you better in your search for the perfect bag.

CIRCA

It is amazing how modern and trendy some old alligator pieces look! Just check out, once again, the featured pieces: a superb, one-hundred-year-old Victorian alligator opera pouch on an elaborate sterling frame; or a marvelous crocodile envelope with a matching silk umbrella, from the flapper era. It's hard to believe that they could be this old!

Unfortunately, it is not always easy to pinpoint the exact age of your treasure. Very helpful for this reason are the back issues of the fashion magazines, *Vogue* and *Harper's Bazaar*, which can be purchased on the Internet.

Another great source to track fashion trends are the merchandise catalogs by Montgomery Ward & Co.—the world's oldest mail order house since 1872—and Sears, Roebuck & Co. Mail Order Catalog. Both provide thorough documentation of the changes in the fashion merchandise traced throughout the decades.

In addition, the specific stylistic and decorative features of your vintage—characteristic to a certain historic period—can also be very helpful in determining its age. Such historic periods are:

Victorian (1837–1902)
Edwardian (1902–early 1920s)
Art Deco (mid-1920s to mid-1930s)
Retro (mid-1930s to late 1940s)
"New Look" (1950s)
"Mod" (1960s)

Victorian Style (1837–1902)

The Victorian style reflected the sentimental taste of Queen Victoria, and the merits of the English Industrial Revolution. Newly rich professionals and proprietors demonstrated their wealth through luxurious possessions. Their favorites included expensive genuine alligator and crocodile accessories trimmed in sterling silver.

Casual styles: *Doctor's bags, travel bags, luggage, trunk cases, shopping bags, satchels, gents' or ladies' pocketbooks, châtelains, and small purses.*

Novelties: *Lady's opera pouches trimmed with sterling silver.*

Sizes: *Over 10" for casual use; small for novelties.*

Skin: *Top-grade crocodile or alligator (smooth or horn-back).*

Features: *Finely fitted; heavy-duty, brass fasteners and latches; leather-lined.*

Retailers: *Le Boutillier Brothers and Gorham MFG Co, Daniell & Sons (NYC).*

Purses and handbags ad, *Sears, Roebuck & Co. Merchandise Catalog* ad, 1897.

Edwardian Style (1902–early 1920s)

Traveling accessories and handbags made of top-grade crocodile and alligator skins became the hallmark of the Edwardian style. Remember, though, that as early as the beginning of the 20th century, they could be also made of imitation materials. Consequently, while dealing with an old travel case, always check its authenticity, as it could be made of embossed leather or early vinyl, not genuine skin.

The key feature of the Edwardian handbags was its frame made of metal or shell (1915-1918). Other novelties in the prevalent Art Nouveau style included large compartment handbags, châtelaine purses, stirrup pouches, and wrist bags. One of their key features was the enameling, as well as a variety of new materials used for trimmings (tortoiseshell, ivory, glass, and gemstone cabochons), often skillfully carved with nature motifs.

Affordable casual handbags were often made of man-made materials.

Casual Bags: "Economy class" travel bag

Material: *Early imitations (embossed goatskin, or "pebble finish rubber"– early vinyl)*
Features: *Cloth-lined, japanned frame, brass-plated trimmings*
Novelties: *Lady's shopping bag*
Size: *large, over 10"*
Material: *Cowhide grained with alligator, seal or walrus pattern*
Size: *medium, under 10"*

Handbags ad, *Sears, Roebuck & Co. Merchandise Catalog*, 1914-1915.

Most desirable collectibles from the Edwardian period are made with genuine skins of one-piece shell frames–quite difficult to come by in excellent condition. In 1918, Bonwit Teller & Co. and Gimbel Brothers were the first retailers to promote the fantastic alligator shoppers with the new shell frames. Today, they could cost about $500 - $3,000 depending on the model.

Type	Material	Features	Size	Circa
Gladstone travel bag	Top-grade leather, gator-, croc skin	Leather-lined	12"+	1902
Oxford travel bag	Same as above	Steel frame, brass lock, sliding catches	18"+	1902
Châtelaine shopper	Fabric, skin, leather, suede	Ornamented metal frame, catch, chain, belt attachment	Petite, 4" x 4"	$950 today, $1.25 in 1902
Stirrup pouch (pear, trapeze-shaped)	Soft, pleated leather; textured skin	Single-loop top stirrup, leather lined, covered frame, w/watch	10.5" x 8"	1902
Wrist bag	Gator-, seal skin	Nickel frame, vinaigrette	11" x 7"	1903
Compartment handbag	Brown alligator	Powder puff, hairpins	7" x 6"	1903
Satchel, shopper	Horn-back crocodile	Riveted frame (nickel or gold-plated), spring clasp, multi compartments	10"x 6"	1908
Daytime vertical pouch	Textured leather, skins	Welted seams, doubled straps	Petite	1914-1915
Vanity box-purse	Leather, fabric	Inside mirror	Petite	1914
Special occasion handbags	Leather/skin	Moiré or poplin lining, mirror, coin purses, scent bottle, brush, hanging mirrors, card-case	11" x 8"	1915
Daytime bags	Smooth skins, centered horn-back inlay	Safety latch, piped seams, top handle, leather frame	12"	1915
Shoppers (current price $400-$1,200)	Baby-alligator claws	Coin purse, double-locking frame	13"	1916
Tailored bags	Skins, suede	Shell frame	8"-12"	1918
Fitted envelopes imported from France and England	Leather or skins	Inlaid frames (shell, marcasite, mosaic medallions, black onyx or cameos). Silver or gold clips.	Small, delicate	1919

Art Deco Style (mid-1920s to mid-1930s)

The diverse Art Deco style produced an abundance of streamlined, sophisticated designs. In fashion, interest had shifted to refined symmetry and balance, straight edges and vivid hues.

A clutch, or an underarm purse, invented in France and introduced in New York in 1925, appeared in various versions: a framed pouch with a back-strap or no strap; a framed flat envelope; a frameless folded envelope with a front flap; and a handbook with a flat handle on top. Particular attention was paid to craftsmanship.

Depending on the usage, thousands of Art Deco handbag styles were divided into four major groups: daytime bags (leather, skin and fabric), formal afternoon or evening bags (silk, embroidered, beaded), gifts or novelties, and travel accessories.

Type	Material	Features	Size	Circa
Envelope, framed pouch, finger purse	Skins (lizard, ostrich, gator, croc), leather combinations	Tailored, single-, double-handled; lack of structured bottom; under-frame pleating	Various, from 5" to 11"	1925 - 1930
Vanity cases	Leather, skin	Silk-, leather lined	Small	1925
Underarm	Gator, croc, python, lizard	Clever back strap instead of top handle; pretty frames; neat welting; extra pockets; fitted moiré interior	Slim, flat	
Handbook	Leather combinations, baby croc, shark, etc.	Lavishly embossed; flat adjustable top handle; vanity compartment; new zipper opening	Small	Late 1920s – early 1930s
Hatbox (novelty)	Gator, croc, leather, vinyl	Removable hat forms; solid locks; velvet lining	Large, up to 18" in diameter	1920s-1930s
Mallette (Hermes)	Croc, gator, leather	Multi-pouches for papers; secret jewelry box	Large	1925
Vanity box (France)	Gold leather, gator or lizard	Inside mirror	Small	Early 1930s
Matching travel sets	Imitation leather	Hatbox, suitcase, overnight bag		Early 1930s

Newly developed *composition materials* became the cornerstone of the Art Deco period of the 1930s. French Galalith that looked exactly like tortoise, rose quartz, or ivory, and especially Prystal—imitation crystal in polished, frosted, or carved effects—were favorites for making amazing clasps and handles.

Together with Bakelite, those trimmings revolutionized the bag industry of the 1930s.

Key features of the Art Deco handbag are the trimmings and frames.

Feature	Finish	Types	Function	Circa
Plain or jeweled metal frames	Covered with leather, polished, engraved, etched, or inlaid with natural/faux gems (pearl, jade, amber, quarts, tortoise, onyx, carnelian)	Gold-, nickel-toned. Gold gilt. Various pulls, trimmings, plaques: jeweled, enameled, beaded (steel, glass, crystal), cloisonné, carved gems, rhinestones	Focal point	1925-1935
Multiple frames w/ separate clasps	Gunmetal	Double, triple, quadruple; turn-lock safety frame by Jemco	Practical	1920-1930
Plastic frames	Molded	Accented with Art Deco motifs	Substitute of metal	1920-1930
Bakelite, Galalith, Prystal handle	Circle-, square-, ring-, or bar-like	Structural, top handles & frames	Decorative	mid 1930s
Doorknocker or bar-catch clasps, clasp ornaments	Metal or skin	Encrustation, faux or real gems, beads, monograms	Decorative	mid 1930s

Handbags ad, *Montgomery Wards Merchandise Catalog*, 1928-1929.

The innovations included the greatest variety of new leathers, skins and decorative accents.

Skins: *Buffed or horn alligator, crocodile; lizard, cobra, ostrich, seal, sharkskin, broadtail.*

Leather: *Pigskin, buckskin, capeskin, saffian, seal, doeskin, sheepskin.*

Leather Combination: *Smooth goatskin with Galuchat grain; glossy calfskin with alligator or reptile skin; ostrich with shark grain; and alligator grain with smooth leather.*

Finishes: *Suede, patent, glazed, brushed, washable, frosted, or grained with animal patterns.*

Lining: *Silk, moiré, or leather.*

Colors: *Jeweled tones, pastel tints, dark costume colors; predominant black; red; shades of red; black/white combination – the hallmark of the Art Deco period.*

Key Features: *Frames, Handles, Clasps, Decorations.*

Handbags ad, *Montgomery Wards Merchandise Catalog*, 1928-1929.

Retro Style (mid-1930s to late 1940s)

Rich in creativity and novel ideas, the Retro style had been constructed on the solid foundation of Art Deco and preserved its classical symmetry through a decade. The visible changes of the silhouette became apparent in about 1935, when less severe, smoothed-out silhouette emerged to complement the romantic flair of summer silks and winter tweeds. Practical femininity replaced the strong, masculine notes of Art Deco. Generous pleating and shirring were incorporated into every design to increase the capacity of the bags.

1930s

Casual styles: *Large, soft clutches; smaller frame bags, satchels.*
Size: *Large for casual use; medium – for daytime; tiny – for evening.*
Features: *Simple and undecorated; zippered top-closure.*

Novelties: *Vanities, cigarette cases, satchels with rounded bottoms, muff bags.*
Handles: *Bracelet-, hoop-, braid-, bow-, and loop-handles.*
Leatherwork: *Shirring, tucks, pleats.*
Trimmings: *Prystal; Bakelite; rhinestones, beads, faux gems; carved cinnabar, marcasite.*
Skins: *Snakeskin for afternoon handbags; baby alligator (Tailored Woman, 1943); Mexican baby alligator, lizard, and ostrich.*
Leathers: *English Morocco; alligator-grained or lizard-grained calf; ostrich-grained cowhide; lizard-grained goatskin; French antelope suede; Scotch pigskin; rough-grained Austrian leather; genuine patents; and Alaskan seal.*
New styles: *Roomy envelope, swaggers, zippered bags, framed bags – made of alligator.*
Innovations: *Eel skin, Lucite, metal zipper.*

Generally, the late 1930s were marked by the existence of two variably different casual styles: a squashy jumbo bag in pliable leather and a structured framed bag in sturdy alligator or leather.

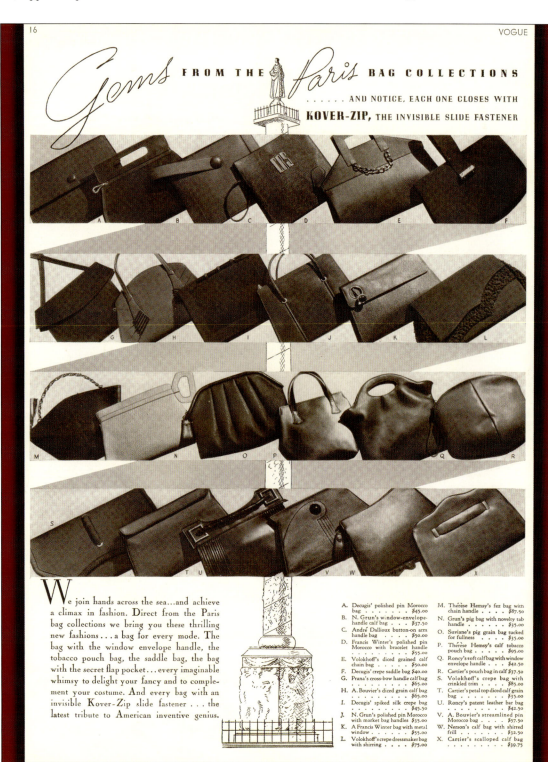

Retro handbags ad, *Vogue* 1936.

1940s

Key Styles: *Large hand-free shoulder bag; huge, soft double-handled dressmakers and clutches.*

Casual Bags: *Portmaneau, attaché case, drawstring and mailman's pouch.*

Sizes: *Large, over 12" long.*

New Casual Styles: *Enormous shoulder bag (1944) worn slung across the shoulder, skin envelopes and frame bag.*

Novelties: *Baskets, whistlet boxes.*

Handles: *Wide over-arm handles; shoulder straps; wristlets, loops.*

Skins: *Soft Mexican alligator (Harry Rosenfeld), polished African crocodile (Mark Cross).*

Decorations: *Faux amber clasps and frames; plain and carved Lucite, Bakelite.*

Frames: *Tubular, metal bar-clasp, massive double-, triple-, quadruple-frames; exotic wood.*

Colors: *Cocoa brown, honey, fudge brown, burnt maple, red, wine, green.*

Lining: *Leather or natural water snake.*

Innovations: *Matching alligator shoes; affordable South American export; and plastic zipper.*

Wards finest handbags... 6.95 to 15.50

[1] **Classic Envelope** in fine polished Calf. The style for town tailored outfits. Smartly styled with pleats in front for interesting detail. Clever slip-through flap holds bag tightly shut. Deep leather gussets make it roomy. Fittings include a zipper compartment, large wall pocket, coin purse, and mirror. Rayon lining. Size: 11¼ x 7½ in. Colors: Navy, Turf Tan, Cherry Red. State color.
D30 A 1407–Ship. wt. 1 lb. 2 oz....Each 6.95

[2] **Top Handle Pouch** . . . your favorite soft, chunky type Handbag in fine Calfskin. Excellent for dressy or tailored costumes. Full shirrings caught in an expensive leather covered tubular frame. Distinctive plastic clasp. Wide leather gussets for roominess. Inside fitted with a zipper compartment, coin purse, mirror. Rayon lining. Size: 15¾ x 7 inches. Colors: Turf Tan or Navy. State color.
D30 A 1543–Ship. wt. 1 lb. 7 oz....Each 6.95

[3] **Underarm Frame Pouch** in fine smooth Calf. Its feminine lines designed to complement both tailored and dressy outfits. Soft shirring gathered into leather covered tubular frame. Gold-color metal knob clasp. Wide leather gussets make this handbag roomy. Fitted with a zipper compartment, coin purse, mirror. Fine Rayon lining. Size: 15¾ x 6¾ inches. Colors: Turf Tan, Navy. State color.
D30 A 1542–Ship. wt. 1 lb. 5 oz....Each 6.95

[4] **Genuine Cordé by Weeda.** A superbly styled dressmaker Envelope to complement your feminine costumes. Fine Rayon Cordé looks so elegant yet wears so well. Softly draped front. Clever gussets designed to preserve the bag's shape, hold contents securely. Large zipper compartment, wall pockets, coin purse, mirror. Rayon Satin lining. Size: 16 x 6½ inches. Colors: Black or Navy. State color.
D30 A 1544–Ship. wt. 1 lb. 8 oz....Each 9.95

[5] **Genuine Snakeskin by Lesco.** Fine skins with lovely natural markings in a wonderfully soft and puffy handbag. Carry it whenever you want a brilliant color accent. Wide opening covered frame with metal clasp. Handsomely fitted: compartment with flap, wall pocket, coin purse and mirror. Fine quality Rayon lining. Size: 15 x 6½ in. Colors: Golden Brown, Red, Bright Green. Please state color.
D30 A 1545–Ship. wt. 1 lb.......Each 9.95

[6] **Top Zipper Underarm Handbag by Lesco.** In polished butter-soft Calf, magnificently tailored. Attached envelope compartment is both useful and decorative. Wrist loop on zipper. Superb fittings . . . compartment with flap, and wall pocket on one side; wall pocket and mirror pocket on the other; coin purse, mirror. Fine Rayon lining. Size: 13¾ x 6¾ in. Colors: Golden Brown or Black. State color.
D30 A 1546–Ship. wt. 1 lb. 4 oz . Each 11.50

[7] **Tailored "Practique" by Bienen-Davis** with the marvelous patented frame that springs open and snaps shut easily, securely. Handbag in finest hand-crushed Goatskin, softly draped with expensive Lucite ornament in front, convenient back handle. Very roomy. Zipper pocket, wall pocket, coin purse; Compartments for comb, mirror, lipstick. Rayon lining. Size: 13½ x 9 in. State Color: Turf Tan, Navy or Red.
30 A 15⁴⁹–Ship. wt. 2 lbs. 2 oz. . . . Each 15.50

[8] **Streamlined Envelope by Bienen-Davis.** Mirror-bright Patent worked in dramatically simple lines. Made of the finest Leather. A bold accessory accent that will enhance every outfit. Zipper closing hidden under flap; handsome Lucite bar pull. Loads of room inside. Smartly fitted with wall pocket, attached coin purse and mirror in pocket. Finest quality Rayon lining. Size: 16½ x 7¾ inches. Color: Black.
D30 A 1548–Ship. wt. 1 lb. 8 oz...Each 12.75

[9] **Dressmaker "Practique" by Bienen-Davis.** Favorite underarm style with the convenient patented frame that springs open and snaps shut smoothly, securely. Comes in exquisite polished Calf. Skillfully draped "canoe" corners. Simulated tortoise shell ornament. Wall pocket, attached coin purse, mirror, and compartments for lipstick, comb, mirror. Rayon lining. Size: 18 x 7 inches. State Color: Brown or Navy.
D30 A 1547–Ship. wt. 1 lb. 4 oz...Each 13.95

bienen davis — Handbags 7, 8, 9
LESCO — Handbags 5, 6
Genuine WEEDA Cordé — Handbag 4

Time Payment information may be found on the Inside Back Cover. Use your account to buy best quality for superior styling, materials, workmanship.
Note: All the Handbags shown on this page will be mailed to you from Chicago; however you only pay postage from Wards nearest Mail Order House.

WARDS 173

Retro handbags ad, *Montgomery Wards Merchandise Catalog, 1943.*

"New Look" Style (1948 to late 1950s)

The 1950s were the era of big fashion and big ideas. A stunning variety of bold shapes and proportions—a happy marriage of utility and femininity—filled the needs for the bag for every occasion. It became the most important part of the outfit, and the most wanted gift.

Key Styles: *Sleek, trim silhouette – "Battle of the bulge" (by 1950s).*

Sizes: *Practical proportions (daytime); tiny (evening); oversized over 14" Argentine export.*

Leather: *Calf, rawhide, saddle leather, rustic textured leathers, Morocco, pigskin.*

Skins: *Cobra, genuine ostrich, lizard (or lizagator), gator, French Madagascar crocodile.*

Imports: *France (Saks-34th, B. Altman & Co.); Argentina, Brazil (Franklin Simon).*

Other Brands: *Bienen-Davis, Milch, Phelps, Whilshire, Josef, etc.*

The alligator was in its zenith! Huge, supple and rich, the magnificent bags of this decade were accessorized by matching sets of coin purses and mirrors. The best of all gifts, they were cherished as diamonds, minks, and the Rolls Royce.

Key Skin Styles: *Slim, slightly tapered gator or croc casuals.*

Handles: *Bright metal (gold- or silver-tone depending on costume and line), top skin handles.*

Innovation: *Not to match alligator handbag and shoes.*

Fur Novelties: *Fox tote, broadtail cosmetic case, zebra billfold, mink cigarette case, African leopard bag.*

Casual Styles: *Fitted boxes and lunch-boxes, satchels, barrels, pouches; huge frames bags made of the variety of skins.*

Travel Styles: *Oversized carry-alls with watches and secret compartments (Koret, 1955-1959).*

Size: *From 12" to 18" wide (cost astronomical $250 in the '50s!).*

Colors: *Light hues of beige and brown (parchment, toast, amber, honey or tan).*

New Makers: *Susan Gail for Henry Bendel, 1954; Wilcof (exclusive alligator "buckets") and Nat Lewis (glorious snake clutches) for Bergdorf Goodman, 1955; Moris Moscowitz (tailored dinner bags in snake) for Lord & Taylor, 1957; Mayer (classic alligator bags) for Arnold Constable, 1958; Theodor of California (stylish skin bags) for B. Altman & Co., 1959.*

The trend for commodious alligator handbags continued through 1959, when it gradually wound down to visibly smaller, sensibly sized casuals. Eventually, the designers and manufacturers started paying more attention to the interests of the young adults between sixteen and twenty-five years of age. It appeared that the teen fashion promised to become big business in the upcoming 1960s.

Handbags ad, *Montgomery Wards Merchandise Catalog, 1954.*

Handbags ad, *Montgomery Wards Merchandise Catalog, 1954.*

"Mod" Style (1960s)

The teenage MOD look became the biggest moneymaker for the fashion industry in the 1960s. *"We're trying to make handbags a fashion accessory rather than a functional accessory,"* announced Murray Resnick, president of the National Handbag Association.

The bag's size became the major feature defining the fashion of the 1960s. The radical change in fashion leaning towards girlish looks and extremely short hemlines promoted a trend for *tiny purses* of Lilliputian proportions.

Key Feature: *Large (early 1960s). Small (mid-1960s). Miniature (late-1960s).*

Shoes: *Classic, narrow pumps (early 1960s). Flat-heeled, wide oxfords (mid-, late-1960s).*

Novelties: *Reptile accessories for daywear or evening wear; anteater skin.*

Evening Skin Bags: *Mid-size gator and croc evening bag w/jeweled clasps ($125 in 1961).*

Travel Skin Bags: *Large Alligator travel bag with lock and key ($275, 1961).*

Handles: *Bamboo (Gucci).*

Colors: *Total volume colors (plum, violine group, red hues, cobalt, teal, orange), 1963.*

Casual Styles: *Totes, satchels, clutches, boxes coordinated with shoes in color and material.*

New Feature: *Accordion pleats to assure more discreet room in smaller bags, 1964.*

1960 was proclaimed a year of alligator, and their prices became bigger than life. At Bonwit Teller, for example, the finest handbags for travel cost an incredible $495.

In 1967, the handbags became dangerously small—*almost doll-size*—yet quite roomy. It was a matter of proportions, as a spokesman for Lesco Lona, Inc. said, whose three-in-one turtle pouch was one of the season's best sellers: *"A woman would look pretty silly carrying a large bag with a short skirt."*

When miniskirts were worn by millions of women, handbag producers turned out mini-bags as complementing accessories. A year later, when dresses got slightly longer, the handbags also grew moderately larger.

By 1969, the strong protests against poaching of mammals and reptiles for fashion skins resulted in bans and restrictions on Ceylon leopard, elephant and American Alligator. As a result, alligator handbags went out of style for several decades.

MOD handbags ad, *Sears, Roebuck & Co. Catalog,* 1963.

CONDITION

I must admit that it is not easy to find a valuable vintage bag in original, truly mint condition. Very few qualify as mint: flawless pieces in original packaging with no traces of use, repair, or restoration. Most vintage bags that survived to this day do have some minor or major flaws. That is why it is so very important to know how to assess their condition and establish the correct price.

Remember that the value of vintage always depends on its condition. The better it is, the more expensive the handbag is!

Slight wear, scuffing, or insignificant soiling is almost inevitable and can be easily corrected by expert cleaning and polishing. Dry rot, cracks and tears, broken seams, discoloration or darker spots, broken or missing parts, bad repairs, damaged or dirty interior, musty odor or cigarette smell, as well as any other significant damage, are serious flaws to avoid. That is why it is important to inspect the bag before buying, especially if you are not an expert.

Unfortunately, the worst damage—dry rot caused by time, use and elements—cannot be seen from a distance or in pictures. To detect it, you must physically touch and feel the skin to be sure it is flexible, soft and pliable. Do not buy a bag if the skin is brittle with dark dry spots that peel or flake. Skins damaged by dry rot are fragile. On contact with moisture or heat, and also on impact, dry spots can crack and break. Dark spots on brown or colored skins can be an indication of dry-rot damage.

Generally, the handle is the most fragile part of the bag and gets damage first. Even a minor stress mark can later become a break, which undermines the value. Multiple surface cracks that hide inside wear-spots between the scales are also considered serious damage and cannot be ignored.

Always confirm whether the handle is original to the bag. A replaced handle is okay if you intend to wear the handbag. However, if you are buying a collectible for investment, the replacement will affect its value. Carefully inspect a chain strap. Most likely, it is a replacement, unless it is a small evening bag by Lucille de Paris or Koret. Note that large shoppers by Vassar with replaced metal chains are not as valuable as the same handbags with original handles.

If you see a vintage piece with a remarkably "alert" handle, most definitely it is a replacement. Sometimes, such replacements could be made of belts—often, vinyl or embossed leather, not genuine skin.

The original leather-backed skin handles are usually slightly misshapen due to years of storage, which is normal. Unless, of course, it is a rolled handle by Bellestone supported from inside by a tube-like rubber core; or a semi-rigid handle by Lucille de Paris with an internal metal band. In this case, the handle must be in a perfectly arched shape.

Make your judgment taking into consideration the fact whether the bag is collectible or not. The replacement significantly affects the value of a fine collectible, but is perfectly acceptable in vintage casuals for everyday use. If you like the handbag with a damaged handle and you plan to use it, don't be afraid to buy it. With a little effort, you can easily "get a handle on the situation". Replace it with the new one made of skin or embossed leather, or a metal chain-strap.

Unfortunately, it is not easy to match the color of the replacement when it comes to colored or brown bags. While deciding on the replacement, coordinate it with the original design, style and proportions. Yes, your personal taste always matters. However, it is recommended to stick to the original design, as closely as possible—to preserve its historical appeal and not to lose on value—especially when dealing with collectibles.

Don't forget to check the interior. Even though nobody but you can see behind the "closed clasp," a clean interior is always preferable. Major flaws—such as significant soiling, spots, scuffing, dye loss, odor, pen marks, lipstick, nail polish, water stains, broken zippers, torn pockets, etc.—undermine the bag's functionality and appearance, and definitely reflect on its value.

Avoid bags with bent, corroded, or broken frames or clasps. They cannot be mended.

Note that jeweled alligator handbags were made primarily per order, thus they're quite rare and expensive. Most of them were created by Rosenfeld, Lucille de Paris, Koret, or Martin Van Schaak—so, if you have found one of those gorgeous pieces, don't ever let it go!

Craft & Quality

Over centuries, a handbag has evolved from a simple necessity into an important fashion element. As a reflection of a woman's intimate world, it has been an object of interest of many celebrated designers for decades. However, no designer's vision can be realized without a skilled artisan. If you take the time to carefully examine a fine vintage handbag, you will notice how much skill has been put into its creation. Attention to detail is essential. The thought, time, work and craftsmanship is noticed when people see fine vintage for the first time; they always sigh in admiration, "Oh, they don't make them like this anymore."

The culture of mass-produced fashion—intended to be disposed of the next year—affects the quality and style of the products we buy. That is why 'going vintage' is a fun and affordable way to personalize your fashion choices. Be unique and special, for less!

What makes a fine vintage purse so attractive is its handmade quality, which never comes cheap. Why some bags are considerably more expensive than others depends on the same reason diamonds cost more than rhinestones: quality! Two parameters—the quality of the craftsmanship and the quality of the skins—influence the value and price.

If you are new to collecting, start by purchasing signed brand-name pieces, to be sure that you are buying best quality. It is also important to know that early exotics were rarely authenticated or signed by their makers, until the 1940s-1950s. Thus, most vintage bags produced by smaller makers for the domestic market, in the United States or overseas, were not signed, except for the bags by Rosenfeld, Lucille de Paris, Coblentz, Koret, Vassar, and Sterling U.S.A. Also, South American caiman handbags were often mislabeled as alligator, as mentioned previously.

To assess the condition and quality of vintage handbags and determine a correct market price, see the tips provided below.

CRAFTSMANSHIP

Vintage exotics are handmade products made in strict accordance with ancient procedures. The basic tool that aided craftsmen in the process was the knife for cutting and shaving.

A handbag begins with choosing the right hides that were tanned, glazed and lap polished to bring out the sheen. Then, to have a prototype made, a pattern-maker transferred the design of the handbag model—drawn on paper—to cardboard. The skill of a pattern-maker consists of the optimal use of natural markings of the hides. Proper selection of matching hides with similar patterns is quite a difficult task. Meticulous centering of the skins to achieve symmetry is another important goal that takes a lot of skill to master.

Next, the precut skins were either backed or padded for support, ready to be stitched. Stitching techniques varied and sometimes included piping or hand-perforation and hand-stitching with waxed thread.

Once the form was sewn together, the bag was inverted. The pre-sewn lining was inserted, then stitched to the exterior and finally framed. Lastly, the fixtures, the handles and the clasp were attached. The bag was finished!

Top Design Features
- Well-balanced proportions and interesting construction
- Uniquely shaped handle, gussets or bottom
- One-of-a-kind frame fixtures or clasp decorations (make sure they are original!)
- Application of unique materials (plastic, wood, or fur)—must be original to the bag
- Unusually fitted interior with accessories, extras, secret compartments, etc.
- Lock closure with a key
- The more complex the construction is, the higher is the level of the workmanship.

Top Craftsmanship Features
- Skins are superbly matched, symmetrical and centered.
- Seams are piped for added durability, or stitched outwards (French handbags).
- Stitching is strong and even, sometimes in contrasting colors.
- Corners are crisp and well defined.
- Frame is fully covered with skin or decorated with ornaments, embossing, or studs.
- Original frame is made of Lucite or Bakelite, wood or other unusual materials.
- Handle is rigid or semi-rigid, with strong padding and support.
- Hinges are draped in leather, or of unusual construction (Vassar floating hinges, etc.).
- Solid brass or gold-plated metal fittings are well polished and finely crafted.
- Interior is fitted with top-quality suede, kidskin, lambskin, goatskin, silk, or moiré.
- Interior features a built-in wallet or a swivel mirror.
- Interior compartments of unusual construction: duplet, duple, triple, etc.
- Unique original decorative accents: 24-karat plating, sterling frames, etc.
- Clasps encrusted with rhinestones, precious gems or glass beads; decorated with colorful enamel, braided leather or Lucite/Bakelite ornaments—must be original to the handbag.

- Original accessory kits: coin purse, mirror in leather or plastic casing, comb, perfume bottle, lighter, lipstick case with lipstick, etc.

Quality of Skins
"Alligators are like women," an old, wise man said, *"the best ones are soft, supple and nonbelligerent."* If you shop carefully and take your time, you will find the best one that will provide honorable service for a lifetime.

Prices of exotic skins are primarily based on their quality, which depends on their origin. The most valuable, thus expensive are highly pliable Porosus Crocodile skins. The most affordable are South American caiman due to their relative brittleness.

Start your inspection by running your fingers over the skins. The best ones will have a sculptured effect achieved by a special French method of tanning, when each scale is domed separately by hand. If the surface is flat, a less expensive tanning method was applied. The finer the skin is, the more it yields when you press your thumb against it.

Then, examine the scales. They can tell you the story about where the alligator lived, how it lived, and whether it is worth spending. While scrutinizing the grain, ask yourself the following questions:

1. Does the front match the back in pattern and symmetry? In the finest goods, both sides are virtually identical.
2. What is the size of the scales? The smaller the scales, the finer the quality. Most valuable are the underbelly cuts of baby Porosus crocodile and baby American Alligator, with the tiniest scales. Uneven, coarse-grained South American caiman cost less than one-fifth the price of the Porosus crocodile. Remember that several large-scaled crocodiles from Africa—Nile crocodile and New Guinea crocodile—are also quite valuable, but not as much as Porosus crocodile.
3. Can you see the center line that divides the pattern into two parts mirroring each other? If yes, you made the right choice.
4. Are there any bruises and scars often seen on inferior skins? If the skins are free of such, you're getting the best quality.

In addition to their origin, skins are valued based on their grade, cut, pattern, and finish.

Grade: Alligator and crocodile skins selected for manufacturing are graded by 5 categories and judged by the shape of the skin, presence of scars, cuts, scratches or holes, and "buttons" (osteoderms). The fewer the flaws, the higher the grade is. Look for bags with a fine, even surface texture that does not have any scars or "buttons" (thicker spots).

Cut: The underbelly skin is considered to be the primary leather for making bags. It consists of two cuts: a central-pattern cut and an outside-of-pattern cut. A neat, central-pattern cut is divided into three main areas: belly, head and tail. A belly cut is the most desirable because of its superb symmetry. It usually features an umbilical scar, which is often displayed prominently on the front of the handbag. Flexible head cuts composed of smaller scales are used for gussets. Tail cuts with tile-scales arranged horizontally are for the bottoms. The outside-the-pattern cuts—head and tail—are less valuable because of their random scale patterns.

Luxurious, large-scaled African crocodile skin satchel, suede-lined. Supple, thick and cushioned skins, with distinct scale patterns. A great example of how different cuts are used on a premium-quality handbag, to emphasize its value and uniqueness. **Top left:** The front is made of the central belly-cut of high symmetry that features a neat, even scale-pattern, and the umbilical scar displayed prominently right in the center, under the front-pull. (Remember: Not only alligators have umbilical scars, but also crocodiles, yet they are usually less defined). **Center right:** The back is made of the outside-of-pattern, belly-cut that features a random pattern of rounded scales. **Bottom left:** The smaller parts of the handbag, such as its decorative accents (pull, clasp encrustation, etc.) are all made of the flexible head cut, composed of smaller, rounded scales.

The example how various cuts are used on the same handbag. **Bottom left:** Both handle and frame are made of the flexible head-cut, with small scales. **Right:** The gussets are made of the tail-cuts, with tile-scaled pattern. **Bottom:** Usually, the bottom is made of less expensive tail-cut. Not on this one! To emphasize its value, its bottom is crafted of the expensive, central belly-cut. No shortcuts on quality here!

Pattern: Symmetrical central patterns indicate the highest quality. Off-centered patterns have lesser value. Random patterns are least desirable. A bag made of perfectly matched, symmetrical patterns on both sides represents the best quality.

The example of a highly symmetrical, central belly-cut (top quality). Please note how the scale-pattern is running vertically, with the symmetrical left and right parts separated by a central cord right in the middle.

The example of an outside-of-pattern belly-cut (lesser quality). There's no symmetry in the pattern, and it is positioned on bias. Please note how the random scale-pattern is running from left to right – on diagonal – not vertically.

Finish: For decades, tanners around the world have struggled to master the perfect finish that ads that final magic touch to the splendor of exotic skin. Depending on the decade and the country of origin, different technologies and methods have been used to create three basic types of finishes: glaze, bombe and matte.

Glazed finishes can vary in intensity and brilliance, depending on the maker and tannery. Lucille de Paris, Deitsch, Evans and Coblentz favored a medium-shine glazing. Tasteful and elegant, it was never overwhelming. A highly reflective glaze was developed for the Bellestone brand which became its signature feature helpful to authenticate their unsigned pieces. South American caiman handbags boast the brightest "glass-like" gloss. On the other hand, expensive French handbags are often treated with low intensity glazing—to slightly pick up the tone of the dyed skin and leave the rest to the imagination. Subtle and intimate!

The example of glazed finish (crocodile skin).

The example of matte finish (crocodile skin).

Matte finish is a subtle treatment with a soft glow used primarily by French and Italian masters. Quiet and delicate, it has the appeal of discreet, casual luxury. Vintage models by Hermes and Gucci are often treated with this expensive, elegant touch. Every older crocodile purse treated with a matte finish is a valuable find, quite contrary to the popular belief that the glossier the bag, the better.

Bombe finish (pronounced 'bombay') is a well-fixed, brilliant gloss that catches the eye and reflects the natural sheen of the individual markings of the skin. It is achieved by applying heat to flat, polished skins and by slightly raising the center of each scale. Juicy, plump scales of high definition are the effect of the bombe—the incomparable, full-aniline glazing mastered by the finest tanneries of Europe and America. Gorgeous Rosenfeld bags made in West Germany often sport this glamorous finish.

The example of bombe finish (alligator skin).

Quality Tips

Alligator or crocodile: Generally, the handbags by Harry Rosenfeld, Nettie Rosenstein, Lucille de Paris, Lederer de Paris, Mark Cross, Koret, Rendl, Judith Leiber, Coblentz, and Deitsch—made of American Alligator or various crocodiles—are more valuable than the products by Lesco, Bellestone, Vassar, Escort, or Sterling U.S.A.

Baby alligator: Expensive skin from juvenile alligators is at the top of the quality spectrum. A miniature version of a full-sized alligator, their skins with small tight scales, arranged in a perfectly symmetrical central pattern, is extremely flexible and supple. Beware of cheaper lizard bags misrepresented as "baby alligator". Lizard has a completely different appearance. It has nothing to do with the expensive, real baby-alligator skin.

Caiman: Handbags of inferior caiman made in Argentina, Uruguay, the United States, Italy or Germany are low-grade products. The caiman skin lacks flexibility; the color can be patchy and uneven; the scales are large, bony and rigid, with sharp, lifted edges. Flank cuts have smaller, round scales of uneven sizes and spaced scales.

Turtle skin: Turtle handbags by Rosenfeld or Lucille de Paris are collectible, but less expensive than alligator or croco-dile. Rosenfeld handbags are always marked as *Genuine Turtle*. Beware of misrepresentation of turtle as crocodile or gator. Remember that turtle scales are angled, arranged in random, circle patterns. Cheap turtle-embossed cowhide or vinyl bags are not collectible.

Ostrich: Full quill bags are generally more expensive than smooth- or leg-cut bags.

Embossing: Remember that a lot of embossed bags were manufactured starting from as early as the turn of the 20th century—to imitate genuine skins. Regardless of the bag's age, always double-check its authenticity. Embossed vintage is not collectible.

Patching: Generally, patching is very undesirable when it comes to the quality. Patched purses are way less valuable than the ones constructed from the whole skins, unless the patching is used as an important stylistic feature to add interest to the design, such as some older pieces, from the 1940s. Especially desirable are the delightful little baskets and clutches by De Lumur—a little shop in Florida—assembled by hand into wonderful collages from dozens of skin squares encased in plastic, metal, or wood frames.

Artistic, genuine alligator clutch assembled from squares of skin encased in plastic. Zippered top; fabric interior; wallet. (W 12-inch by H 6 ½ -inch by D 1 ¾ -inch). Made by De Lumur, Florida, U.S.A. 1949.

Color

It is amazing how much the ability to see color influences our perception of the universe. In art, the spirit of the time has often been expressed through specific color combinations. In fashion, avant-garde designers tend to reflect their revolutionary vision in creating new, startling shades and hues. A notion of a designer color fist came to life in the 1930s, when Elsa Schiaparelli introduced her legendary trademark, 'Shocking Pink.'

Similarly to other collectible, the color of vintage exotic skin handbags is an important factor influencing their value and price. Pieces in popular colors and shades are always more desirable, hence expensive. The demand generally depends on the location of the market, the season, and the type of buyers. It is also based on the general color-trend prevalent in the current fashion.

Lovely, genuine alligator frame-bag in collectible ivory, by popular Lucille de Paris. Tailored leather interior; brass trim. (W 10-inch by H 10-inch by D 2 ½ -inch). Signed: Lucille de Paris Made in U.S.A. American, ca 1964.

Super rare, designer, alligator satchels by Lucille de Paris, in custom-tanned, flamboyant cobalt-blue and California tangerine. American, ca 1960s.

In today's vintage market, demand for a casual alligator bag in black among first-time buyers outweighs any other color. It reflects on the price of a black bag, which is on average about 20 percent higher than a similar one in brown, regardless of the maker.

Common brown and its variations—coffee, chestnut, raisin, Hershey, chocolate, mocha, redwood, and mahogany—represent the base price, color-wise. It is relatively stable, except for the fluctuations due to the season, the market, and the vendor. Fall and winter quite often yield higher prices from end consumers; spring and summer is a season when dealers restock their inventory. The New York, Los Angeles, Florida, and Texas markets are noticeably more expensive than other locations.

Light shades of brown (brandy, caramel, honey, tan, taupe, etc.), as well as other light neutrals (beige, cream and ivory) are quite desirable, and usually cost more in spring and summer. Therefore, off-season is the best time to purchase expensive brand-name handbags in collectible light shades, if you're looking for a deal.

One of the most rare colors in alligator handbags is pure white. Most skillful tanners, who mastered the complex process of tanning darker skins into pristine snow white, were commissioned by Nettie Rosenstein, Lucille de Paris, Koret, and Martin Van Schaak to produce their outstanding pieces in white or cream. Each bag in white alligator or crocodile, by the above-mentioned brands, is quite a valuable addition to any comprehensive collection, worth upwards of a thousand dollars if in mint condition.

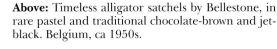

Above: Timeless alligator satchels by Bellestone, in rare pastel and traditional chocolate-brown and jet-black. Belgium, ca 1950s.

Collection of desirable Martin Van Schaak exotics in designer colors: lipstick-red, classic-mauve, sunflower-yellow, and snow-white. American, ca 1960s.

Purses in mass-produced red, green and navy blue, as well as their numerous shades and hues—and especially in novel pastels—bring top dollars from customers who own several pieces in basic colors.

Interesting, plastic-encased arm-purses in collectible emerald-green, ruby-red, and coffee-brown. American, 1949.

Rare, designer colors tanned per order (e.g. yellow, pink, fuchsia, lavender, orange, baby-blue, royal blue, purple, teal, turquoise, chartreuse, lime, etc.) are in the highest demand among savvy collectors and bring top dollars, often thousands of dollars, for a mint quality piece in alligator or crocodile. Virtually impossible to find because of a limited supply, each piece is an exceptionally prized possession.

Gleaming evening bags from the 1960s—made in gold or silver alligator, lizard or ostrich by Lucille de Paris or Rosenfeld—are always more expensive than similar ones in casual colors.

Cheerful exotics by Judith Leiber – in designer turquoise (alligator) and fuchsia (karung). American, ca 1980s.

Delicate, silver alligator-print leather cocktail purse, with bar-handles, two outside compartments, self-covered frame; and a dusty-pink satin interior. Looks so real, you wouldn't know it is faux unless you examine it with the magnifying glass! Silver-tone trim. Shown with a removable rhinestone clip. (W 7 ¾ -inch by H 7-inch by D 2 ¾ -inch). Signed: Rosenfeld. Ca 1968-1969.

Antique travel bags, doctor's bags, châtelaine purses, claw watch-fobs and ladies' pocketbooks—made of horn-back alligator and ornamented with claws or entire bodies of baby alligators—came predominantly in brown, or the shades of amber and tan; and very rarely in black. Therefore, if you've come across an "early-looking" handbag in modern bright colors, think imitation.

In addition, the color of a vintage handbag can give you a hint about its age. And it is my hope that the following overview of the color trends—according to decades—will help you to determine the age of your treasure.

Passionate Hues of the Twenties

The dynamic 1920s were marked by the great diversity in the color scheme resulting from the development of new aniline dyes – the first synthetic dye extracted from coal tar in the mid-19th century. Skins treated with new aniline pigments had bright and even coloration, which did not fade under the influence of elements.

Sensual hues of dramatic earth colors were in vogue, alone or in combination with other shades of the same color. They complemented the fluid, slim silhouette and the supple accessories of the 1920s. Often mixed with the prevalent black, they accentuated the crisp lines of the well-balanced Art Deco designs.

Red became a particular craze in 1926, especially in crocodile clutches: wine, crimson and scarlet. Those ultra-chic evening bags were crafted of precious java-lizard and lustrous red crocodile. So delicious!

Extremely collectible are the pieces from the superb gift collection of colored crocodile handbags imported from France by Saks Fifth Avenue in December 1926: *"When crocodile bags turn to soft pastel shades, it's not only news – it's good news!"*

1920s fashion and color ads. **Top left:** *Montgomery Wards Catalog,* 1928-1929. **Top right:** *Harper's Bazaar,* March 1924. Bottom left: *Vogue* 1926. **Bottom right:** *Vogue* 1926.

Saks Fifth Avenue colored alligator handbags ad, *New York Times,* December 7, 1927.

Museum-quality, Art Deco crocodile clutches from 1924-1925, in status black and red.

The assortment consisted of astounding, totally decadent soft pouches, clutches and envelopes in luscious green, immaculate beige, and luminous silver-gray crocodile. Lined in peach satin, framed in gilt, and outfitted with gem clasps, tiny watches and extra vanity pockets—with generously sized coin purses and mirrors—they cost a fortune in the 1920s, from $58.50 to $95!

Poetic Pastels of the Thirties

Realistic by day and romantic by night, the mode of the 1930s moved to a relaxed dress in pastel chiffons and linens. The season of 1937–1938 became a trendsetter, insisting on radiant palettes for day and night. Softly bright, unafraid colors of spring flowers were transferred onto printed silks and cottons, in Europe and America, by Chanel and Lanvin. Tantalizing Fuchsia Pink and Butter Yellow combinations by Molyneux; Sky-Blue and Red-Wine by Hattie Carnegie; as well as a whiff of Russian Violet and a tinge of Mimosa by Patou and Lelong—all looked very attractive. Especially romantic was the combination of black with pink, a tender young shade of sweetheart roses—Schiaparelli's favorite.

Echoing the trend, a demand had developed for pastel-colored skin handbags. A remarkable domestic maker, Koret, Inc., took the lead by introducing a vast collection of new, chic crocodile handbags in festive colors. Crocodiles, once exclusively a fall and winter fashion, became a year-round classic. *"One of the smartest ideas to pop out of Palm Beach this season was wearing of polished colored crocodile,"* paired with matching crocodile shoes and belts, as advertised by Koret, Inc. The company was very passionate about the new trend: *"…No other leather takes such true, rich tones…Neither spring showers nor strenuous wear dims or dents their hardy hides."*

1930s fashion and color ads. **Top left:** Patou dress ad, *Vogue* March 1, 1938. **Top right:** Chanel suit and hat ad, *Vogue* January 15, 1937. **Bottom left and right:** Fashion ads, *Vogue* March 15, 1938.

Koret colored alligator handbags ad (Bonwit Teller, Spring 1935 Shades Collection). Presented are Cruiser Blue, Flowerpot Red, Grass Green, English Parchment, Tunisian Brown, Demi-tasse Brown.

Between 1935 and 1938, Bonwit Teller sold about sixty different styles by Koret made of supple Mexican crocodile in unbelievable designer colors: Cruiser Blue, Wine, Flowerpot Red, Grass Green, English Parchment, Midnight Navy, Tunisian Brown, Mahogany-Red, Classic Beige, Spring Maple, Maple Sugar, Fancy Blond, Brick Rose, Cornflower Blue, Cherry Sauce, Butternut Brown, Light Brown, and classic black. Particular attention was paid to a chic Poison Yellow, which nicely harmonized with any other color: *"A golden shade in the new brown-beige. Incomparable with black, brown, wine. Good with gray – sheer poetry with green. More practical even than black."* That wonderful collection included double-zipper underarms, softly shirred dressmaker bags, top-handles, link chains, and enormous Schiaparelli-types with leather linings, sold for affordable $10–$58 a piece. Today, those gems are priceless.

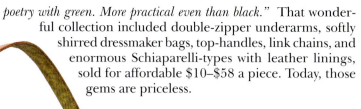

Fun, multi-colored exotic skin barrel-bag. Picturesque combination of natural water-snake, olive java-lizard, yellow ring-lizard, and orange-coral leather. Great presence! Leather-lined. Fine quality! (W 9-inch at the widest points, 6 ½ -inch wide body by H 5 ½ -inch by D 5-inch). Ca 1930s.

"Unexpected Colors in Unaccustomed Places" of the Forties

In February 1940, Carmel Snow—editor of Harper's Bazaar—broadcasted from Paris: *"There's a new kind of coquetry – the utmost feminine guile to hold the eyes of one man, rather than catch the eyes of many."* That new, "gentlewoman" look was captured by Bonwit Teller in their disarming accessories created in a quiet, ultra-sophisticated palette. The new darks— deeply muted earth tones and plumage colors—were truly marvelous. Sophisticated, shiny crocodile bags in warm, subdued gray, brown and beige—large and soft, generously draped with pleats in a multitude of ladylike styles—appeared to underline the simple elegance of a newly narrow silhouette.

Yet, the somber color withdrawal caused by the turmoil of World War II did not last long. In September 1940, a group of leading retailers—Saks Fifth Avenue, Neiman Marcus, Bonwit Teller, and Lord & Taylor— originated a new trend of wearing bold-red, all wrapped up in a spacious alligator satchel. Navy became particularly fashionable in 1941, in a mix with red and yellow. Smashing crocodile handbags in fabulous Epaulet Yellow or Carnation Red were designed by Mark Cross to accompany those navy outfits: *"Wear them with navy blue, like a smart young officer on dress parade."*

1940s fashion and color ads. **Top left:** Schiaparelli fashion ad, *Vogue* March 15, 1940. **Top right:** Fashion ad, *Vogue* 1944. **Bottom left:** Fashion ad, *Vogue* October 15, 1941. **Bottom right:** Fashion ad, *Vogue* September 15, 1940.

The combination of black with brilliant rainbow colors was another popular concept of the 1940s. Purses, gloves, belts and sling-back platforms (in fire orange, hypnotic red, paradise pink, or ming-blue) were thrown together with dark-colored garments – to shock you outright! Our lavish Mexican crocodile handbag from that era, built around a stunning faux tortoise frame, is quite impressive on its own. But, go on, open it—and, surprise, surprise! Fully lined in outrageously "loud" fuchsia leather, it is so decadent! Crafted per order for an important customer, it cost a fortune over sixty years ago. Today, be prepared to shed thousands for it!

The mid-1940s literally exploded with a burst of color. Fashion magazines showed loads of affordable exotics from South America in vibrant colors, as Macy's advertised in 1944: *"Spring colors – brilliant as gems! Each wonderful, slithery skin has been polished until it looks back at you. Imagine being able to reach out and touch it – for 19.98!"*

1950s fashion and color ads. **Top left:** *Nettie Rosenstein dresses ad, Vogue* September 1, 1950. **Top right:** Fashion ad, *Vogue* March 1954. **Bottom left:** Fashion ad, *Vogue* March 1 1952. **Bottom right:** Fashion ad, *Vogue* March 1, 1950.

Right: Super rare, museum-quality, genuine alligator arm-purse, adorned by a distinct, molded Bakelite frame, with a front adornment. Unique, split arm-handle; bold, intriguing design. Loud, Schiaparelli-fuchsia leather interior! Gold-trimmed interior, complete with accessories. (W 11-inch by H 8 ¼-inch without handle by D 3-inch). One-of-a-kind, indeed! Ca 1946-1948.

Color Drama of the Fifties

By the early 1950s, the "Genie of Color" was let out of the bottle. Amazingly, during that period of the Cold War, which was full of dark fears and paranoia, fashion was saturated with a cacophony of colors.

Fashion editorials shared how particularly electric the 1950 couture was: the shock of color from Schiaparelli; Ripe Apricot from Nettie Rosenstein; and delicious Pink Champagne—as the premier evening brilliance. Breathtaking evening gowns in couture pink, turquoise and tangerine came along as the ultimate night-time glamor, matched with pastel exotics.

White became the "after dark" color, shown in Dior's collections: *"Purely chalk white. No colors, no contrasts, no interruptions."* Lucille de Paris and Nettie Rosenstein offered a new assortment of swan-white ostrich and croc wonders.

Strong, glamorous colors appeared side by side with delicate pastels in Dior's 1952 collection of crepe sweater-dresses, completed with a pair of kid gloves, a brimless straw hat and satin mules—all in a matching, solid color—and accompanied by a roomy alligator handbag in a soft, pastel shade.

In 1958, red became as important as ever: *"Fifties style was red in everything but its politics"* (Anna Johnson). New shades of Revlon Fire or Chevrolet Red were worn with great panache.

Collection of colorful handbags, from the 1950s. **Pink:** Lovely, suede-n-snakeskin frame-bag, with a top skin handle and gilt trim, leatherette-lined. (W 11-inch by H 7-inch by 3-inch). Signed: Stylecraft Miami. **Turquoise:** Sleek, genuine karung clutch. Retractable top handle, lined in champaign satin. (W 12 ½-inch by H 6-inch by D 3-inch). Signed: Palizzio Very New York. **Black:** Different, tegu-lizard satchel, lined in sunflower-yellow leather. Molded, hard-shaped body. (W 11-inch by H 7-inch by d 3-inch). Signed: Sydney of California. **White:** Fashionable, leather clutch printed with lizard pattern. Huge gold-nugget detail, accented with a large, faux pearl. Removable, metal-and-plastic shoulder strap; Leatherette-lined. (W 9 ¼-inch by H 7-inch; nugget is 2 ½-inch by 2-inch). Signed: Martin Van Schaak New York. **Navy Blue:** Silk cocktail purse, with bejeweled silver frame. Signed: Martin Van Schaak New York. **Coral:** Roomy, genuine alligator satchel. Leather-lined, accessories. (W 11 ½-inch by H 8 ¼-inch by D 3-inch). Signed: Andrew Geller.

THE STREAK DRESS OF TWEED... SHORT YOUNG SUIT WITH A BUTTON SWITCH

New suit mainstay.

Black & White – status symbol '68

Best & Co.
FIFTH AVENUE · NEW YORK

PALE WOOLS FOR DAY — OVERBLOUSED, SIDE-BUTTONED

1960s fashion and color ads. **Top left:** *Vogue* September 15, 1964. **Top right:** *Harper's Bazaar* Sept 1968. **Bottom left:** *Vogue* 1962. **Bottom right:** *Vogue* Sept 15, 1964.

Brilliant Palettes of the Sixties

In the 1960s, the color drama of previous decades was transformed into richness of saturated palettes—to emphasize the simplicity of its uncluttered, architectural flare. Designers were mixing solid colors into unexpected combinations of new, complex shades.

Simply adorable was the color group called 'Violine'—not a musical instrument, but rather a glowing spectrum of amethyst notes running from rosy violet to misty lavender, from ripe plum to dark eggplant. In 1960, Bergdorf Goodman sold stunning Lucille de Paris alligator satchels in royal purple for $225.

Skins were produced in a remarkable array of greens and blues—bright to mist—and their intriguing new mixes, such as Bermuda Teal by Lucille de Paris. The new darks in handbags included Cardin's black tulip—the darkest green-to-black. Among newcomers, a tender willow-green as well as a shocking peacock-green made their debut.

Noted once again was the undying power of red. Used alone or in new fascinating mixtures, it ranged from ruby red to raspberry; autumn red to berry-red; screaming azalea pink—Judith Leiber style—to the softest shade of Chanel geranium pinks.

The color grouping was very innovative. Red tweeds were accessorized by Lesco handbags in brown, amber and gold. Greens were matched with gold purses. Alligator in reds were terrific with amethyst and emerald tweeds. The subtle interplay of brown and black was the autumn mood of lavishness; whereas the elegant, immaculate look in monotone beige was prevalent for spring.

The fresh look of Twiggy and Courreges haute couture blazed onto the fashion scene in the mid 1960s. It brought the purest colors; the prettiest lines; and over-the-shoulder bags in the newest turtle skin gleaming in young cornflower blue and raspberry, along with turquoise and coral.

Classic black-and-white duo, by Martin Van Schaak, from the 1960s. **Left:** Elegant, white lizard-print leather tote. Four jeweled ornaments (gold-plated, off-white enamel, with dozens of glistening rhinestones). Spectacular! Leatherette-lined. (W 9 ½ -inch by H 14-inch). **Right:** Timeless, black shark-printed leather, with patent-leather handles, accented with two gold-plated ram-ornaments. Amazing, 3-D effect, and handmade quality! Leather-lined. (W 10 ¾ -inch by H 15-inch with the handles).

The pristine, classic combination of black and white hit a note of harmony in 1968, and became the very spirit of the fashion of the 1960s.

Group of spectacular 1960s exotics, in rainbow colors. **Left:** Pretty, genuine alligator skin Kelly-style purse, in petal-pink, with long shoulder strap, a lock and clochette with a key. Lined in metallic-pink leather. (W 8 ½ -inch by H 11-inch by 3 ½ -inch D). Signed: Sharif USA Genuine Alligator. **Center top:** Unique, teal crocodile satchel by Lucille de Paris. **Right:** Burgundy crocodile frame-bag, France. Center bottom: Dramatic, royal-purple caiman clutch, lined in matching leather, with gilt trim. Labeled: Olop, Milano Italy.

CHAPTER SIX
THREE HOW-TO'S

"Don't Judge A Book by Its Cover"

HOW TO BUY

Buying collectible vintage from reputable sources has always been the safest option, yet the most expensive one. Not long ago, the supply of fine vintage was limited exclusively to live auctions, estate sales, antique stores, and vintage boutiques run by experts. Today, when vintage has become a fashion necessity, buying opportunities are endless.

You can find a gorgeous alligator bag at a flea market or a garage sale, a thrift store, a charity store, or a consignment shop. Or, buy it online. Unfortunately, you cannot always rely on the opinion of an online seller, especially when it comes to the value or the condition, because very few of them specialize in vintage exotics.

Regardless of whether or not you're a serious collector, a fashionista looking for a funky piece to wear, or a dealer searching for good inventory at affordable prices, what you need is a buying strategy—and, simple safety tips:

Tip 1: Preferably, buy brand-name bags to avoid imitations.

Tip 2: Inspect the bag for authenticity to make sure it is genuine skin, not embossing.

Tip 3: Inspect it for flaws to assure best possible condition, which determines the price.

It is safer to buy vintage in person. Online auctions and sales are usually non-refundable. Thus, it is almost impossible to correct a judgment mistake after the fact. Since people see things differently, it is unlikely that an online dealer has the same standards as you do. To avoid disappointment and to match your expectations, be prepared to ask a lot of questions.

Popular collectibles are often over forty years old; therefore, it is unrealistic to expect the pieces advertised as 'mint' or 'excellent' to look "like new." Needless to say how important it is to know the condition criteria and inspection tips —in order to make the correct buying decision. The following criteria will help you to properly assess the condition of the bag when buying online.

Condition Criteria

Mint: rare; no visible signs of use or age; no repair; no odor; original packaging or tags

Near mint: quite rare; clean, intact; no visible flaws or repair; minor clean-up; odor-free

Excellent: no noticeable wear or flaws; if any, very minor; refurbished; clean, no odor

Very good: minor wear and flaws; no cracks/dryness/rips/tears/odor; clean interior

Good: some wear; few minor flaws that have been mended; interior may have marks

Fair: wearable with flaws; may have mended or replaced parts; cleanable; faint odor

Poor: dry rot, tear, significant wear, broken parts, odor; beyond repair

The price you pay should always reflect the condition of the bag. Do not buy lesser than 'excellent' for your collection, or lesser than 'good' for use. Before making your buying decision, double-check the seller's standards by asking her specific questions about the condition, using our inspection tips provided below.

Inspection Tips

Exterior

- Check the shape of the bag for damage. Does it stand on its own? Does it stand straight? Is there any deformity?
- Check for missing or altered parts (handle, clasp, decorations, and accents).
- Inspect the front and back skins for dry rot and surface damage (glaze loss, pealing or bubbling, rubbed spots, edge wear, cracks, tear, breaks, etc).
- Inspect the skins for darker spots or discoloration. If you see obvious, massive darker spots on brown skins, it could be dry rot—leather cancer. **Note:** Old, dried-out glue often leaves darker residue on light-colored skins on the bottom or edges, which is acceptable if they are minimal and do not affect the general appearance of the bag.
- Inspect the edges and corners for wear, separation, dye loss, cracks and tear.
- Inspect the seams and stitches for strength, separation, or breaks.
- While the bag is opened, thoroughly inspect the gussets (sides) from inside out. Major problems like dry rot or tear very often occur on those parts.
- **Important!** If you see bad wear spots, gently flex the skin to check for cracks between the scales. If the skin is torn, cracked or feels dry, most likely the bag is damaged by dry rot and cannot be "rescued." Do not buy it!
- Check the bottom to see if it is intact.

Handle

- Check the handle for wear, tear and cracks, especially at the base where it is attached to the body by D-rings. The handle that is visibly torn at the base undermines the value and must be repaired or replaced.
- Insignificant wear (loss of dye) on the edges does not hurt the bag.
- Thoroughly inspect every wear spot for surface cracks by gently flexing it. A handle with only one significant crack undermines the value and must be repaired or replaced.
- Check the rivets and D-rings to see if they are intact.

Interior

- Check the clasp to see if it's in perfect working order. Open and close the bag several times for confirmation.
- Thoroughly inspect the frame for bends, corrosion, or any other damage. Check the hinges to see if they work properly.
- Inspect metal fixtures for rust and loss of plating.
- Check if the interior is fresh. Musty and cigarette odors are difficult to get rid of.
- Inspect it for wear, stains and spots.
- Check every pocket and zipper to see whether or not they are intact.

Do not feel uncomfortable using these inspection tips and condition criteria when buying in person or online. Ask questions of the online sellers to confirm whether their condition description matches your expectations. Be an educated buyer and use caution, and you will not be disappointed with your purchase.

In addition, if buying online, ask the seller to pack the bag properly and carefully to assure its safe delivery by mail. Vintage bags are fairly fragile and can be easily destroyed in transit, if packed insufficiently. Below, please see a list of common shipping problems and some recommendations on how to avoid them by assuring proper packing.

Shipping Damage
- Collapsed or crushed body due to lack of stuffing or outside protection
- Freshly broken seams due to lack of stuffing and outside protection
- Freshly broken handles due to insufficient protection
- Bent handles due to tight shipping box

The most secure way to ship is to double-box the bag in a strong, two-piece box padded with peanuts in a larger shipping box. If not available, follow the packing procedures developed over the years specifically for mail order service.

Packing
- Slightly stuff the bag with tissue to preserve its shape and protect from collapsing or crushing in transit. **Important**: Do not use heavy paper or newspaper. Do not overstuff!
- If there is no dust bag, carefully wrap the bag in several sheets of acid-free tissue, and then cover it loosely with bubble wrap to give additional protection. **Important:** Never use plastic bubble wrap directly on the skin without tissue paper. It can fuse into the skin and damage it badly, if shipping during the hot summer.
- Pick a large shipping box with a lot of room left on each side of the bag.
- Put the bag flat and pad it with peanuts to protect from crushing or heat damage.

You can ship by traceable Insured USPS Priority with delivery confirmation, UPS, or FedEx. Regardless the carrier, be sure to have your precious bag insured and packed properly and securely, to protect your investment in full.

Alteration and Counterfeit
If buying online, beware of altered vintage and counterfeit. Remember that original vintage by prominent designers is normally stamped by the brand's logo. Some handbags could also have a fabric label with the name of a store. Such fabric labels are usually sewn into the interior seam, not glued. If you see a glued-on label, check the name against the list of makers and department stores provided in this book. The only well-known maker to use glued-on labels in alligator bags was Sterling U.S.A. If the name you're checking is not listed or sounds unfamiliar, most likely the label was added later, and the handbag is not original vintage.

Once in a while, you will come across a handbag crafted recently with the idea to imitate original collectible vintage. It can

be a new handbag made to look like vintage; or an inexpensive second-hand changed to look like a valuable collectible. Pieces of accenting skins (new or cut from old, unrepairable bags), or other materials, such as fur and feathers, could be glued or stitched to the existing parts of such a bag originally made of leather, plastic, metal or fabric.

Some vintage handbags can also have replaced handles or adornments. Metal and plastic chains or belts, as well as faux alligator belts are often used to replace broken handles. A number of decorations—pins, watches, rhinestones, or faux gems (new, vintage, or antique)—can be glued directly to the skin, the frame, the handle or any other part. Sometimes, such decorations could be used to distract from existing flaws.

To see if the accents on your handbag is original or not, check how it is attached. On originals, rhinestone or beaded decorations are usually bezel-, prong-, or pave-set on a frame or a clasp (Harry Rosenfeld, Koret, Lucille de Paris, etc.). Only the handbag jewelry by Martin Van Schaak is attached directly to the skin. Although, not by glue, but rather by means of special holders on the back of the ornament, inserted through the perforated opening in the skin, prior to stitching the exterior and interior together.

It is important to understand the difference between original vintage and altered vintage, because any alteration usually reduces the price and could compromise the classic appearance of original vintage. It is up to you to decide whether to buy it or not. Some customers, especially inexperienced ones, find such bags attractive. Dedicated collectors and fashion experts believe in preserving the purity and stylistic integrity of original vintage. They value its historic importance and appeal, and do not compromise.

Unless an altered handbag is something really fantastic and special, its value is lower than that of a true vintage in original, unmodified condition. For educational purposes, we have put together a couple of examples of handbags with replaced handles and added accents. Enjoy viewing them and studying.

Right: Unfortunately, when I found this roomy Lucille de Paris alligator satchel, its handles were badly cracked and broken; and its corners and edges showed some wear associated with age and use. To bring it back to life, I refurbished it with the Apple leather cleaner and conditioner, and also polished its dull, tarnished hardware. After cleaning and conditioning, I applied a touch of Meltonian brown polish to the corners of the bag, to restore some loss of color. Now, it looks smooth, pliable, and healthy! I also replaced the broken skin-handles with the beautiful vintage plastic-n-brass straps. It took a while to find several perfect necklaces and belts, in order to create the straps that complement the handbag in style, color, and quality. But, in the end, I'm quite happy with the final result! (W 11 ¼ -inch by H 9-inch by D 2 ¾ -inch; 31-inch long straps).

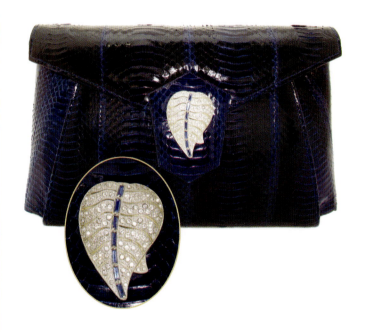

Opposing page:

Top left: I bought this genuine vintage ostrich piece several month ago, for a very good price, without knowing its brand. What attracted me was its classic style of a 1950s frame-bag; and also the desirable color of the skin: bridal white!
You can only imagine how pleasantly surprised I became when I opened its classy-beige leather interior to find a famous Deitsch-dragon logo. Unfortunately, the handle didn't really look very well in person, there were small tears at the base. They were the type that, so innocent-looking at first, would later turn into serious cracks and tears. Since the handbag was initially intended as a summer-wedding piece, I decided to replace its damaged handle with a beautiful, beaded strap, and accent it with a matching front jewel, in order to create an elegant, special-occasion look. I spent about a week searching eBay for the right vintage pin, in white-and-black, with matte surface and no shine – to go well with the matte texture of the ostrich skins. I was very lucky to find strands of glass beads in different colors, with shiny brass hardware. I braided three black strands with three white strands together, into a luscious, 20-inch-long beaded shoulder strap. How divine! Very carefully, I attached the pin to the front relief seam, right under the frame. Here we go – a new, trendy purse is born! (W 10 ½ – inch by H 8-inch by D 3-inch).

Top Right: It happens so often that exceptionally strong, well-made, vintage skin handbags can be found today with badly damaged handles. Such a disappointment! Like this gorgeous, top-quality, very well-cared-for piece from the 1950s, possibly by Lesco, that was so well-preserved when I found it. It even included the original, unwrapped mirror, and a coin purse. Such strong, pliable, healthy skins on its body, with not a touch of dryness, whatsoever! But, the handle was so badly destroyed that there was absolutely no chance to save it. The brightly-polished, shiny hardware of the piece, as well as its unusual shade of brown – both difficult to match if replacing with a metal strap, or a skin belt – gave me an idea to look for an unusual replacement, such a strap made of wood. I spent some time searching for the 1970s "hippie-look" belt, and finally I'd found this impressive, wood-link belt that was long enough to have a strap made of it. Outstanding quality! This wonderful, rescued handbag measures W 11-inch by H 6 ½ -inch by D 3 ½ -inch, with 29-inch long strap. Such an interesting, unorthodox look!

Bottom Left: Quite often, you can find a variety of flamboyant snakeskin handbags made by J. Renee in Hong Kong or China. The company has been in operation since the late 1970s, and their current production can be purchased in various stores all across the country. Their older pieces from the 1980s are quite popular on eBay, but not collectible, as yet. Very often, they're sold with various pins added by a seller, like the featured sapphire-blue cobra clutch. It has a vintage, 1950s rhinestone pin attached by superglue to the skin of the pull. Quite impressive, it was sold as vintage "Art Deco", which, of course, is not the case, because it was made in the 1980s, and its vintage pin was added in 2009. (W 12 ½ -inch by H 7 ½ -inch by D 2 ½ -inch). Signed: J. Renee Made in Hong Kong. Ca 1980s.

Bottom Right: This trendy, tegu-lizard shopper by Palizzio is an example of a creative and effective approach to refurbishing vintage. Made in the early 1960s, this capacious, yet stylish shoulder bag looks quite modern! Clean lines of its uncluttered design are complemented by the textured look of the added leather-n-metal belt. Quite a successful marriage of function and style! Lined in tan leather, with an original coin purse. (W 12-inch by H 8 ½ -inch by D 3 ¾ -inch).

Where to Buy
"Where There's a Will, There's a Way"

As discussed, you can buy an older skin handbag at vintage or antique retail stores, wholesale outlets, estate or garage sales, live or online auctions, and Internet sites. In this book, however, you will not find any specific recommendations or promotions. I firmly believe that it is up to a buyer to decide which source is the best for her. But, I'll be thrilled to share a couple of tips that could be helpful in your search for a perfect bag for the right price.

Because it is crucial to feel and touch the skin before purchasing a handbag—to be absolutely sure that it is authentic, healthy, flexible, and free of dry rot—the best practice is to buy in person. Scout local estate and garage sales, flea markets, vintage trade shows, charity and thrift shops, antique stores, and vintage boutiques—all the places where you can carefully inspect items for damage.

Take your time while checking the skins for cracks and tears, and make your decision based on the condition criteria and inspection tips provided in the previous chapters. The prices are fairly affordable (in comparison with thousands of dollars you would pay for a new alligator purse in a fine department store or a designer boutique, and often you can find a bargain. Check your local stores periodically, as they restock weekly.

Consult one of the best sources on vintage and designer resale boutiques in the United States: *Retro Chic*, a book by Diana Eden and Gloria Lintermans. It provides short profiles and contact information on hundreds of highly reputable domestic dealers.

Additionally, some leading vintage boutiques operate specialty Internet sites, where they offer a wide variety of quality merchandise for safe online purchasing. They offer a wonderful selection of affordable, authentic vintage and antique merchandise at great prices, as well as expert advice accessible by computer from any part of the world.

While buying online from specialty sites, remember that one reason to buy vintage is its relative affordability. Check their merchandise to determine if it is priced fairly. Most online dealers buy their inventory on eBay, for less. So can you.

Quite often a handbag purchased on eBay requires some repair, but you can always find a great bargain, as dealers do. After basic TLC, such bags are frequently resold for about 2- to 5-fold of their eBay price. Why pay $2K for a common, mass-produced bag if you can buy on eBay a similar one for about $400? Professional refurbishing would cost you additional $100, but in the end you could have a beautiful, classic piece for $500. That's a bargain.

Internet auction sites merely provide cyberspace to various individuals to list their items. They do not verify the authenticity of their merchandise, and do not guarantee their promises. Some auction sites have a feedback forum with individual comments left by buyers. Be aware that some positive reports could be "planted" by the sellers' associates and the negative comments by their competitors.

Be especially cautious when dealing with individual sellers from overseas. Always pay by a credit card. Under federal law, you can dispute a charge in cases of non-delivery or gross misrepresentation. If you do decide to try anyway, be prepared to ask as many questions as possible to determine the true condition of the handbag and its authenticity. Do not rely on the product description blindly. Quite often, vendors do not have enough knowledge or they are simply unable to provide an objective description. Therefore, authenticity could be misrepresented and the flaws could be significantly understated. Mint condition is an incredibly rare occurrence. In reality, a handbag advertised as "mint" could probably be of lesser condition.

Be skeptical of auctions that describe ordinary-looking bags as "rare". Check the seller's credentials and the provenance of the item to confirm its rarity.

Online auction prices are absolutely unpredictable and vary from vendor to vendor. It is not easy to navigate the online auction waters. There are many nuances and selling strategies you must be aware of. Some sellers list with no reserve, others with very high reserves. There's also a Buy Now option.

It is important to know the approximate value of the item before you bid; do not to get carried away in a bidding war. Online auctions can easily become a playground for gambling, if you don't know exactly what you are looking for.

If a valuable vintage piece is offered for a low opening bid, find out if the seller is a specialist. A low opening bid could be a selling strategy to attract bidders a; or it could be a "too-good-to-be-true" deal.

To tell the difference, you need to see how the bidding is going and know the bag's value and the seller's credentials. Don't get too excited when you see a "popular" bag with a lot of bids. Numerous bids do not necessarily mean the bag is a catch.

Before placing your final bid, be sure the handbag is a valuable investment by asking questions and doing your homework. The real bidding war starts a couple of hours before the auction ends, sometimes in the last minutes or even seconds.

If you want to get a valuable item, stay cool and do not get overly excited. Set a limit—the highest amount you can pay at the moment. Online auctions work like gambling. There is always a danger to overextend yourself by bidding too high.

Check Internet sites that provide automatic bidding services for a small fee. Use common sense along with the online auction tips and price guide.

Before placing your bid, make sure that the-

- Vendor specializes in vintage exotic skin bags and has the feedback reflecting that
- Bag is genuine skin, not embossed leather or vinyl
- Bag is genuine alligator or crocodile skin, not turtle or lizard
- Bag has an original handle and accents
- Bag has not been altered (no glued-on pins, replaced handles, etc.) unless stated otherwise
- Bag has not been extensively repaired to "fix" serious flaws (minor cleaning and refurbishing is okay)
- Vendor is willing to answer your questions quickly, honestly and professionally

HOW TO CARE

"Better Safe, Than Sorry"

Classic leathers are gorgeous, luxurious, precious, and very tough. But even a strong vintage skin bag must be treated with care and stored properly to prolong its life and protect your investment.

This is a funny story by an unidentified contributor to an internet blog:

In 1958, when I left for college, my father presented me with an elegant black alligator box purse. I felt so sophisticated and loved to open it as the lining was bright red leather. Years later when alligators became endangered, I put the purse away…And there it stayed until the afternoon I found it in the toilet bowl. The result of my efforts to potty-train my young son? The bottom of the purse had turned white. But to my considerable surprise, it cleaned easily. Forty years have passed and my alligator purse is still elegant on my closet shelf.

Good for her! She managed to rescue her treasure from the toilet, just in time. If you personally do not want to take any risk with precious handbags, follow our useful tips on how to take care of them properly.

If you keep your collection at home, consider including them in your homeowner's insurance. Determine replacement value and take pictures to document items in detail.

Store your bags flat, in strong two-piece boxes, wrapped in clean flannel dust bags. Do not bend the handles! Let them lie flat, fully extended. Slightly stuff the bags with clean, acid-free tissue to preserve the shape. Keep the boxes with bags away from heat, moisture, freezing temperatures, direct sunlight, and dust. Do not use plastic bags for storage. Like furs, skins need air space. Deprived of oxygen, they might go through color change.

The general care rule is to leave your alligator bags alone. Most of them have a protective finish and merely need occasional wiping and conditioning, plus professional refurbishing every couple of years. Polishes, even the gentlest ones, build up on alligator skin and dull the finish. If you just can't resist polishing, use special neutral cream designed specifically for alligator skin care.

It is important to dust your bags regularly and wipe off oily fingerprints after use. Dry rot—leather cancer—occurs when greasy dust clogs up the skin pores and traps bacteria and moisture inside, enabling mildew or rot to grow and cause deterioration of the skin.

On colored skins, it shows in the form of darker, brittle spots. On black ones, it is virtually invisible. But don't get fooled by its "innocent" appearance. Contact with moisture or an impact can cause it to break and leave ugly tears and cracks, which cannot be mended. Once the bag is damaged by dry rot, it's gone. That is why it is crucial to inspect every bag before purchasing. You can easily detect brittle, damaged areas by touching and flexing the skin.

Avoid extreme temperatures, especially in hot summer or freezing winter, along with excessive dryness or moisture from rain. Doing so will help retain the skin's flexibility. Remember that dryness can cause it to crack. Avoid moisture because it will cause the skin to swell, mildew and eventually stiffen as it dries out. Water spotting is a particular problem on high-gloss finishes. If your alligator bag does get wet, wipe it dry fast with a soft cloth and allow it to air-dry naturally, away from any heat source.

Never load your vintage bag heavily. After all, it was not intended to "haul" half of your household. Also, do not throw it around, because seams weakened by age could easily break on impact. In short, treat it gently, with respect. It is worth doing so!

When displaying your collection in curio cabinets, use low-wattage bulbs to avoid heat damage. Remove the bags before you clean the display glass with a product such as Windex, to avoid spotting. Wait until the cabinet airs out before you put the bags back.

Once in a while, your bags will require cleaning and conditioning. Avoid using saddle soup for cleaning. It is not good for alligator or crocodile skins. Never use Windex spray or any other household cleaners that contain chemicals—they will destroy the finish by leaving ugly dull spots. The damage from Windex is permanent and cannot be remedied.

Don't underestimate how important it is to clean the bag before conditioning. In gentle, circular motions, wipe it off

with a soft dry cloth to get rid of dust and oily fingerprints. Take your time and be as thorough as possible. Don't forget metal parts and fixtures.

Wipe the interior with a clean cloth to eliminate dust and dirt, and then refresh it with a leather conditioner. Use a suede-cleaning spray and a brush on suede interiors. However, be very careful when applying any type of spray to your skin bag, as it could damage the finish.

A great trick to loosen a stuck zipper is to rub candle wax over it.

As soon as you are done with the cleaning of the exterior skins, use a conditioner designed specifically for reptile and exotic skins. I like the Apple Leather Care cleaner and conditioner, as well as the DYO reptile conditioner—both can be purchased online. They are free of wax and silicone, and protect skins from drying and cracking without impeding their ability to breathe. Use only a dot of it, by rubbing evenly with the softest cloth you can find. Leave conditioner on for one minute and slightly polish off.

Never use any creams designed for smooth leathers—they could leave streaks on the glossy finish.

Remember that Mink Oil is not recommended for reptile skins. With time, it oxidizes and turns into whitish solid grease, which could clog the pores, and, in turn, promote dry rot. Avoid buying bags treated with mink oil—it is virtually impossible to remove the mink oil deposit from the grooves between the scales.

Never use any household grease to condition your skins—no olive oil or butter, please! I almost had a heart attack when a customer said an "expert" had recommended her to use butter on her skin bag. My first reaction was, *"Salted or unsalted?"* But, seriously, it is not a laughing matter, especially when dealing with such an expensive material.

If you need to slightly freshen up the color of your vintage skin handbag, use the Meltonian shoe polish, which comes in a great array of easy-to-match colors. This excellent, premium-quality product is designed for both smooth-surfaced and grained leathers. To achieve best-lasting result, please use it sparingly.

Cherish your exotic skin purse, clean it, store it properly, and don't ever let your pet or toddler chew on it or play with it—and it will last for generations!

Refurbishing and Restoration

If you found an affordable piece with condition flaws, such as a broken handle or dull skins, don't shy away. A skillful restorer can bring it back to life by replacing the handle and refreshing the skin.

Carefully inspect the body of the bag—especially the gussets—for dryness, separation, peeling and cracking, by checking worn stress points. Gently flex them to see between the scales. Avoid handbags with torn gussets; they cannot be repaired. Pay close attention to the most vulnerable areas where the handle is attached to the bag. Stay away from dry and brittle skins. If the skins are soft, pliable and full of life—with no cracks, tears, or breaks—buy it.

Tarnished brass hardware can be cleaned and polished. However, it is not recommended buying handbags with corroded or bent frames, or broken clasps and closures. Broken handles can be replaced with new ones made of matching skin or leather, or updated with a stylish chain strap.

One customer shared an interesting story about the beautiful vintage crocodile handbag he purchased for his wife:

Let me share this with you. I bought a '40s Bellestone purse from you for my wife. She complained that

the handle was "old style" in the pocketbook fashion and that wasn't the style nowadays. So after much reflection I looked through my belt rack and found a real croc belt I've had for more than 10 years. After much research I came across a Russian shoemaker. He didn't even speak English, but his wife worked with him in their shop. He took my belt and cut it both in length and width to match the original handle. In fact, when I was relaying my wishes to his wife, she had me spell and pronounce the word "width" several times for her.

The purse looks astounding. The belt matches in every way (color and grain). It now hangs from her shoulder. I tell her friends how it came to be and then turn the strap over to show them the "40" imprinted on it and explain that that is my waist size and now when my wife carries this bag she's carrying a little bit of me with her.

I thought you might enjoy the story and thanks again. I'm sure we'll do business again, God willing.

What a lovely story, indeed! Follow your own sense of style when deciding on a replacement, and be creative.

If replacing the handle of an important handbag, stick to the original design to preserve its historic appeal. Dramatic modification reduces its value considerably.

For skin restoration, hire a person with proven experience. Dull skins can be freshened up, polished, re-dyed, or re-glazed. However, it is important to remember that re-glazing should be used as a last resort, and done by a professional. Applied improperly, directly on dirty skin, the shiny film could soon peal off.

Luckily, the art of restoration has been around for decades. In 1943, women were so conservation conscious that the shoe repair shops across the country were swamped with orders to repair, dye or refurbish older handbags. It was noted that the ladies from the affluent Park Avenue sometimes were waiting in lines to have their imported alligator purses refreshed right next to their "domestics" who also wanted to take care of the purses given to them by their employers a couple of years earlier.

In the 1960s, numerous repair shops, such as Leathercrafts at 62 West 56th Street in New York City, offered refinishing services needed to maintain the beauty of exotic skins. Working from the inside out, they could reline the bag, supply it with a new frame and clasp, or completely restyle it for $7.50, including treatments for drying and cracking, tinting and re-glazing. Today, expert care can be found in every city, in every part of the country; simply check the Internet or the phone book for the best leads.

HOW TO WEAR

"Beauty is in the Eye of the Beholder"

Fashion trends come and go, and it is always a matter of your taste and financial means whether to follow them or not. For years, trend setting has been a prerogative of the wealthy, celebrities and renowned designers. The time has finally come when every woman can be her own designer by wearing quality vintage with her modern wardrobe—to create her personal look. To wear vintage properly, the major rule is not to overdo and use only one or two vintage elements at a time. Avoid looking like a character from a period movie.

Lucille de Paris crocodile Porosus cocktail-purse. 24K-gilt leaves; Venetian silver-glass beads, and sparkling rhinestones (vintage, ca 1958). Chanel black wool-n-chiffon jacket (ca 2002). Swarovski crystal chandelier-earrings (ca 2003). Versace sunglasses. Cache stretch-satin low-riders (ca 2000). Mosell 24K-gilt leaf necklace and bracelet (vintage, 1950s). Coach gold-leather Goddess sandals (2009). Vintage crystal-bead necklace (ca 1950s).

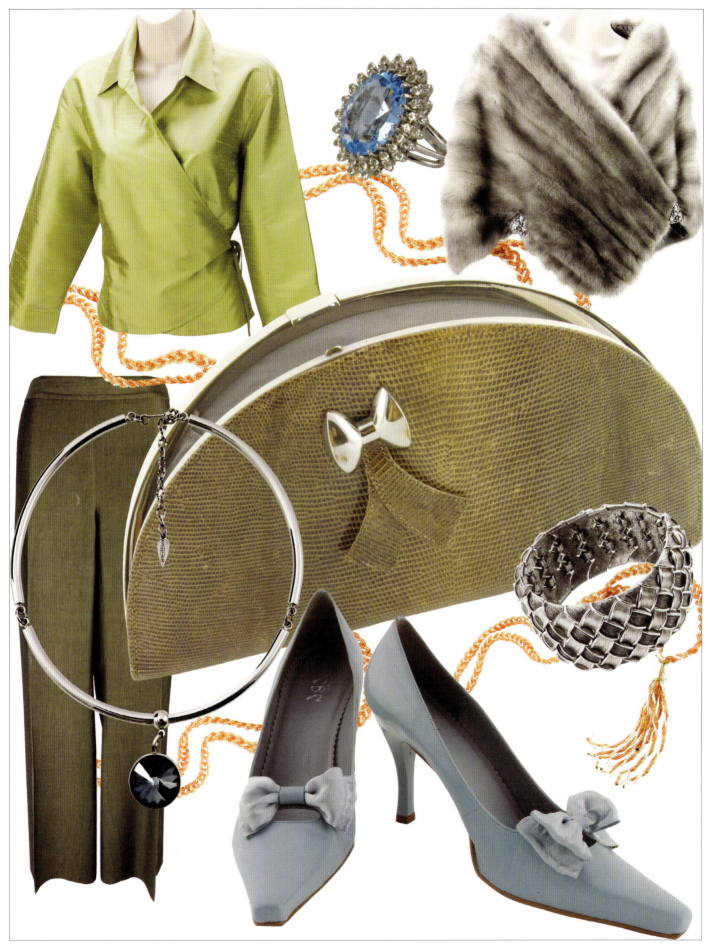

Olive, java-lizard clutch lined with blue satin (vintage, ca 1920s). Ann Taylor raw-silk top and khaki low-riders (ca 2003). Silver-blue mink stole, with 2 jeweled fur-clips (vintage, ca 1940s). Boucher braided cuff-bracelet (vintage, ca 1940s). Panetta sterling aquamarine cocktail-ring (vintage, ca 1950s). BCBG powder-blue leather heels (2004). Whiting & Davis circle choker, with a huge faceted blue rhinestone (vintage, ca 1950s). Long, flapper beaded necklace, with a tassel (vintage, ca 1920s).

To wear vintage properly, the major rule is not to overdo and use only one or two vintage elements at a time. Avoid looking like a character from a period movie.

Rosenfeld black crocodile briefcase, lined with red leather (vintage, ca 1958). Schiaparelli wool-n-leather riding hat (vintage, ca 1960s). Express white wool coat (ca 2005). Hermes silk scarf (ca 2002). Manolo Blahnik leather boots (ca 2005). Hermes leather bracelet (ca 2004). Vintage Cartier sterling-silver watch, with sapphire cabochon and alligator band.

Most important, do not try to match vintage accessories with modern garments; rather, mix and blend. Tasteful coordination of styles from different epochs can be tricky. Therefore, a whimsical touch is always the best icebreaker when unsure.

Rosenfeld chocolate crocodile clutch, with a Bakelite detail (vintage, ca 1940s). Mark Cross yellow crocodile clutch (vintage, ca 1940s). Gucci brown jacket (ca 2001). Pierre Cardin 14K-gold sculptural ring with a genuine gem (vintage, ca 1970s). Murano glass floral necklace and earrings (2001). Michael Kors riding leather boots, Italy (ca 2000). TJ Max floral skirt and brown stretch-satin culottes (ca 2005). Brocade floral top, Italy (ca 2002).

Originality is important. Personally, I feel compelled not to stick to the mainstream when it comes to accessories. The idea of shedding dollars for a purse that any girl can get from a store, regardless of how big of a brand it is, does not excite me at all. If huge, soft handbags were filling the pages of fashion magazines, I would be definitely prancing around with the tiniest, structured one, until it was back in style, only to be swiftly replaced by another one—in complete contradiction with the trend.

When it comes to the purity of the original vintage, there are plenty of options to choose from. Among my favorites are the bags from the late 1950s and early 1960s: sleek and smart, in a great variety of sizes, colors, shapes, and forms. I mix them with Armani, Gucci, and Chanel— just to add spice to their sporty elegance.

My favorite, huge, black alligator frame-bag by Lucille de Paris, ca 1950, is shown with a substantial, yet sophisticated vintage rhinestone dress-clip. It can be safely removed, if you are going for a clean, day-time look, or clipped back on the front pull – to create a sparkling look for a special occasion, or a night out. To accent the elegance of the smooth alligator skin even further, wear it with the heels in textured lizard or snake, in contrasting colors. Absolutely fabulous!

You can also "recycle" beautiful vintage jewelry and use it as handbag jewelry. In order to create a special mood for a special occasion, pick the right clip (fur, dress, scarf, or shoe) and put it on a handbag. It is a fun yet safe way to change the look of a handbag without damaging it. Especially handy are fur and scarf clips, which don't leave any marks on the leather of the handbag. A couple of examples appear here.

A group of vintage skin purses is shown with removable, vintage clips – a great, safe way to spice up their look for special occasions. **Top left:** Saks Fifth Avenue python satchel, (ca 1960s), is marvelous with a whimsical, beetle fur-clip (ca 1930s). **Top right:** Slim Palizzio pouch – in bubblegum pink faux-lizard – from the 1950s, looks opulent with a large, sterling dress-clip accented by faceted amethyst rhinestones (ca 1940s). **Center:** The enormous, quilted red alligator clutch by Deitsch, (ca 1940s), is absolutely stunning with a huge, flower fur-clip, appointed with dozens of shimmering rhinestones, and a bold, ruby glass-jewel (ca 1940s). Bottom left: Rosenfeld ostrich satchel, (ca 1960s), looks quite refined, ornamented by a simple, gilt scarf-clip with a Celtic motif. **Bottom right:** Rich, black crocodile frame-bag, by Saks Fifth Avenue, (ca 1960s), is even more spectacular worn with a rare, black-current Bakelite fur clip, from the 1930s.

When looking for the right handbag, think about the general flavor of the historic period you want to use. They are the Flapper Twenties, Ladylike Thirties, Practical Forties, Glamorous Fifties and Youthful Sixties.

A group of collectible skin purses shown with removable, original vintage clips – a "green" way to utilize your vintage jewelry, in order to create a special, personal look. **Top left:** Petite turtle satchel, by Lucille de Paris, in unexpectedly bright pink, (ca 1960s), looks oh-so-very-pretty, adorned by a glowing moon-glass fur-clip (ca 1950s). **Top right:** This very unusual, "hat-box" wristlet from the 1940s – made of water-snake and black lace – is a gem by itself. But, accented with a rare, antique, Victorian floral clip, made of embossed brass and matte sapphire glass– it becomes a piece of art! **Center:**

Tremendous, ca 1950s shopper by Nettie Rosenstein – in butter-soft, black crocodile – is simply perfect, as is. Yet, in the evening, I dare adding even more character to it. I clip on an enormous, over 6-inch-long, vintage Bird-of-Paradise fur clip by Coro (ca 1940s). **Bottom left:** A classy, pliable brown alligator clutch, (ca 1940s), is jazzed up with an elegant, emerald-rhinestone fur clip. Quiet and sophisticated! **Bottom right:** A trendy, azalea-pink cobra clutch by Palizzio, (ca 1960s), is spiced up by a pair of rhinestone shoe-clips, from the 1920s – for a happy night out!

To create unique style that cannot be replicated, mix the bags of your liking with vintage jewelry, gloves, scarves, or hats from other periods. Beauty is in the eye of the beholder, indeed!

Size Also Matters

In addition to other aspects influencing the value of vintage handbags, there is also the matter of the size. Alligator and crocodile skins are the only leathers sold by the inch or centimeter, and they are valued like diamonds—the larger, the better. The widest part of the skin is measured to establish the price of the handbag.

But not every large alligator bag is automatically more expensive than a smaller one. What also matters is the origin of the skin. Some species are considerably more valuable than others. As a result, a tiny purse made with precious Crocodile Porosus or American Alligator will be more expensive than a briefcase made with inferior caiman.

Two important factors to consider are the skin's pattern and the cut. A symmetrical, central underbelly cut is more expensive than the out-of-pattern, random cut—despite its size. Hence, a smaller bag made with matching symmetrical cuts is more expensive than a larger bag made with random cuts.

The most valuable handbag is made from a central underbelly cut of a valuable species, perfectly matched in grain size and pattern. It could take many years to find in the wild two animals with matching patterns!

Several decades ago, when alligator and crocodile skins were harvested strictly in the wild, genuine skin bags were manufactured in three general sizes, based on the width of the hide: large, over 12-inches; medium, 10- to 11-inches; and small, under 9-inches.

In 1962, a premier domestic maker, Lucille de Paris, produced handbags in five prime sizes: an oversized, 14-inch travel bag for $305; a large, daytime 12-inch shopper for $260; a medium, 11-inch daytime handbag for $185; a demi-sized, 8-inch purse for $99.50; and a petite, 7-inch evening bag for $79.50.

Since the early 1980s, the supply of classic leather no longer depends solely on the wild harvest. The tightly controlled and regulated farming industry has eased the limitations on large, flawless skins needed to create a superior product. Presently, domestic tanneries process alligator skins in six major sizes, from 18 centimeters (7-inch) to 45 centimeters (18-inch) wide.

Adorable, miniature, American Alligator Kelly bag in metallic pink, with gold-plated accents, leather interior and original accessories. Complete with a shoulder strap, lock and clochette with two keys. (W 8 3/4-inch by H 7-inch by 3-inch). Signed: Sharif Made in USA Genuine Alligator. Ca 1980s.

CHAPTER SEVEN
VALUE AND PRICE

One of the most important factors influencing the price of a collectible vintage is its value, which is based on several features outlined below.

More Valuable Features	Less Valuable Features
Genuine skin	Embossed leather or vinyl
Authentic vintage	Recent (after '70s) mass-produced
Original vintage	Altered vintage
Fine collectible	Casual handbag for everyday use
Rare, unusual piece (design and features)	Common, mass-produced vintage
Signed by a recognized designer/maker	Unsigned
Documented provenance*	No provenance
No name of a previous owner **	Stamped by the name of an owner
Excellent original condition	Lesser condition
Rare designer color	Standard black or brown color
Black	Brown
Oversized or miniature	Common medium- or small-sized
Crocodile/alligator skin	Caiman skin
Crocodile/alligator/caiman skin	Lizard skin
Crocodile/alligator skin	Turtle skin
Underbelly skin	Horn-back skin
Belly cut	Tail or flank cut
Symmetrical central cut (Pattern cut)	Outside-the-pattern cut
Whole skins	Patched skins
Suede or leather-lined (day bags)	Leatherette or fabric-lined (day bags)
Satin or moiré-lined (evening bags)	Faille or fabric-lined (evening bags)
Original handle	Replaced handle
Structural, padded handle	Soft handle
Skin-covered frame	Metal frame
Skin gussets	Embossed leather gussets
Skin bottom	Embossed leather bottom
Metal zippers	Plastic zippers
Original condition	Refurbished or repaired condition
Acquired from a specialist	Acquired from a general dealer

*In vintage fashion, a collectible piece with a provenance (documented history of origin and ownership) is more valuable than an ordinary, mass-produced bag without a history. Documented provenance of a vintage handbag may include an original marketing ad, or a purchase receipt with the name of a store, the date of purchase and the original price. It usually increases its selling price.

**Unlike a work of fine art, a vintage handbag stamped by the name of a previous owner is actually less valuable than an unmarked piece, unless it belonged to a celebrity or a dignitary. The reason being is that, in the 1920s-1960s, it was quite common to monogram or sign valuable personal belongings to prevent theft.

PRICE TABLE

As we learned in Chapter 5, the price of a collectible skin handbag depends on the 4 *C*s (condition, circa, craftsmanship/maker, and color), as well as its size. What also matters is where you buy your handbag, because the price from an expert is always higher.

When determining the price of a handbag, compare the features of your handbag with the features presented in the table above. The fewer valuable features your handbag has, the less expensive it should be. If your handbag has most of the 'more valuable features,' outlined in the left column of the table, you have found a treasure. Enjoy it.

The price table below reflects the online and retail prices for vintage designer handbags in mint to excellent condition, purchased from a specialist. The data was accumulated over the last ten years. Less valuable pieces, in lesser condition, purchased from Internet sites, may cost below indicated values.

Note: Prices are in US dollars.

Maker	Skin	Features	Online	Retail
Hermes	alligator, crocodile	rare styles	3,500+	7,000+
	ostrich	novelty	2,500+	4,500+
Gucci	alligator, crocodile	black, brown	850+	1,500+
		colored, novelty	950+	1,700+
	lizard	colored	550+	900+
Judith Leiber	alligator, crocodile	black, brown	750+	1,400+
		colored, jeweled	850+	1,700+
	ostrich	jeweled	700+	1,000+
	lizard, karung	colored	500+	900+
Nettie Rosenstein	alligator, crocodile	black, brown	650+	1,300+
		colored, novelty	750+	1,500+
Rosenfeld	alligator, crocodile	all sizes	600+	1,300+
		novelty	750+	1,500+
	ostrich	any color	450+	800+
Lederer de Paris	alligator, crocodile	all sizes	650+	1,300+
		novelty	750+	1,500+
Lucille de Paris	alligator, crocodile	all sizes	600+	1,300+
		colored, novelty	750+	1,500+
	ostrich	all sizes	400+	800+
Mark Cross	alligator, crocodile	all sizes	600+	1,200+
	ostrich	colored, novelty	500+	1,000+
Koret, Deitsch	alligator, crocodile	black, brown	550+/500+	1,000+
		colored, novelty	600+	1,200+
Coblentz, Rendl	alligator, crocodile	all sizes	600	1,200+
		novelty	650+	1,300+
Evans, Finesse	alligator, crocodile	w/accessories	650+	1,200+
		w/no accessories	500+	950+
Manon	alligator, crocodile	all sizes	500+	950+
		novelty	600+	1,000+
Novelty Bags	alligator, crocodile	signed, unsigned	550+/400+	1,000+/800+

continued on following page

Maker	Skin	Features	Online	Retail
Designer/signed	alligator, crocodile	novelty, colored	450+	900+
	ostrich	novelty, colored	350+	650+
	lizard	novelty, colored	250+	450+
	snakeskin	novelty, colored	150+	300+
Store Brands*	alligator, crocodile	all sizes	400+	900+
	ostrich	colored	300+	600+
	lizard	colored	200+	350+
Bellestone	alligator, crocodile	Belgium	350+	700+
Lesco, Dofan	alligator	novelty, colored	350+	650+
Vassar	alligator	large	450+	950+
		novelty	550+	1,000+
Sterling U.S.A.	alligator	all sizes	300+	600+
		novelty	400+	750+
Prado, Mexico	alligator	black, brown	350+	700+
		colored, novelty	500+	950+
	baby gator, crocodile	novelty	550+	1,000+
South American Import**	caiman, alligator	black, brown	250+	450+
		colored, novelty	300+	600+

Store Brands: Saks Fifth Avenue, Neiman Marcus, I. Magnin, Bonwit Teller, Bergdorf Goodman, etc.
**South American Import: Argentina, Uruguay, Cuba, Brazil*

Important: The prices of some items featured in this book, which are mostly rare, one-of-a-kind objects, are not included in the Price Table above. The level of such prices is established by the condition of the market and the demand. Such museum quality objects are priced at a level higher than the price range of more ordinary examples.

Glorious, alligator cocktail-purse. Accentuated by sixteen garnet cabochons, with gold-plated trim. Single, whole belly-cut of superb symmetry. Leather-lined. (W 7 ¾ -inch by H 5 ½ -inch by D 2 ½ -inch). Signed: Michael's Genuine Alligator. Ca 1980s.

BIBLIOGRAPHY

Books

Bertram, Anne. *Life is Just a Bowl of Cherries (And Other Delicious Sayings)*. NTC Publishing Group, 1997.

Dooner, Kate. *A Century of Handbags*. Schiffer Publishing, Ltd., 1993.

Dubin, Tiffany, and Ann E. Berman. *Vintage Style*. Harper Collins, 2000.

Clayton, Larry. *The Evans Book*. Schiffer Publishing, Ltd., 1998.

Johnson, Anna. *Handbags: The Power of the Purse*. Workman Publishing Company, Inc., 2002.

Sussman, Jeffrey. *No Mere Bagatelles*. New York: Judith Leiber LLC. 2009.

Tolkien, Tracy. *Miller's Handbags: A Collector's Guide*. Octopus Publishing Group Ltd., 2001.

Wilcox, Claire. *Bags*. V&A Publications, 1999.

Wilcox, Claire. *Century of Bags (Icons of Style in the 20th Century)*. Chartwell Books, Inc., 1997.

The Louisiana Fur and Alligator Advisory Council (FAAC)

Export/Import Checklist of HS Codes and Product Codes, AHTN 2007: CITES Section, Wildlife Regulatory Service, Import & Export Division, Agri-Food and Veterinary Authority (AVA)

Periodicals (various back issues)

The New York Times

Vogue

Harper's Bazaar

Merchandise Catalogs (back issues)

Montgomery Ward (1928-1929, 1943, 1953-1954, 1964)

Sears (1897, 1902, 1914-1915)

Sotheby's ("Nothing to Wear" Auction, New York City, April 8, 1998)

INDEX

Abtik, Mexico 187

Alligator Skin, American 3, 37, 96-97, 101, 107, 125-128, 131-136, 141-147, 172-175, 194, 204, 264. Baby 39, 46, 88, 105, 167, 243. Mexican (Baran) 39, 177, 187. Faux (grain, print) 26, 63, 70

American Handbag Designer Award, 79

Andre Courreges 72

Andrea Pfister 67

Andrew Geller 250, 262

Ann Taylor 259

Anna Johnson 11, 250

Anteater Skin 71

Armani 262

Arnold Constable 28, 61, 126, 236

Asprey 66

Authenticity, replica, reproduction, 28. Test 3, 226. Dual signature 146; hallmarks 13; monograms 25, 27, 53

B. Altman & Co. 17, 28, 46, 48, 61, 70, 77, 86, 90, 126, 174, 187

Bag: Aubusson needlepoint 24; boudoir 34; box 48, 112; broken bottom (accordion bottom) 18; carriage 17; club 13, 18, 87; daytime 13, 18, 65, 97, 141,230; dressmaker 185, 235; hobo 178, 202; jewelry box 17, 50; zipper 106; briefcase 90, 133, 161, 179; carryall 17, 108; drawstring 11, 105, 123; Oxford 230; pleated 34, 38, 39, 46, 185; pocketbook 18, 19, 37, 66, 70, 83, 91, 100, 127, 164, 199, 228; portfolio 45; quilted 43, 81, 104; saddle 51, 59, 101, 132, 192; shopper 18, 147, 160, 204, 206, 230; shoulder bag 38, 44, 60, 81, 91, 103, 176, 235; suit 48, 25; swagger 24, 40, 192, 234; swagger pocket 93, 173, 176, 179; tailored 56, 230; trapeze 78; novelty 267

Bakelite 19, 27, 31, 39-40, 42-44, 46, 47, 61, 70, 83, 87, 93, 132, 167, 175, 199, 204, 232, 261, 263

Bass 43

Bellestone 3, 75, 87, 88, 190, 191, 243, 245, 267. Bellestone Bags, Inc. 191127, 175

Bonwit Teller 19, 28, 61, 46, 72, 77, 78, 88, 91, 103, 125, 126, 140, 174, 193, 249

Bergdorf 17, 46, 53, 51, 77, 90, 91, 135, 139, 140, 161, 190

Best & Co. 61, 94

Bienen-Davis 56, 225

Bloomingdale's 17, 46, 61, 8

-Boucher 259

Caiman Skin 3, 7, 31, 42-44, 49, 58, 137, 187, 214, 243

Cartier 7, 36, 260

Celebrities: Audrey Hepburn 6. Bette Midler 109. Elizabeth Hurley 109. Elizabeth Taylor 67. Marlene Dietrich 150. Mary Tyler Moore 109. Naomi Campbell 109. Cindy Crawford 109

Chandler's 46

Chanel 7-9, 26, 28, 30, 33, 73, 74, 248, 258, 262. Coco Chanel 6, 26, 38

Christian Dior 7, 50, 68, 72, 115, 135

Coblentz 3, 38, 76, 46, 62, 69, 72, 75-78, 88, 174, 190, 243, 267. Coblentz, Louis J. 76, 78, 79

Colombetti Milano 223

Construction: Accordion 58, 115; hard-body 98, 118; semi-hard, -rigid 54, 159; tailored 54. Floating hinges 42, 119, 205, 239. Lock, push 40; squeeze 62, 142; slide fasteners 87, 103. Clasp, bamboo 101; wood 49; enameled 93, 94; filigree 88; flip 148; lift 45; lever 79, 94, 141; locking luggage-type 42, 87, 119; brass 204, 206; jeweled 194; Inner-Grip 34. Closure, belted 89; flap-and-belt 133; no-metal 83; pin-closure 186; push-botton 115; side-pull 90; snap 37, 43, 88, 101; zipper ("Hermes closure") 56, 102; folding 52. Bottom 44, 240, 266; expandable 100; felt 47; folding 103; hidden compartment 102; platform 83, 89, 133, 137; protected 77, 78, 88; rocking 61. Front, scalloped 60, 103; flap 85, 142; expandable 132; locking 123; pleated 107, 83. Gussets 24, 28, 34, 36, 240; 4-piece 89; accordion 44, 59, 79, 100, 132, 161; expandable 88, 91; folding 40, 49, 53, 100; leather 201; molded 77, 88, 130, 142, 160, 193, 201; sculptured 78; tailored 90, 147, 162; triangular 85; square 46. Interior 27, 37, 40, 239; chamois 87; lambskin 101, 105; tailored 100, 196, 89; kidskin 118; three-compartment 88; wide-split 170; taffeta 44, 47; suede 49; vinyl 49; rayon faille 36, 47, 96, 125; built-in mirror 27

Convention for International Trade in Endangered Species (CITES) 212, 216

Corde 39

Council of Fashion Designers of American Lifetime Achievement Award 106

Courreges 251

Craftsmanship 3, 239

Crocodile Skin 3, 99, 108, 112, 129, 195, 212, 248. Nile 17, 18, 160. Porosus 25, 47, 57, 62, 77, 84, 90, 100, 115, 129, 135, 146, 151, 201. Baby Porosus 89, 103, 116, 120, 130, 150, 162. American 208. African 49. Javanise 119. Madagascar 119. Hornback crocodile 13, 18, 28, 233; faux 57; crocodile-grain 28, 94;

Crouch & Fitzgerald 92, 138

Darby Scott 10

De Lumur 47, 243, 246

Deauville Bags 93; Deauville, Inc. 113

Decorations: Timepiece 56, 58, 96, 114, 118, 121; carved glass 19; gemstones 19, 36. Ornaments 34, 42, 239; jeweled 163; marcasites 23, 29, 116, 130, 146, 234; rhinestones 27, 70, 136, 194, 202, 258; cloisonne 22, equestrian motif 183, 192.

Deitsch 3, 43, 50, 75, 80, 82-86, 88, 92, 131, 191, 223, 243, 254, 263, 267. Deitsch Brothers 46, 80. Deitsch Brothers Leather Goods Corporation 81. Deitsch, Edward J. 81; Deitsch, Alan 81, 85

Dofan 3, 92-94, 109, 225, 267

Dotti 10

Doyle Auction House 74

eBay 255, 256

Emanuel Ungaro 73

Emilio Pucci 100

Escort 190, 243. Escort Bag 200

Evans 3, 95, 46, 267. Evans Case Co. 95. Evans Elegance 95, 96, 97, 98. Alfred F. Reilly 98

Finesse 190, 201, 202, 225

Finish, 242: Matte 97, 98, 101, 169, 242. Glazed/gloss 87, 194, 242. Bombe, 242

Foreign Suppliers: Argentina 31, 34, 43, 49, 57, 185. Belgium 57, 61, 84, 85, 87, 174. Brazil 39, 44, 185, 213. Cuba 45, 186. England 25, 27, 39, 57, 221, 223, 225. France 25-28, 32, 39, 57, 59, 61, 71, 78, 79, 92, 93, 102, 117-123, 131, 135, 138, 147, 174. Germany 7, 11, 24, 34, 47. West Germany 173. Switzerland 42, 58, 62

Frame bag 119, 125, 136, 164, 201, 234. Frames: brass 82; collapsible 83, 112; concealed 78, 141, 143; domed 84; etched 29, 34, 141, 167; embossed 57, 69, 161; enameled 23, 57, 62, 115, 130, 153, 169, 173; encrusted 59; filigree 29, 104, 59; japanned 229; jeweled 116, 202; polished 108; with rhinestones 104; riveted 87; scalloped 108; bejeweled 116; self-covered 54, 77, 93, 106, 135; wood-inlay 151; etched 56; wood 45; gate-frame 58; riveted 40, 42; tortoise shell (mock, faux) 19, 25, 37, 40, 47, 229

Franklin Simon 61, 126, 127, 190, 205

Frog Skin 107

G (Grimaldi) Paris 66

Galalith 26, 27, 29, 31, 37, 232

Gimbel Brothers 19, 28, 43, 46, 61, 86, 87, 90, 127, 185. Gimbel, Adam 87

Gucci 3, 7, 8, 10, 73, 74, 99, 100, 101, 217, 261, 262, 267. Gucci, Adolfo 99. Gucci, Aldo 99, 100. Guccio Gucci 99. Gucci, Maurizio 100. Gucci, Vasco 99

Handbag Designer of the Year Award 106

Handbag: Bar-belle 78; barrel 48, 54, 78, 82, 125; basket 47; bracelet 34, 37, 57, 83, 152, 178; hatbox 231; messenger 56, 152; dress suitcase 19; Pullman 103, 152; tote 18, 83, 105, 237; Bugatti Bag 102; doctor's bag 77, 88, 130, 155, 171, 193, 201; duplet 39, 180; Gladstone 15, 17, 230; It bag 36; matching set 27, 50, 126, 164; pouch 24, 35, 45, 54, 93, 101, 228; triplet 49; valise 17; vanity 27, 31, 44, 84, 96, 185, 234; vanity box 18, 230; English Kit Bag 40; Lantern Bag 32; mallette 58, 102, 114, 118, 231; satchel 20, 35, 42, 72, 85, 111, 125, 132, 142, 151, 228; Kelly Bag 103, 123. Kelly-bag style 57, 119

Handbags & Accessories Magazine 94, 133, 142

Handle: Architectural 84; back 24, 35, 40, 57; bamboo 73, 86, 101, 160; bow 234; bracelet 54, 90, 234; braided 39; brass 139; folding 85; hoop 234; loop 234; luggage 87; retractable 166; rolled 42, 45, 87, 193, 196; semi-structured 62; stationary 113; structured 57, 90, 119, 173; swivel 85; top handle 35, 63; wire 91, 105; cuff 48; double 43; hook 48; twisted 42, 44; wristlet 48; woven brass 111; braided 39; plastic 96, 254; drop-in chain strap 104, 105, 108, 202; swivel 170, 197

Harper's Bazaar 21, 40, 50, 55, 64, 69, 72, 76, 80, 90, 95, 97, 110, 139, 149, 158, 163, 247

Hattie Carnegie 52, 86, 248

Henry Bendel 61, 72, 91, 217, 236

Hermes, House of Hermes 3, 4, 7, 8, 36, 71-74, 99, 102, 103, 219, 260, 267. Hermes Museum of the Faubourg Saint-Honore (Paris, France) 103. Thierry Hermes 102. Emile-Charles Hermes 102. Jean R. Guerrand-Hermes 102

Holzer 41, 56

How to care, 256. Condition 3, 238, 252, 257, 266. Alteration and counterfeit 253. Inspection tips 253. Mink oil 257. Packing 253. Refurbishing and restoration 257. Shipping damage 253

Hubert de Givenchy 115, 116. Givenchy 73

I. Magnin & Co. 86, 138; 91, 111

Imitation, embossing 3, 224, 243. Embossed leather and vinyl 224-254, 229

Imports, 25: European 27, 45. South American 3, 45, 50, 184-189. Spanish 57, 70. West Germany 57

Industria Argentina 31, 43-45, 49, 185, 187, 188,

ISO (integumentary sense organ) 212

Italy 7, 27, 57, 61, 67, 71, 73, 99, 100, 174

IUCN Red Book of Threatened Animals 2008 28, 36, 39, 43, 82, 86, 207

Jacomo 19, 71, 86, 217. Heidener Laurenz 71. James Kaplan 71

Jana 46

Jemco U.S.A. 28, 34

Jolles 48

Josef, Bags by Josef 46, 57, 94

Judith Leiber 3, 4, 72, 104-109, 219, 243, 246, 267. Gerson Leiber 105, 109. The Leiber Museum (East Hampton, New York, U.S.A.) 109

Kenneth J. Lane 182

Koret 3, 35-37, 46, 50, 54, 59, 74, 86, 92, 110, 131, 174, 219, 243, 245, 249, 267. Koret American 116. Koret Classics 116. Koret Givenchy, Inc. 116. Koret USA 116. Koret, Inc. 110-116. Koret, Inc. of California 116. Koret, Richard 105

Lanvin 25, 28, 61, 67, 248

Lederer de Paris 3, 6, 73, 74, 86, 88, 117-122, 243, 267

Lederer, Ludwig 118, 123

Lesco 3, 50, 75, 124-127, 243, 251, 254, 267. Lesco Lona, Inc. 127. Lesco, Ltd. 127

Lewis 35, 36

Lizard Skin 3, 22, 34, 86, 108, 119, 126, 220, 233. Lizard pattern 165; lizard-calf leather 25; lizard-grain, faux 25, 60, 119. Ring lizard 137, 155, 221. Tegu 35, 82, 164, 194, 197, 201, 206, 221. Iguana 25, 221. Java 14, 37, 67, 81, 100, 119, 150-153, 155-157, 161, 220

Lord & Taylor 28, 46, 61, 78, 86, 91, 174, 187, 190, 249

Louis Vuitton 7, 8, 115

Louisiana Fur and Alligator Advisory Council (FAAC) 210

Lucille de Paris 3, 5, 51, 59, 69, 74, 86, 88, 89, 92, 128-139, 146, 174, 190, 219, 234, 243-246, 252, 253, 258, 262, 264, 267. Lucille Bags, Inc. 128. Lucille de Paris, Inc. 213. Charles Hahn 131. Claude Hahn 133. Lucille A. Hahn 131. Peter Hahn 133, 213

Lucite 31, 35, 40, 44, 47, 49, 65, 125, 126, 157

Luminaries: Barbara Bush 109. Baron and Baroness Philippe de Rothschild 157. Jacqueline Kennedy Onassis 6, 67, 68, 150. Nancy Reagan 108, 109, 150. Raisa Gorbachev 108. Hillary Rodham Clinton 109

Macy's 17, 40, 44-46, 61, 65, 89, 91, 187, 190; R.H. Macy & Co. 28, 86

Madeleine Pegs 187, 188

Manolo Blahnik 260

Manon 3, 140-143, 190, 267

Marcel Boucher 182

Mark Cross 3, 16, 17, 19, 46, 74, 88, 131, 139, 144-148, 212, 243, 249, 261, 267. Henry W. Cross 144. Edward Wasserberger 146. George Wasserberger 146, 212, 217. Sarah Lee 148

Marshall Fields & Co. 91

Martin Van Schaak 3, 65, 74, 149-157, 245, 250, 251

Materials: Broadcloth 44; brocade 29. Feathers, peacock and pheasant 67. Furs, broadtail 233; pony 27; leopard 236; faux leopard 72. Leather, antelope 25, 31, 34; box 103; calf 25; embossed 14, 94; Morocco 19, 97, 234; saddle 61; patent 116; seal 19, 25, 233; walrus 19. Vinyl 31, 60, 119; embossed 266; leatherette 59; keratol (first man-made vinyl material) 15

Mayer 236

Menihan 46

Mexico 186, 221

Meyer's 60

Michael Kors 261

Molyneux 28, 248

Montgomery Ward & Co. Merchandise Catalog 21, 24, 225, 233, 235, 236, 247

Morris Moscowitz 56, 57, 105, 225, 236

Mosell 127, 258

Museums, 106: The Los Angeles County Museum of Art, The Museum of the City of New York. The Smithsonian Institution (Washington D.C.) The Victoria and Albert Museum (London, England). Metropolitan Museum of Art, New York 67, 175.

Musi 62

Nadelle 54

Nat Lewis 236

National Authority for the Ladies' Handbag Industry (NALHI) 54, 76, 81, 94, 112, 127, 133, 140, 167, 173, 191, 204

Neiman Marcus 91, 99, 101, 107, 249

Nettie Rosenstein 3, 46, 52, 55, 63, 86, 54, 74, 105, 109, 158-162, 175, 243-245, 250, 264, 267,

Oleg Cassini 52, 68

Oppenheim Collins 61, 125, 187, 190

Original by Caprice 54, 60, 68

Ostrich Skin 3, 53, 54, 56, 97, 103, 107, 108, 112, 128, 136, 142, 170, 180, 218, 233, 243, 254

Palizzio 3, 163-166, 250, 254, 263. Palizzio, Inc. 163. Palizzio Shoes, Inc. 165

Paloma Picasso 215

Panetta 259

Patou 26, 28, 248

Pichel 50

Pierre Cardin 73, 115, 251, 261

Pisk Buenos Aires 44

Plastic, Celanese plastic 44, 81, 168. Composition materials 31, 40, 232

Prado Bags 186, 189

Prestige 190

Prystal 20, 25, 31, 37, 40, 44, 175, 232, 234

Pucci 73

Purse: Arm 35, 36, 54, 186; boat 54; bucket duffel 52, 83; canteen 37; chain 38, 94; envelope 20, 35, 230; figural 37; finger 231; handbook 28, 231; lunch box 56, 83, 113, 170; mailbox 63, 83, 139; mesh 22; micro-beaded 27; Permasuede, cashmere 78; cocktail 27, 59, 116, 130, 152, 167, 195; coin 24, 39, 53, 77, 84, 114, 170; needlepoint 29, 69; opera pouch 15, 228; reticule 11; swivel coin 28, 29; trim box 56; underarm 24, 25, 43, 231; chatelaine 13, 18, 19, 106, 228, 230; double-decker 34, 63; evening (jeweled) 59, 66, 105, 152, 130, 146, 172; wristlet 29, 34, 44, 83, 90, 168, 185, 230. Clutch 25, 31, 43, 56, 83, 97, 101, 118, 127, 145, 155, 234, 264; convertible 91

Rendl 75, 174, 219, 267; Rendl Original 3, 167-171

Revitz 61, 89, 190

Roberta di Camerino 74

Ronay 58

Rosenfeld 46, 62, 74, 217, 260-263, 267; Rosenfeld Imports, Inc. 177; Rosenfeld Original 44, 47, 174

Rosenfeld, Harry 3, 46, 92, 94, 125, 172-183, 243, 246

Royalty: King Edward VII of England 16, 17. Prince of Wales 103. Princess Grace Kelly 6, 103, 144. Princess Margaret 134. Queen Victoria 16

Ruth Saltz 222

Sacha, Madam Sacha 90, 91

Saks Fifth Avenue 18, 25, 37, 46, 53, 61, 78, 87-90, 96-98, 115, 127, 134, 159, 161, 219, 249, 263. Saks - 34th 47, 190. Saks Herald Square 28, 87

Salvador Dali 32, 33

Schiaparelli, Elsa 30, 32, 33, 38, 40, 55, 127, 133, 129, 248, 249, 260

Sears, Roebuck & Co. Catalog 15, 16, 20, 126, 203, 224, 229, 228

Skins 3, 34, 77, 207-223, 239, 266. Cut 239, 240; hornback cut 36, 70, 87; belly 25, 35, 77, 103, 135, 146, 241, 266. Grade 239. Pattern 239, 240. Symmetry 241, 266. Cleaning 256. Patching 40, 200, 243. Conditioning 257

Snake Skin 3, 25, 37, 222, 234. Anaconda 143. Cobra 35, 48, 93, 125, 151, 165, 233, 264; king cobra 223. Whip 108. Water snake 34, 59, 68, 264. Karung skin 13, 104, 108, 166, 197, 222. Python 38, 54, 56, 60, 71, 85, 101, 116, 154, 165, 177, 202

Sotheby's Auction House 74

Sterling Handbag Co. 198. Sterling U.S.A. 3, 190, 198, 243, 267

Stern Brothers 28, 46, 61

Style: Art Deco 21, 23, 27, 34, 60, 71, 156, 227, 231. Art Nouveau 19, 229. Edwardian style 3, 16, 17, 19, 227. Glamorous Fifties 3, 51. Ladylike Thirties 3, 30. Practical Forties 3, 41. Flapper Twenties 3, 21, 32. Mod 3, 64, 227, 237. New Look 50, 54, 227, 236. Victorian 3, 12, 71, 227. Retro 39, 42, 227

Stylecraft Miami 250

Supreme Original 63

Susan Gail 72, 236

Sydney California 61, 250

Tailored Woman 46, 61, 190

Talon fastener (zipper) 35, 37, 40. Zipper 44, 234, 266; plastic 40, 46. Pull 29, 47, 56

Tano of Madrid 70

The Fashion Institute of Technology 106

Theo Rendl 92; Theodore Rendl Co. 167

Theodor of California 236

Tiffany & Co. 13, 61, 177

Tom Ford 6, 101

Town & Country 41, 98, 144, 145

Tracy Tolkien 149

Travel bag 19, 42, 53, 102, 114, 121, 228; case 13; satchel 18; set 231; trunk case 18, 228; Passport-and-Travel 53; Passport-Tickets-Money 114. Treatment: accessories 34, 96-98, 111, 194, 239; clochette 57; embroidery 29, 37; lacing 28; protective feet 49; stitched seams 66, 137, 239; contrast 49, 77, 90, 239; saddle (Hermes) 102; trapunto 49, 82, 120, 193; trim 27, 83, 91, 109, 118; riveted 88; silver 104; welted seams 28, 36, 46, 54, 70, 130

Trifari 133

Triomphe 89

Turtle Skin 3, 70, 91, 137, 181, 216, 243, 264

U.S. Fish and Wildlife Service 212, 216

Varon, Bags by Varon 223

Vassar 3, 75, 190, 203, 243, 267. Vassar Bag Co. 204

Versace 258

Viki Original 35

Vintage, altered 254, 253; vintage, original 266

Virginia Pope 158

Vogue 21, 30, 36-38, 40-42, 46, 48, 50, 58, 64, 69, 76, 80, 92, 111, 122, 136, 140, 159, 234, 247-251

Whiting & Davis 22, 259

Wilcof Original 53, 56, 236

Wilshire Original 38, 48

Yves Saint Laurent 73